h
2-7-07

Palgrave Foundations

A series of introductory texts across a wide range of subject areas to meet the needs of today's lecturers and students

Foundations texts provide complete yet concise coverage of core topics and skills based on detailed research of course requirements suitable for both independent study and class use – *the firm foundations for future study.*

Published

Biology
British Politics
Chemistry (third edition)
Communication Studies
Contemporary Europe (second edition)
Economics
Economics for Business
Foundations of Marketing
A History of English Literature
Modern British History
Nineteenth-Century Britain
Philosophy
Physics (second edition)
Politics (second edition)

Further titles are in preparation

Communication Studies

SKY MARSEN

First published 2006 by
PALGRAVE MACMILLAN
Houndmills, Basingstoke, Hampshire RG21 6XS and
175 Fifth Avenue, New York, N.Y. 10010
Companies and representatives throughout the world

PALGRAVE MACMILLAN is the global academic imprint of the Palgrave Macmillan division of St. Martin's Press, LLC and of Palgrave Macmillan Ltd. Macmillan® is a registered trademark in the United States, United Kingdom and other countries. Palgrave is a registered trademark in the European Union and other countries.

ISBN-13: 978–1–4039–3998–2
ISBN-10: 1–4039–3998–5

This book is printed on paper suitable for recycling and made from fully managed and sustained forest sources.

A catalogue record for this book is available from the British Library.

A catalog record for this book is available from the Library of Congress.

10 9 8 7 6 5 4 3 2 1
15 14 13 12 11 10 09 08 07 06

Printed and bound in China

Contents

List of Figures, Illustrations and Tables

Figures

Illustrations

Tables

Preface

The aim of this book is to provide a comprehensive introduction to major approaches, methods and concepts in several fields of communication and media studies. Its main motivations are: first, to introduce readers to the subject of communication as an academic discipline and as a professional practice; secondly, to support an eclectic approach, selecting and combining concepts and methods from different areas, thereby helping to bridge the often unjustified gaps between different fields of communication. At the same time, the book also respects the diversity among communication fields and reflects this in the style and presentation of each chapter, which aims to represent the styles of expression characteristic of each field.

Chapter 1 introduces the subject of communication by discussing the kinds of issues and questions that occupy communication research and the different approaches that compose communication theory. The chapter also describes the main subdivisions or subdisciplines of communication studies, showing areas of difference and similarity.

Chapter 2 describes foundational distinctions in communications research, such as the one between quantitative and qualitative methodology. It also overviews the early communication models that form the basis of most recent reformulations and act as background for the discipline of communication studies.

Chapter 3 continues from the previous one, introducing and describing theoretical approaches to communication. In particular, this chapter focuses on linguistic aspects of communication, and the various language strategies that underlie communicative interactions.

Chapter 4 has a stronger emphasis on textual analysis, focusing on semiotics and narratology, which are the writer's specialization. These methods, and the theoretical principles that underpin them, are applicable to most aspects and interactive contexts of communication, and provide a general theoretical foundation to the analysis of texts from diverse fields.

Chapter 5 explores interpersonal and intercultural communication models in relation to business and organizational contexts. It looks at the concept of culture and its relations with business management, principles of team communication ('team' being the equivalent of 'group' in business communication), some issues concerning leadership, project management, and aspects of conflict. In line with the business concerns of effectiveness and testability, as opposed to depth of conceptualization and analytic thoroughness, this chapter focuses on currently popular models that have been proven to be useful for business communicators, and gives advice on practical strategies for communication in professional contexts.

Chapter 6 describes and analyses approaches to mass communication. It begins with definitions of the audience and the role in communication research of factors relating to the public, such as 'public opinion' and the 'public sphere'. It then proceeds to discuss major approaches to the relations between media texts and audience responses, concentrating on the approaches known as 'media effect', 'diffusion of innovations' and 'uses and gratifications'. The focus of this chapter on mass communication makes it necessary to take into account the technical means through which this type of communication takes place.

Therefore, to reflect this, the chapter includes descriptions, in independent boxes inserted in the main discussion, of the development of radio, television and computers, as well as of the salient elements of the audience.

Chapter 7 focuses on one mass medium: film. Film holds a central position among media for a variety of reasons: first, film narrative forms the basis of other texts, such as television series, and interactive multimedia texts, such as computer games, and many terms originating in film are used in other media; secondly, film has been the object of study of many textual analysts, and a vast amount of theoretical literature exists on it; thirdly, film is one of the most popular and influential media world-wide, as audience participation and business investment testify. These reasons justify an inclusion in this book of an independent chapter on film. This chapter discusses the changes in theoretical approach since the first structuralist film analyses of the 1960s and 1970s, and describes the stages of filmmaking. It ends with a discussion of major artistic movements that have found expression in film, and the ideologies associated with these.

Chapter 8 examines the aspects of the media that are related to business organization and internationalization. It discusses the structures of the media industry, focusing on the regulation of television in certain countries. It then proceeds to discuss developments in international connectivity through the media, and describes the effects of the internet and of the phenomenon known as 'globalization'. This chapter also includes a description of the hierarchical organization and professional roles of media businesses, relevant especially to those readers interested in pursuing a career in the media industry.

Some thoughts for the reader

What do I think you know? This book is an introductory analysis of communication and the media, and so I assume no prior theoretical knowledge of these subjects. However, I do assume that you use media tools and objects (watch television, surf the internet, etc.), and engage in communication activities (belong to groups or professional associations, and interact socially). Your own experiences in such areas will be very useful in understanding the technical and theoretical concepts described in the book. At the same time, I assume that you have an enthusiastic approach which will enable you to persevere through the many models and concepts described and to pursue some of them in more depth. I give names of relevant authors and finish all chapters with a list of titles so that you can follow up areas of interest.

Although using an accessible style, I have not attempted to oversimplify complicated issues or to translate into layman's terms all technical terminology. I believe that any learning involves some degree of stress and effort, and have tried to respect this in the style and organization of the book. In addition, it is an accepted fact that acquiring new knowledge allows you to become insiders in the groups that possess this knowledge. Using appropriate forms of expression and specific terminology is an indication of insider status; since the book aims to be an initiation to communication and media research, on both academic and professional levels, the style in which it is written should show the way.

Who do I think you are? The structure of the book is well-suited for one-semester courses in communication. Therefore, I assume that you are likely to be a university student taking a module in communication and/or media studies. You could also fall into another category of reader, including: a graduate student who has studied a different discipline and who is now doing a graduate degree that includes communication studies; a student in an inter-disciplinary area who is taking a component of his/her studies in communication; or a student of semiotics, rhetoric or cultural studies who wants to see the broader context of communication. You could also be a professional working in the media industry or in a corporate position that involves complex communication tasks (such as human resources or public relations), and you want some useful ideas to develop your skills and abilities.

What will you gain from this book? I can make three promises about how this book will benefit you: first, you will understand the complexity of factors involved in communication, and become more resourceful and confident as communicators in both professional and social contexts; secondly, you will learn about the kinds of questions asked and the methods of analysis used by specialists in several areas of communication and media research; thirdly, you will be able to write about and discuss relevant issues and major areas of debate using accepted theories, concepts and terminology, thereby giving your arguments more credibility.

How does this book differ from others in the field? As noted above, the book's main char-acteristic is its eclectic approach, selecting and synthesizing methods and ideas from differ-ent schools of thought. In addition, its distinctive aspects lie in two other features. First, it discusses theoretical and practical aspects of communication, making it relevant to both academics and practitioners. In this respect, it differs from many of its predecessors, whose approach was often critical of commercial practice. Secondly, it covers a wide area by including chapters in several seemingly disparate sections of communication and media studies, including text analysis, professional communication and film. In this way the book is a concise but comprehensive resource of material in communication theory and media studies.

Sky Marsen, 2006

Acknowledgements

I extend warm and sincere thanks to all those who helped in any way with the writing of this book, whether it was through practical advice or through moral support and encouragement, or both. In particular, I would like to acknowledge the special assistance of the following people: the Faculty of Humanities and Social Sciences, Victoria University of Wellington, who funded my travel to Los Angeles to interview key figures in the media industry; Robert Gustafson, Director of the Entertainment Industry Institute, at California State University Northridge, for his kind help in contacting specialists in the media and entertainment world, and for our illuminating discussions on the workings of the media industry; Barry Collin, founder of the Association of Independent Feature Film Producers, for his encouragement and support throughout the project, as well as for his valuable insider perspective on independent film-making; Steve Leblang, Senior Vice-President of Strategic Research and Planning at FX Networks, for discussing with me current trends and developments in the television world, and issues of audience research from a media practitioner's perspective; Joseph Soukup, General Manager of CBS Studios, Los Angeles, for taking the time to guide me around the studios and patiently describe media management issues and the facilities used in media production; Alan McKee for his true collegial spirit in giving me moral support and practical tips on how to write an informative book for non-specialists – and to keep it interesting; Pippin Barr, my model reader, for reading through drafts of the book and offering valuable insights from a student's perspective; Stephen King, for permission to include his article, 'Why We Crave Horror Movies'; Zentropa Productions, for permission to include the Dogme 95 'Vow of Chastity'; and last but certainly not least, Suzannah Burywood, my publisher, for her continuous support, consideration and help in all matters relating to the complexities of publishing.

Every effort has been made to trace the copyright holders but if any have been inadvertently overlooked the publishers will be pleased to make the necessary arrangement at the first opportunity.

Introducing Communication

Consider this situation. You visit a country for the first time. One of your first impressions is a newspaper article with the headline 'Mother gets prison sentence for slapping three-year-old'. The article is a news story about a woman who slapped her three-year-old child in a supermarket and was charged with violence against a minor. Even before analysing the situation you spontaneously sense something about this event, and this sentiment influences your attitude towards the country and colours your experiences there. You may feel amused, disappointed, curious, surprised, perplexed, angry, pleased, or may have any of a million other possible reactions. To what degree the story influences your attitude will depend, of course, on your individual orientation and personal expectations. However, the story will have some effect on you because of the psychological faculties of 'attention' and 'judgment' that will come into play (i.e. your attention was attracted and your sense of judgment activated). Here are some possible reactions you might have:

1   You might feel disapproval or anger towards the mother and adopt a righteous, authority-supporting perspective. In this respect, you might read the story with a 'human affairs' type of interest, following the thread promoted by the headline passively, without resistance.

2   You might feel disappointed that you are in such a silly place where trivia make headlines. You might think that this is a primitive place which is not likely to challenge your intellect or excite your senses. You might feel let down that a story that 'hit the headlines' was not a more serious, intriguing or glamorous one.

3   You might feel indignant for the mother who has received such a strict punishment for what seems like a minor misdemeanour. Consequently, you might fear that this is an oppressive, 'stiff' and overly severe place where one cannot get away with much, and where everything is taken 'too seriously'.

4   You might feel tenderness and compassion for the child. The place might start to seem to you to be a child's haven, where the authorities protect the innocent and helpless and

1

where justice can be sought. You might feel that this is a civilized place with a developed understanding of ethical issues.

All these reactions have one thing in common: you have responded to a set of signs (words telling the story, attention-capturing headline, possibly pictures) that make up a message (the events of the story), expressed through a medium (the newspaper). The message communicated some ideas about the world and you communicated your response to these ideas (even if you expressed your communication only in intimate thought, 'intrapersonally', and not in material form).

In addition, the ways in which you responded, although apparently totally different, also share common characteristics. In situations 1, 3 and 4, you identified with a character in the story and approached the recounted events from this character's point of view. In situation 1, your identification with the authorities that imposed the punishment was probably a direct result of the way the story was presented. The opposite extreme would be situation 2, where you resisted identifying with any character and instead focused on the presence of the story – the act of communication rather than the content. In situations 3 and 4, you did not accept the perspective of the authorities, but instead related the characters to your own assumed ideas about social roles and 'how things should be' – notions of personal identity, both your own and that of the characters, became prominent in this case.

In all cases, meaning was created in the interface between what was given, the text, and your interpretation. In this meaning-creating process, factors at play include *assumptions* made by both sender (the writer of the article) and receiver (the reader) and the *expectations* to which they lead *subject positions* (to whom you attribute a sense of self, and whose point of view you adopt), and agency (whom you consider an independent agent responsible for an action).

Now consider an actual event. On 28 January 1986 the high-profile space shuttle Challenger project turned into a disaster when the shuttle exploded seconds after it was launched, killing all the crew. The accident was witnessed by millions who were watching the launch on television. Minutes later the stock market reacted to the disaster. Investors dumped the stocks of the four main contractors who had participated in the Challenger project: the company that built the shuttle and its engines, Rockwell International; those who managed ground support, Lockheed; the manufacturer of the external fuel tank, Martin Marietta; and the company that built the solid-fuel booster rocket, Morton Thiokol. As news spread about the reasons for the explosion, the work done by Morton Thiokol came out as having been defective. Thiokol engineers had evidently known that there could be problems but had not communicated their fears appropriately to parties who could postpone the launch and prevent the disaster. The result? Many Thiokol employees lost their jobs, the company itself suffered a severe loss of reputation, and the Thiokol stock crashed and remained down, even when the other companies started to recover.

What does this incident show? Among other things, it shows that news travels fast and that the mass media, such as television, play a major role in how we gain knowledge about the world. In addition, it shows that the knowledge that is communicated, through the media or other means, does not remain as abstract information, but has concrete and far-reaching consequences: it becomes translated into material forms, and produces a chain reaction affecting social and financial factors. Also, it shows that important decisions are made in anticipation of such factors as public opinion. Finally, it shows that even technical

defects do not remain in the sphere of technology, but actually involve some fc
communication in how they are managed.

Both situations described above illustrate areas in which communication plays a role.
They show how communication processes are at play in the ways in which we perceive and
interpret information, in the means through which information is transmitted and also in
the effects of information on social behaviour. Keeping these situations in mind, we can now
attempt to delimit and describe the concept of communication as it is used in academic and
professional contexts.

1.1 What is communication?

Here is how some scholars have defined communication (listed chronologically):

1   'social interaction through messages' (Fiske 1990: 2);

2   'a process in which participants create and share information with one another in order
    to reach a mutual understanding' (Rogers 1995: 35);

3   'an activity in which symbolic content is not merely transmitted from one source to
    another, but exchanged between human agents, who interact within a shared situational
    and/or discursive context' (Price 1997: 5);

4   'a process whereby people in groups, using the tools provided by their culture, create
    collective representations of reality' (Trenholm 1999: 31);

5   'a process in which there is some predictable relation between the message transmitted
    and the message received' (Graber 2003: 2).

Some of these definitions emphasize the social and cultural aspects of communication
(definitions 1, 3 and 4); others focus on behavioural and cognitive aspects (definitions 2 and
5). This distinction between culture and cognition actually grounds the main differences in
theoretical approaches to communication. Thus, to put it simply, contemporary communication theory is divided into two broad groups of approaches: those that draw their inspiration, and some methodological practice, from psychology and behavioural sciences, and
those whose theoretical inclinations place them closer to cultural studies. This dichotomy is
bridged by a third group: those approaches that look at communication in terms of textual
strategy. This group studies communication activities through the techniques that participants in a communicative interaction use, and traces these techniques in the structures of a
text, i.e. in the ways a text is put together. This situation is conceptualized graphically in
Figure 1.1.

These groups are also affiliated with national traditions, although it should be emphasized that these affiliations are very general and that there are many scholars who work
across nations. The behavioural approach to communication is generally associated with
American theorists, and examines statistical trends, psychological processes and measurable
methods of analysis. As an academic discipline, communication studies developed in the US
mostly in response to the aim of investigating the effects of political campaigns and the
changes in public opinion, especially in relation to such campaigns.

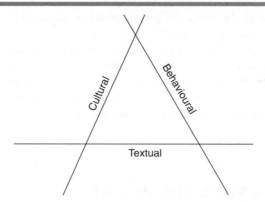

Figure 1.1 Trends in communication studies

In contrast, the culturalist trend is generally associated with British, Commonwealth and, to some extent, German approaches, and explores ideological issues of identity and power as these manifest themselves in cultural institutions. In Britain, communication studies started in the form of interdisciplinary ventures, drawing from sociology, philosophy and literary studies, many informed by Marxist theory. For example, the group of researchers in the Centre for Contemporary Cultural Studies (CCCS) at the University of Birmingham was instrumental in developing communication studies in Britain in the 1970s. The Frankfurt School, under the leadership of Jürgen Habermas and Theodor Adorno, although developing separately from the CCCS, followed a parallel neo-Marxist approach aimed at investigating the ideological overtones and undertones of communication and media activities, especially as these relate to political factors, governmental regulation and public policy.

The textual approaches developed to a large extent in continental Europe, especially France, with an echo in Scandinavian countries, such as Denmark. Textual studies were initially strongly language-based, and in many institutions they were (and often still are) integrated as a branch of linguistics or anthropology. They are closely associated with the work of structuralist semioticians, who compared a variety of texts, in both oral and written forms, to distinguish common underlying patterns that might not be obvious at a surface level. These approaches combined linguistic analysis with rhetoric and concepts from the philosophy of language to examine how the ways in which people make sense of the world are inscribed in language. Since the beginnings of textual approaches in the 1960s, many scholars have pursued their analysis from linguistic texts to non-verbal behaviour, such as dress, advertising and ritual, as well as film. Such approaches cut across the other two branches of communication studies in that they are interested in both universal, cognitive aspects of communication (i.e. how the human mind works) and the cultural manifestations of these aspects (i.e. what gives each text its particular take on the universal, or its unique 'flair').

Interestingly, many culturalist approaches were influenced by textual studies. French structuralist scholars, such as Roland Barthes, Louis Althusser and Michel Foucault, have strongly influenced the study of ideology and power in social life by British culturalists. In fact, the writings of philosopher Michel Foucault have arguably been more influential in Anglo-Saxon countries than they have in France. However, much continental textual analysis remains more 'technical' and abstract than the British contributions, which emphasize social and contextual factors.

At this stage, it is fair to note that the writer of this book also comes from a textual tradition, with a background in semiotics, and experience in the analysis of written text and film. However, this book does not attempt to take sides, but to provide a comprehensive introduction to major methods, concepts and issues that are associated with communication studies across approaches. A main tenet running throughout the book is that selecting and combining ideas from various sources is not only possible but also, indeed, helpful in shedding new light on questions about how communication works.

In many ways, since its inception, communication as an object of study and analysis has sought to synthesize technological and mechanical categories with human and social practices. The model of cybernetic theory first advanced by Norbert Wiener in his 1948 publication *Cybernetics: Or Control and Communication in the Animal and the Machine* proposed many ideas that were to become foundational in the development of the discipline of communication studies. Wiener defined cybernetics as 'the study of messages as a means of controlling machinery and society', thereby making a direct link between message exchange and the pursuit of control. He took up the concept of control again in his 1954 publication *The Human Use of Human Beings*, where he also emphasized the function of feedback as a primary evidence of communication. Feedback, particularly when interpreted as 'positive' outcome to a message, could be considered in terms of communication effectiveness or in terms of behaviour change and persuasion. As Wiener argued (Wiener 1988: 16), 'when I communicate with another person, I impart a message to him, and when he communicates back with me he returns a related message which contains information primarily accessible to him and not to me ... if my control is to be effective I must take cognizance of any messages (from him) which may indicate that the order has been understood and has been obeyed'.

More recently, the Canadian communication specialist Marshall McLuhan again took up the question of the relationship between human intention and the technological means through which this can be expressed. In their book, *The Laws of Media* (1988), McLuhan and McLuhan noted how understanding the ways in which media technologies evolve and the activities that they enable can throw light on what the concept of communication includes at any point in the history of society. They proposed a set of four questions that should be asked of any medium, which can lead to an understanding of how communication strategies are implemented through media technologies (McLuhan and McLuhan 1988: 7):

- What does it enhance or intensify?
- What does it render obsolete or displace?
- What does it retrieve that was previously obsolesced?
- What does it produce or become when pressed to an extreme?

They formulated these questions by starting with a working hypothesis posed as a question: 'What general, verifiable (that is, testable) statements can be made about all media?' (the hypothesis being that such verifiable statements do in fact exist).

This recurrent phenomenon of attempting to link technology with content in the history of communication research points to the inherent affinities between communication as an intentional activity of an individual or group, and the media through which it is channelled.

Marshall McLuhan (1911–80) was very influential in drawing attention to the pervasive role of the media, not only in their social function as information regulators, but also in their cognitive function as enhancers of human perceptual capacity. His description of the media as 'extensions of man' and his saying that 'the medium is the message' have become proverbial in the discourse of communication, and summarize McLuhan's ideas that the media are not only tools through which we perceive the world, but affect both the world that we perceive and the senses through which we perceive it. Rather than being the means to an end, the media are actually part of the end itself.

It also shows the strong ties between communication studies and media research, which this book addresses.

1.2 Fields of communication studies

Communication studies is divided into different fields, depending on the contexts and participants involved. Here is a brief description of major fields, going from the personal to the impersonal.

Interpersonal communication

This occurs when two individuals or a small group of individuals exchange messages in a context of interaction. In many cases, this interaction is done face-to-face, although interpersonal communication includes telephone conversations and e-mail message exchange. Factors that come into play in interpersonal communication include:

- *Assumed values and shared meanings.* Participants in the exchange make assumptions about each other, about what each knows, and about what the aim of the interaction is. In many respects, the effectiveness of the communicative act depends on whether these assumptions are really shared or whether they are one-sided, in which case misunderstandings often occur.
- *Non-verbal and paralinguistic codes.* Even though interpersonal communication could rely to a large extent on the exchange of words, other factors play an important role. These include intonation, or tone of message in the case of written communication (paralinguistic features), gestures, dress and body language (non-verbal codes).
- *Cultural and personal meanings attributed to identity.* Interpersonal communication is the primary means through which we confirm or question issues of selfhood and personal identity, including age, gender and ethnic background.

Group communication

Whether group communication is a separate field from interpersonal communication is a contentious issue. Much depends on the number of participants allowed in a communicative act in each type of communication field. Those that limit interpersonal communication to two would favour a distinction between interpersonal and group fields. In many ways, however, there is rarely, if ever, a communicative act solely between two individuals. Even in cases where two people are having a conversation, the values, assumptions and meanings involved in their interaction point to 'implied others' who need to be taken into account if the interaction is to be contexted and understood. In addition, much communication that takes place in groups makes use of interpersonal factors, such as non-verbal codes and shared values.

If we are to accept a distinction between interpersonal and group communication, however, a key element to use would be 'belonging'. Communication expert Denis McQuail defines the notion of belonging as follows (McQuail 1975: 4): 'To belong to a social group, a society, a culture is to share a common denominator of frames of reference, significant objects, systems for describing the world and facilitating interaction with each other.'

Keeping this in mind, the factors at play in group communication include:

- *A perception of a common identity shared by members of the group.* It is important to exercise care not to confuse the identity and definition that the group accept for themselves, and those imposed on the group by outsiders.

- *A distinction between insiders and outsiders, allies and enemies.* This includes understanding the roles and behaviours that qualify one as an insider and the roles and behaviours that qualify one as an outsider, an ally or an enemy.

- *A shared set of goals, values and general 'way of doing things'.* This can include such factors as group insignia (tattoos, a secret handshake, etc.), written policies or collectively accepted rules, etc.

Intercultural communication

This is in many ways similar to group communication, but the role of groups is taken by ethnic cultures. 'Culture', of course, is not just the domain of nations; it also describes the norms and conventions of groups (e.g. 'gang culture') corporations (e.g. 'corporate culture'), and collectivities with shared knowledge and ideology (e.g. academic culture). However, as it is used in communication studies, intercultural communication tends to describe the relations between members of different ethnic groups and languages, interacting in an international context, such as the United Nations assemblies, or in a context where one culture is dominant, such as in societies with minority migrant groups.

Factors at play in intercultural communication include:

- *Uses of a common language.* Often in intercultural communicative acts, participants use a language, commonly English, that is not their native language. In such cases, problems in translation of terms may occur leading to misunderstanding or limited communication.

- *Degrees of formality and politeness.* Different cultures have their own ways of communicating respect and politeness. Linguistic expressions as well as dress codes and non-verbal behaviour, such as proximity and eye contact, have different meanings for different cultures.

- *Values and world-views.* Cultures attribute different value to forms of behaviour and objects. For example, some cultures may confer more value on material success and possessions, while others may emphasize spiritual factors or family ties. The values and world-views of a cultural group affect the ways in which this group communicates.

Interpersonal and **group communication** look at the factors that become prominent when individuals interact with those with whom they come into personal contact, such as friends, associates, managers, employees and clients. **Mass communication** looks at the factors at play when an organized entity, such as a corporation or broadcast company, sends out messages to an anonymous public. **Intercultural communication** looks at the assumptions that individuals make when influenced by cultural conventions about 'how things should be', and how these assumptions may conflict with 'how things actually are' in contexts where more than one culture is present.

Professional or business communication

This examines the cultures and organizational rules of companies and corporations. It takes into account the role and function of specific corporations in society and their structures as functional units. Business communication examines the ways in which members of an organization interact with each other, how the organization as a whole interacts with its clients and the general public, and how organizations interact with each other in the global arena. In this respect, business communication constitutes a bridge between interpersonal and mass communication. Specialists in business communication favour the use of models in understanding the input of individual initiative and group interaction within an organizational context. Communication activities are studied in order to calculate their effectiveness in achieving specific goals – the famous 'bottom line' of business.

Factors at play in business communication include:

• *The hierarchy and role allocation of the company.* This includes such factors as who reports to whom, and who is held accountable for specific outcomes.

• *The uses of language and non-verbal codes in corporate contexts.* This includes a variety of factors, including how employees are expected to dress, the style and tone expected of them in formal communication, such as report writing, and the organization of meetings.

• *Leadership and managerial attributes.* This describes what makes an efficient leader and team manager, and how this efficiency is reflected in communication styles. It also looks at how promotion and responsibility are achieved and how much initiative and creative input is expected or allowed at lower ranks of the organization.

• *The image that the company presents to the outside world.* This includes public relations techniques, company logos, company websites, product-branding (i.e. names given to products, through which the company comes to be identified) and corporate image as this is communicated through advertising and various Corporate Social Responsibility (CSR) ventures, such as initiatives to reduce pollution and to support cultural activities.

Mass communication

The basic and generally accepted definition of this is communication of the few to the many. Mass communication also involves the technological aspects of information transmission (since communicating to large audiences who are not physically present assumes some technological input) and the institutional practices of the mass media organizations that transmit the messages and own the technological equipment and specialist know-how to achieve this. Impact is a key word in mass communication studies, because the aim of mass communication activities such as broadcasting is to attract and have an effect on large audiences, often internationally. The development of technology in the twentieth century has made mass communication the most modern type, and one that, in many ways, encompasses all others. For example, television series are an excellent way to study interpersonal communication; documentaries and multicultural television provide a window to intercultural issues and conflicts; and many mass media corporations typify big business organization and business communication practice.

Factors at play in the study of mass communication include:

- the interrelationships between technology, ownership and regulation, and media content;
- the development of sophisticated audience analysis and audience measurement techniques and procedures;
- the merging or 'synergy' of different sectors of the media industry, such as comic books with film, and film with theme parks.

Summary

◆ Communication theory looks at how people respond to the *signs* that make up a *message* expressed through a *medium*.

◆ A message is rarely limited to a sender and a receiver, but can have far-reaching consequences in the social and material world.

◆ As an academic discipline, communication studies has taken three broadly defined directions: one leads from behavioural sciences, such as psychology; another leads from cultural and social disciplines; and the other leads from literary and language studies.

◆ The origins of communication studies are closely linked with cybernetics, the science of control in society. Since technology plays a major role in the power to control social processes, communication theory has sought to trace links between technological developments and social behaviour.

◆ Communication studies is made up of different fields, including interpersonal communication, group communication, intercultural communication, professional communication, film studies and mass communication.

Topics for discussion

▶ Communication is part of any human activity. Many disciplines would therefore benefit from understanding communication principles. Discuss the role and importance of communication in disciplines such as sociology, psychology, management or any other discipline you are interested in. Which field(s) of communication would be most relevant and in what ways?

▶ Marshall McLuhan wrote before the advent of the internet. However, in some respects, the internet typifies many of his ideas about the function of the media in society. Using his four questions for media analysis, compare the internet with other media.

▶ Make a list of the contexts in which you communicate and the media with which you communicate. These could include work, school and family situations, interactions with friends and the community, and could involve speaking, writing, dressing in a particular way, etc. How is your style of communication affected by the context and the medium? Describe a situation when your communication strategy (i.e. with whom you communicated and what style you adopted) brought you success, and/or a situation where it prevented you from achieving your aims.

■ References and further reading

Fiske, J. (1990) *Introduction to Communication Studies*, 2nd edn. London: Routledge.

Graber, D. (2003): *The Power of Communication: Managing Information in Public Organizations*. Washington, DC: CQ Press.

McLuhan, M. and McLuhan E. (1988) *Laws of Media: The New Science*. Toronto: University of Toronto Press.

McQuail, D. (1975) *Communication*. London: Longman.

Price, S. (1997) *Communication Studies*. London: Longman.

Rogers, E. M. (1995) *Diffusion of Innovations*, 4th edn. New York and London: The Free Press.

Surowiecki, J. (2005) *The Wisdom of Crowds: Why the Many are Smarter than the Few*. London: Abacus.

Trenholm, S. (1999). *Thinking through Communication*. Boston: Allyn and Bacon.

Wiener, N. (1965) [1948] *Cybernetics: Or Control and Communication in the Animal and the Machine*, 2nd edn. Cambridge, MA: MIT Press.

Wiener, N. (1988) [1954] *The Human Use of Human Beings: Cybernetics and Society*, 2nd edn. Boston: Da Capo.

Methods and Models of Communication Studies

> There are some enterprises in which a careful disorderliness is the true method.
>
> Herman Melville

Communication scholars and practitioners have formulated different models, methods and theories to study the ways in which communication takes place. This chapter looks at some major models and methods that ground the study of communication. It begins with an explanation of some commonly used terms and concepts in the field of communication studies. It then goes on to describe the major models that ground communications research. The last two sections explain and discuss factors involved in miscommunication, and the main methods used in communication research.

2.1 Terms and concepts

A *text* is any object that is used for theoretical analysis or critical inquiry. A book, a piece of clothing, an extract from a conversation, a film, a news item or a drawing can become a text if it is studied in terms of how it produces meaning and/or how it is constructed. The concept of text is so prevalent in some approaches to communication that a number of theorists see most objects as texts. The semiotician Algirdas-Julien Greimas, for example, has famously stated that there is nothing outside the text, meaning that when we understand something by means of our mental faculties (as opposed to, say, intuitively), we turn it into a set of interconnected elements that can be grasped cognitively and talked about – that is, we turn it into a 'text'.

A *model* is a simplified description of the main elements constituting an aspect of the world. A model may be graphic (i.e. diagrammatic or visual) or it may be verbal. It is simpler than the aspect it describes, its aim being to capture some components of this aspect and the ways in which these components are interrelated. A model gives a general picture of the various instances or manifestations of a system or structure by abstracting the formal properties of the object that it describes. It does not refer to or represent reality but, rather, aims to provide an analytical tool with which we can understand and talk about reality.

A *method* is a systematic procedure that is followed to collect and organize information so as to answer a question or test a hypothesis. The question or project that is chosen determines what method would be most effective. In turn, the chosen method determines the techniques that will be used to gather data and the ways this data will be analysed and interpreted.

A *medium* is the means through which a message is communicated from a source to an audience. In many cases, the word 'medium' is used interchangeably with the word 'channel'. If a difference between the two is distinguished, it tends to be that a medium is thought of as more technical or artificial, whereas a channel is more generalized. Media can be divided into three main categories:

- *Natural* media are forms of interaction that transmit information in physiological ways, such as gestures, facial expressions, sensual stimuli, etc.

- *Artefactual* media are forms of interaction that transmit information through artefacts or physical objects, such as books, paintings, carvings, etc.

- *Electronic* media are forms of interaction that transmit information through technologically created devices, such as telephones, televisions, computers, etc.

An interesting distinction between media was made by communication theorist Marshall McLuhan. McLuhan defined the media in terms of their impact on the human senses, and distinguished between 'hot' and 'cool' media. 'Hot' media are defined by their appeal to a single sense and by the linear perception that audiences have of them. Photographs, radio and print are 'hot' media, because they present 'high-definition' information that is grasped through a single sense (eye or ear) and provide all the data needed for receivers to understand them. Cartoons, on the other hand, would be a 'cool' medium because they provide 'low-definition' information, requiring the receiver to use more than one sense to fill in the details. McLuhan argued that the impact of a 'hot' or 'cool' medium depends on the cultural context in which it is introduced. The degree of exposure to the 'hot' media of print, for example, would be a factor in the ability of a culture to adapt to the introduction of other 'hot' media, such as radio (McLuhan 1964: 47).

A *message* is the main information content of an utterance or text. So, even though a text may contain a large amount of information in individual units of meaning, such as sentences or images, a smaller number of messages can be abstracted from this information. In fact, if the aim is to communicate clearly and accurately (as, for example, in technical writing), then each document should contain only one message, even though the message itself may be communicated in a series of sentences containing explanations, examples, etc. The message contained in a set of information would be the core meaning of this information as it was intended by the sender and as it is understood by the receiver (which means that the message the sender sends may not always coincide with the message that the receiver gets).

A *representation* is a constructed pattern or design that describes or stands for something else, such as, for example, a situation, event, feeling, person, etc. Representations are constructed with the use of signs (the topic of Chapter 4). A representation could have a likeness with its object (like a photograph which shows the object depicted) or it could be abstract (like a linguistic description of a scene). Language is to a large extent representational because it creates the object that it describes through words. However, it can also be *referential* when the words used refer to a physical entity in the material world. For example, names are referential because they refer to particular people. If they also symbolize certain qualities, they become representational. This is what happens, for instance, with Robert Louis Stevenson's character Mr Hyde, who *refers* to a character within the fictional world of the novel *Dr Jekyll and Mr Hyde*, but also *represents* certain qualities and behaviours that Stevenson wants his readers to associate with a hidden self. Similarly, a picture of the Eiffel Tower *refers* to the actual building in Paris, but can also *represent* the city of Paris itself through association.

A *code* is the way in which a set of signs are organized into a system. This system regulates, usually according to cultural convention, how the signs may be used to produce meanings. It is important to distinguish between medium and code. On the whole, media deploy different codes. For example, if you decide to convey a message through the way you dress, you choose the medium of non-verbal communication – your body becomes the transmitter of the message. Within this medium, you choose the code of clothes. When a message is put into a code to be transmitted to a receiver, it is *encoded*. The receiver then has to *decode* the message when s/he interprets it. A relatively complicated text, such as a story, can be told through different codes: words, dance, film and even a highly abstract code such as music.

Furthermore, codes may be *broadcast* or *narrowcast* (Fiske 1990). Broadcast codes are shared by a mass audience and are learned through exposure and experience. They involve more 'noise' (defined below) through repetition and cliché. Television soap operas and many Hollywood films are examples of texts that make use of broadcast codes. Narrowcast codes, on the other hand, are aimed at a more limited audience and are often learned with intention rather than through exposure. They tend to involve more subtlety and make use of specialist, 'insider' meanings. Ballet or artistic films would be examples of texts that make use of narrowcast codes.

2.2 Models of communication

The formulation of models in communication studies is generally associated with research in the processes used by the mass media to influence public attitudes. The origins of early models were twofold: first, they reflected the interest of media practitioners to understand the effectiveness of their strategies in the area of public relations, political campaigns and advertising; secondly, they reflected the interest of scholars to understand the modes of interaction between receivers and producers of media messages.

World War II and the concerns it raised over the uses and efficiency of telecommunication provided an impetus to the development of systematic modes of codifying communication processes and thus to the formulation of models. This was compounded by the new economies and technological advancements emerging in the 1940s and 1950s. Two major, foundational models were formulated by the political scientist Harold Lasswell (1948) and the mathematicians Claude Shannon and Warren Weaver (1949) in response to such concerns.

Lasswell's model

Lasswell described the process of communication conveniently and memorably, when he said that an act of communication answers the questions shown in Figure 2.1.

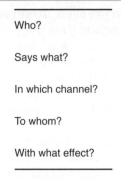

Who?

Says what?

In which channel?

To whom?

With what effect?

Figure 2.1 Lasswell's model

In this model, *who* corresponds to the communicator, *says what* to the message, *in which channel* to the medium, *to whom* to the audience, and *with what effect* to the influence of the message on the audience. Lasswell's model encapsulates the main components of most acts of communication, and is a useful basic tool for conceptualizing and making a schematic representation of communicative interactions. However, it is based on some assumptions that could lead to misleading results. Most importantly, it is a one-way model, assuming that the source of the message intentionally sends out a message that will be received intact and influence a passive recipient. The notions of *interpretation* (what the receiver will 'put in' the message when decoding it) *feedback* (how the sender is influenced by an anticipated or real response of the receiver) and *context* (in what circumstances and settings the exchange takes place) are absent.

Shannon and Weaver's model

Shannon and Weaver were mathematicians working for the Bell telephone company, and their interests in the study of communication had a practical basis: they wanted to know what communication channels could emit the most information, and to what degree 'noise' (intended to mean anything that disrupts clarity and continuity) interfered with the information transmitted. Graphically, their model is shown in Figure 2.2.

In this model, the information source (which could be human or it could refer to a set of technical equipment) produces a message which is transformed into a set of signals by a transmitter. These signals are sent out, via a channel, to a receiver, who reconstructs, or decodes, the message. The received message then reaches the destination. A noise source external to the message can interfere with this process, which means that the message

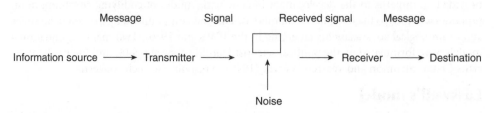

Figure 2.2 Shannon and Weaver's model

> **Feedback** is a mode of assessing if and how one's message has been received. Models based on cybernetics (the science of control) favour feedback because they also favour adjusting a transmission in relation to a response in order to form a stronger relationship with a target audience. Feedback does not have to be intentional. If you talk to someone face to face, his/her expression will give you feedback on how your words are received. If you speak without observing the other person's reaction, you are closing off the communicative act from feedback and relying on message structure only.

reaches the recipient in a distorted form and may cause failures in communication. This 'noise' may be any element that is not relevant to the message but acts as an extraneous factor – in this respect silence could also be 'noise'.

This is a somewhat more sophisticated model than that of Lasswell, making a distinction between source and transmitter and between receiver and destination. Although it has been criticized for not allowing for the influence of anticipated feedback in constructing and transmitting a message, it does provide a useful generalization about the main participants and procedure in an act of communication.

A significant feature of Shannon and Weaver's model is that it emphasizes process over meaning or content and allows logic and efficiency to emerge as achievable objectives, without interference from the human cognitive operation of interpretation and meaning. Therefore, this model highlights the concern of many telecommunications engineers to enhance the functionality of equipment and strengthen the relationship between technology and corporate organizations.

Gerbner's model

The mass media researcher George Gerbner (1956) was one of the first to attempt a model of communication for general use among communication specialists. One of the characteristics of his model was precisely that it could be adapted to suit the purposes of different research projects, which was something that previous models did not do. Gerbner described the model both verbally and graphically. The verbal version is shown in Figure 2.3.

Interestingly, in this model, the process of communication begins with an act of perception, rather than with a disembodied intention, which was the case in the models described previously. In this respect, it brings in a sensory element (or at least a response to an external situation, if the sender is non-human) to the process of communication. This model also includes the category of a perceived event that motivates the act of communication and acts as a contextual, or circumstantial, factor. In addition, Gerbner divides the act of perception into 'transactional' and 'psychophysical'. In the first, the perception is influenced by the perceiver's assumptions, experience, point of view, etc. The result is thus tied to factors inherent to the perceiver and is more subjective and unpredictable. In the second, the perception is influenced by factors pertaining to the event perceived, such as the conditions in which the event takes place, and leads to more predictable responses.

In the next step, the perceiver communicates about the event to another party. This message consists of content and shape or form: that is, the propositions that carry the information and the way in which these propositions are presented. The message is then perceived by the recipient, who, in turn, becomes a potential communicator following a similar process as the one who produced the message.

1. Someone (or 'something', in the case of a mechanical communicator)

2. perceives an event

3. and reacts

4. in a situation

5. through some means

6. to make available materials

7. in some form

8. and context

9. conveying content

10. with some consequence

Figure 2.3 Gerbner's model 1

The model can be represented graphically, as shown in Figure 2.4. This model, then, differs from the ones described above by allowing for more unpredictability, subjectivity and selectivity in message construction and transmission. By positioning the receiver as potential communicator, this model also opens up the possibility of response.

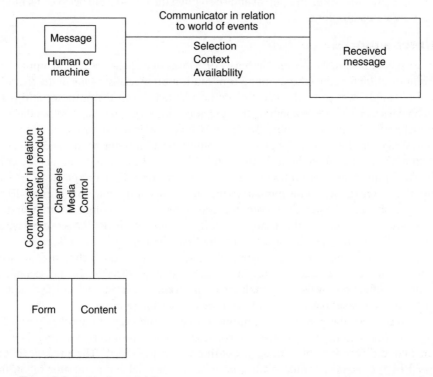

Figure 2.4 Gerbner's model 2

Jakobson's model

A very influential model of communication, especially in the study of oral verbal texts (i.e. spoken interaction), has been formulated by linguist Roman Jakobson (1960). In line with the formalist tradition (described in Chapter 4), Jakobson was interested in finding out the linguistic techniques that artists used to construct their symbolism. His model has subsequently been applied to a variety of texts of different types or genres. Jakobson's model has two layers: the *constitutive factors* of communication and the *functions* of communication. This is how Jakobson (1960: 353) describes the model:

> The addresser sends a message to the addressee. To be operative the message requires a context referred to ('referent' in another, somewhat ambivalent, nomenclature), seizable by the addressee. And either verbal or capable of being verbalized, a code fully, or at least partially, common to the addresser and addressee (or, in other words, to the encoder and decoder of the message); and finally, a contact, a physical channel and psychological connection between the addresser and the addressee, enabling both of them to stay in communication.

The constitutive factors of communication are shown in Figure 2.5.

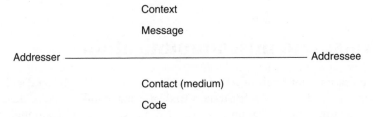

Context

Message

Addresser ———————————————————————————— Addressee

Contact (medium)

Code

Figure 2.5 Jakobson's constitutive model

Simply put, this means: when I communicate, I (the *addresser*) send a message to someone else (the *addressee*). My message is delivered through a contact (the *medium*), is formatted in a *code* (the English language or, in cases of non-verbal communication, my gestures and/or clothes), and is affected by the *context* in which it is given (for example, the topic of 'the meaning of life' would be understood differently in a philosophy lecture than it would at a funeral).

The functions of communication map on to the constitutive factors and are shown in Figure 2.6.

	Referential	
Emotive	Poetic	Conative
	Phatic	
	Metalingual	

Figure 2.6 Jakobson's functions model

The *emotive* function describes the relations between the message and the addresser; if a message is strongly based on this function, it is coloured by the sender's emotive state. For example, romantic poetry typifies the emotive function. The emotive function is I-centred.

The *conative* function, its opposite, describes the relations between the message and the addressee. For example, a set of instructions or a user manual typifies the conative function. The conative function is you-centred.

The *referential* function describes the relations between the message and the world. For example, scientific texts or texts that value objectivity and factual accuracy typify this function.

The *poetic* function describes the relations of the message with itself – the world constructed within the text. For example, texts of fiction and poetry typify this function.

The *phatic* function describes the relations of the message with the connection established between addresser and addressee. The main purpose of this function is to maintain communication between the two parties, even in cases where there is 'noise'. For example, repetitions of a message to make sure it 'got across' and interjections such as 'did you get that?' in oral speech typify this function.

The *metalingual* function describes the relations between the message and the code in which it is constructed. For example, explanations about how a message should be understood ('I mean that . . .') and definitions of specialist terminology typify this function.

2.3 Noise and miscommunication

Miscommunication (not receiving a message as it was intended by the sender) is one of the most salient reasons for, at best, frustration, and, at worst, conflict, and is, therefore, especially interesting to communication theorists. 'Noise' can cause miscommunication when the two parties in a communicative interaction do not 'read' each others' signals correctly, allow their assumptions to shadow the situation as it unfolds, or are unaware of the signals they project. This section looks at two important causes of miscommunication: *message distortion* and *information overload*.

Message distortion

'Noise' is an inherent part of communication. A message is rarely transmitted from a sender to a receiver without some form of interference, whether this interference is mechanical (a 'bad' phone line), or psychological (lack of concentration on the part of the listener). The reasons that a message may be distorted, or the types of noise, include:

- contextual factors, where the message is distorted because of certain elements in the environment in which the communication takes place: examples include attempting to conduct a conversation at a construction site and trying to read a book in extreme temperatures.

- technical factors, where the message is distorted because of faults in the medium used: examples include a distorted signal in a television set, and cases where one party has sent another a message using a digital code that the receiver cannot decode because s/he does not have the appropriate software.

- perceptual factors, where the message is distorted because of the receiver's psychological and/or physical condition: examples include cases where at least one party in the communicative act is under the influence of a drug or alcohol and cases where one party is deaf and the medium of communication is spoken language.

Miscommunication occurs when the message that the sender intended is not the same as the message that the audience received.	Miscommunication is a major source of conflict, and can be due to personal, technical or circumstantial factors.

- cognitive factors where the sender and receiver do not speak the same language or have vastly different systems of reference for the knowledge communicated: examples include communication between speakers of different languages where each has inadequate knowledge of the language of the other, communication between an expert and a non-specialist, and communication between proponents of contradictory ideologies.

These factors are inclusive, which means that a combination of two or more may be present in a communicative interaction. Of course, the more noise factors are present, the more likely it is that communication will be ineffective. When there is noise in a communicative act, the receiver consciously or unconsciously attempts to compensate in order to understand the message. Here are some ways in which receivers attempt to reduce noise. Keep in mind that not all of these necessarily occur in the same message or series of messages:

- *Adding.* The receiver may add details to embellish, fill in gaps and make the message more sensible and plausible, especially in areas that s/he has not completely understood.

- *Assimilating.* The receiver may distort details and/or the order in which they appear to fit in with his/her past experiences, expectancy sets, attitudes and prior input and output.

- *Changing.* The receiver may change details in content and/or emphasis from the original. This is usually done to make more sense of the message.

- *Levelling/deleting information.* Receivers have a tendency to shorten and make more concise a set of information so as to understand and reproduce it more easily. When levelling, receivers use fewer words and retain fewer details.

- *Sharpening.* Receivers tend to select for attention and retention certain elements from the complex set of details in a message. They then highlight and focus on the retained details so that these may take on disproportionate importance. Sharpening is the opposite of levelling.

To minimize the possibility of distortion and to reduce noise, the sender can take some measures, most significantly the following:

- *Analyse the audience.* Knowing the receivers well enough to be familiar with their perceptual filters, vocabulary level, knowledge of specialist jargon, information needs, etc. can be instrumental in designing communication content that will be understood as intended. This is why audience analysis (in other words, finding out what various sectors of the public want) is a major area of interest and research in advertising and the media industries.

- *Control the amount of information in the message.* Complicated information or messages that are densely packed with information are more likely to cause information overload and distort the message. When one needs to communicate large pieces of information, the best way would be to section it into easily manageable chunks, and provide highlighting signals (such as headings or titles, introductory sentences to each section, etc.).

Audience analysis is a fundamental factor in the successful communication of a message. Knowing who will receive the message, their level of knowledge of the topic, their values and beliefs, and the physical circumstances in which they will receive the message help to minimize the risks of miscommunication.

- *Control serial transmission.* If a message has to pass through many links in a communication chain, there is a greater risk of distortion. This can be avoided if links are limited, where possible, by communicating to the intended, or primary, audience directly.

- *Encourage similarity between communicators.* The more similarities exist between sender and receiver, in attitude, knowledge of jargon, experiences, values, consumer tastes, etc., the less likely it is for a message to be distorted.

- *Be receptive to feedback.* Asking for feedback from the receiver allows for possible distortions to be clarified and corrected.

Information overload

Information overload occurs when people or systems receive information at a faster rate than they can process it. As input increases, output may also increase up to a point, but when input is too great, breakdown occurs. As tension within the receivers builds, errors in processing the information may increase. The following are some typical reactive behaviours through which individuals and groups handle overload. Strive to avoid them if you are a receiver of information, but be prepared to deal with them if you are a sender.

Reactive perceptual methods

These are common behaviours that tend to decrease the tension and overload, but may increase the possibility of errors:

- *Levelling*: dropping out information, some of which may be important.

- *Assimilation*: making undetected errors, owing to the process of assimilation and closure, where the information is made to fit, often unconsciously, into a person's frame of reference.

- *Queuing*: ordering information on a 'first come, first served' basis, instead of allowing it to come through all at once before the process of interpretation begins.

Reactive arbitrary methods

These are responses that may decrease the tension, but can be destructive to communication flow:

- *Arbitrary rules*: using random rules to select and manage information. For example, in organizational communication it could be reading only full-page memos, or not looking at any memo that is on coloured paper.

- *Escape*: avoiding the overload, as happens, for example, when one goes to sleep, becomes ill, drinks alcohol, leaves the scene, etc.

An audience can be **proactive** in receiving a message, in which case they will attempt to understand it on its own terms and use the information that it contains effectively, or they can be **reactive**, in which case they will resist any new or challenging information in the message and instead attempt to position it in already-formed categories in order to make it familiar and therefore easier to understand.

In addition to these, there are some 'rational' methods that can decrease the tension and overload while also decreasing the possibility of errors. These are *proactive* methods, and include:

- *Chunking*: grouping things of the same type together, such as the way digits are grouped together in telephone numbers.
- *Filtering*: selecting the highest priority information first and dealing only with pertinent messages. In organizational communication, filtering can also be used to navigate through the hierarchy of an organization in order to address or obtain feedback from the appropriate person.

Knowing that message recipients may chunk and filter the information they receive allows the sender to organize this information in such a way as to make these processing methods more effective. For example, by sectioning information under appropriate headings in a written document, the writer is wisely anticipating the chunking effect.

2.4 Methods of communication research

Broadly speaking, the methods used to study the factors involved in communication tend to fall into two main categories: *quantitative* methods and *qualitative* methods.

Quantitative methods

Quantitative approaches aim to predict social outcomes by analysing society and social interactive processes along rational and scientific lines. Following the lead of natural science, they do this by collecting measurable data obtained through a variety of research techniques. These include questionnaires, surveys, physical experiments and statistical analyses. Quantitative research is rooted in empirical science, and uses mathematical models to measure and classify observed phenomena.

Quantitative approaches tend to be used when there is concern that the results reached will be used to implement changes, or in communities where factual and measurable information is valued (such as many types of scientific communities, for example). As regards social science, quantitative research is often undertaken in the public sector to discover ways to improve the delivery of social policies, the planning of future developments and the maintenance of community infrastructures. In the private sector, quantitative research is often linked to the provision of resources and the development of new marketable products.

Quantitative research tends to be associated with statistical analysis. However, not all quantitative data lend themselves to this. Generally, there are two reasons that a statistical analysis may not be appropriate. One is that statistical tests can only be interpreted in a useful way if random samples have been taken from well-defined populations. In that case, the objective is to find out if the samples are correct representations of the populations or can be attributed to chance. As a whole, for example, research based on case studies does not use clearly defined populations, and so statistical analyses would not be suitable when analysing case studies. The second reason is that statistical tests are only justifiable when the researcher has stated a hypothesis to be tested before carrying out the data collection. By first looking at the data, as, for example, in ethnographic research, it would be difficult to establish statistical significance.

Content analysis

Content analysis is a popular quantitative method used to analyse the composition of texts. It is used to trace the frequency and/or combination of particular words, phrases or images in a text or body of texts. In the words of Bernard Berelson (1952: 18), one of the earlier theorists of the method, 'content analysis is a research technique for the objective, systematic, and quantitative description of the manifest content of communication'.

Content analysis usually takes these steps:

- defining the research problem;
- selecting texts;
- defining analytical categories;
- constructing a coding schedule (used in mass media research);
- piloting the coding schedule and checking reliability (used in mass media research);
- analysing the data.

Defining the research problem will actually show the researcher if content analysis is the best method to use. The researcher begins by posing a specific question that focuses the research and identifies the issues that need to be addressed. This will show what the researcher hopes to achieve by analysing a body of texts – what aspect of communication the proposed research will throw light on. If frequency and extended comparison are important in answering the question, then content analysis would most likely be a suitable method.

Selecting texts follows the decision to undertake content analysis. Since it is impossible and unproductive to analyse all types of text on a given topic, a sample should be carefully selected. Content analysis has the advantage that it can cover an extensive body of texts, but it too needs to be delimited and focused. First, the content analyst selects the media and/or document type on which s/he will focus his/her research, for example newspapers, television, magazines, e-mail messages circulated in a company, etc. Secondly, s/he chooses the period of time that will be covered in the research. Thirdly, s/he selects relevant content from the document types or media that s/he has chosen. For example, if television news is chosen as the media type, a further delimitation could be evening news, daytime news, all news on cable TV, etc. Or, if popular science feature articles are chosen as the medium, a further sampling would specify which magazines carry this content.

Defining analytical categories means describing the dimensions or parameters that will be covered in the research: that is, the aspects of the text that will yield significant information in relation to the research question. At this stage, it is important to concentrate on what can be interpreted within the framework set by the research, and not to include everything that can be counted (as is sometimes the temptation to do). What categories will be chosen depends on the research question. For example, in media studies, common categories used include 'identifier' (the medium or text type), 'date' and 'position' (such as page in print media, or schedule in broadcast media).

Constructing a coding schedule (used in mass media research) is done at the same time as defining the categories. It is the design of a survey-type document listing the categories that will be checked for each item in the corpus. The coding schedule sets out the variables and the values that will be used for the content analysis. The researcher reads through, or views in the case of image-based texts, each text in the corpus and fills in the coding boxes in the schedule.

Piloting the coding schedule and checking reliability on a small sample of the corpus is significant before embarking on a full-scale analysis, because inconsistencies in the categories and media used can become apparent and help to avoid hassles later on. Checking the schedule will help to ensure that the categories used do not mix different levels of classification (so that, say, in a market analysis, 'age' and 'sex' are not mixed by including such categories as 'male', 'female' and 'children'), or that enough differentiation is allowed in the definition of categories (so that, for example, in an analysis of advertising, there is not just a category 'beverages', but a further subdivision into types of beverages).

Analysing the data entails using a software application to sort through the information on the coding schedules so that the researcher can trace patterns and apply a theoretical framework to draw some inferences. In this stage, the material collected can be used to answer the initial question that prompted the research.

As with other quantitative approaches to human behaviour, the 'objectivity' of content analysis must be viewed with caution. Even if content analysts do not explicitly judge or evaluate the data they collect, they still select and classify the textual aspects that they want to examine, and this inevitably involves choice, which carries an element of arbitrariness. In addition, a potential problem of content analysis is that, although it helps to identify the relative prominence or absence of key characteristics in texts, the inferences that can be drawn from its results depend on the assumptions that underlay the analysis in the first place. For example, it would be ungrounded and misleading to assume that the absence of references to the female gender in a number of issues of, say, a sports magazine is enough to claim that the magazine is sexist. As structuralist theorist Burgelin (1972: 319) notes, 'above all, there is no reason to assume that the item which recurs most frequently is the most important or the most significant, for a text is, clearly, a structured whole, and the place occupied by the different elements is more important than the number of times they recur'.

We return to quantitative methods when we discuss mass communication in Chapter 6.

Qualitative methods

Qualitative approaches aim to promote understanding rather than precise measurement. Such methods include ethnographic participation, critical text analysis and the application of critical theory to interpret perceived signs. Qualitative research encompasses factors pertaining to subjective perception of the world and to cultural relativity. For this approach, what matters is how people interpret their perceptions of their environment and how they

Qualitative methods of research define and explore ideas, concepts and experiential observations. Their approach is analytic and often argumentative. **Quantitative methods** of research test a hypothesis by experimental means, reaching conclusions that can be measured on a numerical scale. Their approach is descriptive.

construct, mentally and socially, the realities that guide their behaviour. Qualitative methods recognize that reality can be diverse and open to interpretation and that not all phenomena or ideas have a quantifiable element. Consequently, they are chiefly interested in ascertaining the meanings and patterns of behaviour that are created through human interaction and relationships.

For example, an influential group of qualitative approaches is classified under the title of 'social constructivism'. These approaches maintain that we do not experience the world directly but as our culture reveals it to us. 'Discourse' is a very important part of this process, as it is primarily through discourse that we acquire our world-views or conceptual filters. To accomplish our goals, we choose certain lines of action and follow certain rules laid down by our culture. 'Culture', in this context, does not refer only to national characteristics, such as food and clothes. Rather it refers to condoned and sanctioned forms of behaviour and to sets of values that are present in the interactions of a group or collectivity, such as a company, a group of rock fans, an ethnic minority group or a group of individuals with a particular sexual orientation. Talking about organizations, for example, organizational theorist Geert Hofstede (1991: 180) defines culture as 'the collective programming of the mind which distinguishes the members of one organization from another', and talks of it as the software of the mind (more on culture in Chapter 5).

Social constructivist approaches to communication shift the emphasis from the rationalist, linear model of telecommunications engineers (such as Shannon and Weaver), which privileged efficient delivery of a message, to the shared construction of meaning between sender and receiver. In this respect, the cultural approach understands communication not only as the sending and receiving of messages but also as 'a symbolic process whereby reality is produced, maintained, repaired or transformed' (Carey 1992: 23).

Social constructivism underlies various ethnographic approaches to communication, where the researcher observes behaviour and presents descriptive accounts of it. *Ethnomethodology* and *participant observation* are two such approaches.

Ethnomethodology

Ethnomethodology assumes that people have common understandings that are reflected in the way they reason, or their 'grounds for inference'. This method was developed by UCLA sociologist Harold Garfinkel (1967) with the aim of understanding how people in everyday life give meaning to various events. Ethnomethodology is very difficult to describe, let alone to define, mainly because, in line with its tenets that do not support 'objective truth', it does not use formal models of analysis. Ethnomethodologists observe people's behaviour in everyday interaction and describe how those people, through their conversations and actions, interpret and evaluate the situations in which they find themselves. Ethnomethodologists generally do not explain people's actions with respect to a specific theory, but instead describe the ways those people themselves interpret their actions. Here is how Garfinkel describes the mission of his method in the opening pages of *Studies in Ethnomethodology*:

> The following studies seek to treat practical activities, practical circumstances, and practical socio-logical reasonings as topics of empirical study, and by paying to the most commonplace activities of daily life the attention usually accorded extraordinary events to learn about them as phenomena in their own right (1967: 1).

How do ethnomethodologists achieve this? They take familiar scenes in people's lives and 'ask what can be done to make trouble' and to 'produce and sustain bewilderment, consternation, and confusion; to produce the social structured affects of anxiety, shame, guilt and indignation; and to produce disorganized interaction' (1967: 37-8). This way, Garfinkel claims, we can understand people's definition of normality and the assumptions that underlie human relations. For example, in one case study, Garfinkel asked his students to perform an experiment: to take everything said to them literally and to ask people for clarification even about questions and statements that would generally be considered self-evident. Thus, in one case, when a person was telling one of the students that he had a flat tyre, the student asked what he meant by a flat tyre. In another case, a friend of the student asked him how his girlfriend was feeling. The student asked whether the friend meant how she was doing physically or mentally? In both cases the 'subjects' of the experiment were confused and, in the second case, the 'subject' changed the topic completely.

This approach can be adapted for media and mass communication research. For example, the same questions that ethnomethodologists ask of social interaction can be asked of dialogues and actions in television shows, song lyrics and other media texts. Even though these are fictional constructs created by writers, they still exhibit the same codes and underlying belief systems as natural texts do. The producers of these media texts not only share the perceptions of their target audiences (otherwise their work would have no appeal) but also have the power to influence those audiences by telling a story from a particular angle and thereby directing audience response. By using ethnomethodological methods of analysis for media texts, we can trace not only common assumptions, but also the attempts that people make to influence such assumptions by 'breaking the code', either seriously (as in activist texts) or humorously (as in comedies).

Similar studies have been carried out in the field of natural science. To cite one example, the sociologists Bruno Latour and Stephen Woolgar (1979) entered the Stalk Institute for Biological Studies to study the collaboration of scientists there. How did the scientists determine what counted as truth as opposed to opinion? After months of observation Latour and Woolgar found no genuinely 'rational' way to decide whether one theoretical perspective was more accurate than another. Therefore, they concluded that such decisions were tied to social processes. For example, scientists cite favourably those likely to review their work in the belief that this will increase their chances of publication or other types of 'acceptance', and they often describe the weaknesses of an opposing theory or method without admitting the possibility that their own work can also be seen under a similarly critical eye. This shows the importance of the fact that scientists and other types of investigators exist in communities and that what is taken as truth in these communities depends primarily on social factors such as prestige, negotiation and power.

Participant observation

Participant observation designates a set of 'ethnographic' research practices where the researcher conducts field work in the selected area of study. How much the researcher observes and how much s/he participates depends on the area of study as well as the depth of insight which s/he wants to reach. Even though the participant observers may apply quantitative forms of analysis to the data they collect after they have collected them, during the research period they must rely on their own skills and behaviour rather than on an analytical tool or instrument.

Like other ethnographic researchers, participant observers need three types of skills: skills of observation, skills of interviewing and eliciting information, and skills of retrieving secondary sources (such as scholarly articles and books), which can be used to support explanations of observed data. First, participant observers need to record details of the physical setting in which they work and of the people involved and their reactions to various stimuli. For this they should assume an objective and non-judgemental position, uncoloured, as far as possible, by personal prejudice. Secondly, they need the ability to assess what information is needed in a particular situation and to formulate questionnaires (both formal, as in surveys, and informal, as in coffee-break chats) in order to elicit this information. Thirdly, they need to have done their 'homework' before entering the field situation by consulting existing sources on the topics that are relevant to their research and identifying gaps in the knowledge pool that they may strive to fill, while avoiding what has already been done before. For example, the researcher has to guard against undertaking to prove a point that has already been proven and is, in fact, common knowledge among the scholarly community.

Participant observation methods can be both rewarding and challenging. They can be rewarding because they offer unanticipated insights and discoveries. Since fieldwork is improvised (that is, the researcher has not planned what will happen in the field situation), certain events may be unforeseen and thereby point to directions of interpretation that the researcher may not have expected. Participant observers remain relatively open to on-site developments and impromptu lines of inquiry, whereas those undertaking forms of textual analysis may rely more on models and a theoretical framework in their interpretations.

For similar reasons, these methods can also be challenging and may lead to misleading or erroneous results. Avoiding preconceived ideas is no easy matter, and participant observers will often judge the behaviour they see, even if it is just by classifying it in a specific semantic category. For example, classifying an activity as 'deviant behaviour' carries certain assumptions that colour the interpretation of that activity, even when no explicit criticism of the activity is made. Another reason that data gathered through participant observation has to be received with care is that the sample studied is of necessity quite small. The researcher is physically limited to observing a restricted number of people in specific circumstances, and is subject to the constraints of time and space. Conclusions drawn from such observations can add to the pool of 'case studies' on a given topic, but cannot be used to make far-reaching inferences about the 'state of things' and should not be used for practices with serious consequences, such as policy-making.

Participant observation usually takes these steps:

- design
- access

- field relationships
- collecting and recording data
- analysing data
- write-up.

Design includes knowledge about the topic, an explanation of the reason why this topic is important, the methods that will be used to gather data on the topic, time limitations, and what further action will be taken on the data collected. In fact, in matters of design, research based on participant observation is no different from any other type of research.

Access denotes availability of resources needed to undertake the research, including money, people and documented information, such as archives and records. Access depends a lot on the status of the researcher. In cases where s/he is an insider in the field s/he is observing, it is easier to gain access. In such cases, however, the question arises of where the allegiances of this person lie, or should lie. For example, if the participant observer conducts his/her research in the organization where s/he works, in order to divulge information about the organization to an external source, then this becomes a form of spying and it is open to ethical questions. Similarly, if the participant observer remains loyal to his/her organization by not enabling all relevant information to be made public, then the research will be biased. In cases where the researcher is an outsider to the field, s/he needs permission to access resources. In those cases, it is important to determine the interests of the organization in granting this permission and to make sure that there are no hidden agendas.

Field relationships need to be established as soon as access has been granted. These involve getting to know and forming links with the people the researcher will be observing/working with. Gaining trust and assuring co-operation are very important tasks at this stage. Another task is to dispel any suspicions that may be present. In many cases, people do not like to be studied or to have their behaviour observed and documented, unless they can sympathize with the reason and see that the results will benefit them and/or the common good. For example, since the publication of 'media effects' research, which suggests that the media are largely responsible for increases in violence and aberrant behaviour in society, media-based organizations are reluctant to co-operate with researchers for fear that these researchers may be disparaging of media practices.

Collecting and recording data involves noting down what is observed. At this stage, field notes should aim principally to record by describing what is observed, not to interpret or theorize. They should record data for subsequent interpretation and analysis, and, ideally, they should be written from basic observation notes and memory prompts, within a day or so from the actual observation. Recording data can also be done with a tape recorder, keeping in mind that such recordings can become very long and cumbersome to transcribe and analyse, because of the indiscriminate nature of tape recording.

Analysing data is what the researcher does when s/he has gathered enough information that can be structured and interpreted using selected theoretical principles. Having collected field notes, transcripts and other sources of documentation, it is time to sort through what is there and to identify the material that will be shaped into the final presentation.

Write-up happens at the same time as analysing the data. Writing interpretations and explanations of collected data shows what is missing or is unclear from the information, and, consequently, which sources need to be revisited and which theoretical principles can be employed in the presentation. This stage follows the guidelines of any writing project. The writer writes a draft first and then follows this by revising and polishing the style and reorganizing the information to enhance clarity and readability. The writer should be familiar with the tone and style conventionally adopted in the type of document s/he is producing and with the ideas and concepts that informed readers would expect to see mentioned.

Both ethnomethodology and participant observation are ethnographic methods, where the researcher is physically present in the field s/he is studying. In fact, many writers consider ethnomethodology to be a form of participant observation and use the two terms interchangeably. Confounding the two, however, would be misleading. Ethnomethodology has a stronger subjectivist and relativist inclination. Ethnomethodologists attempt to present their work with minimal intervention, ideally through the testimonies or narratives of the people involved. Participant observation, on the other hand, is not as averse to using quantitative or statistical methods of classification, often producing work that is evaluated with critical distance and objective criteria.

As a final note to this section, it should be pointed out that qualitative and quantitative research methods are not exclusive. They can be used together in one study, for different purposes. Ethnographic research, for example, which consists mostly of describing observed behaviours of a collectivity and is fundamentally qualitative, does use quantitative measurements for some aspects of its collected data. This is how Saville-Troike (2002: 119) describes the balancing of the two methods:

> Quantitative methods are essentially techniques for measuring the degree of consistency in behaviour, and the amount and nature of variation under different circumstances, but if quantitative methods are to be used, they must first be developed and validated by qualitative procedures. Quantitative procedures may in turn serve to determine the reliability of qualitative observation, which is apt to be casual and uncontrolled, and the validity of generalizations which may be made on the basis of a very limited sample.

In any case, the choice of method should reflect appropriately the purposes and objectives of the study to be carried out. In addition, practical factors, such as access to resources and time/money limitations, play a role in determining how to approach a particular issue. We return to qualitative methods when we discuss text analysis in the next two chapters.

2.5 Post-modernism

The set of approaches grouped under the term 'post-modernism' are not easy to describe or to classify, and, in fact, cannot be defined as research methods in the accepted sense; rather, they are closer to attitudes about the world and about the nature of knowledge. The decision to include this section after describing quantitative and qualitative methods comes from the fact that post-modern attitudes are deliberately eccentric, refuting or ignoring many of the research procedures followed by non-post-modernist writers and opting for a more anarchic orientation. Therefore, they provide an alternative to methods such as those described above, justifying the positioning of this section as a conclusion to the above discussion.

The semiotician Umberto Eco gives an interesting (and post-modernist) definition of post-modernism, in the postscript to his novel *The Name of the Rose* (1983: 67). In this he describes the post-modern attitude as 'that of a man who loves a very cultured woman and knows he cannot say to her "I love you madly" because he knows that she knows (and that she knows that he knows) that these words have already been written by Barbara Cartland'.

Post-modernism designates a set of attitudes towards the nature of knowledge – how we know things and how what we know is influenced by what we believe. It is for the most part based on the idea that the world does not function according to rational laws and that the most challenging of human issues are beyond the grasp of scientific approaches. For post-modern writers, identity is not fixed, and ethical concepts, as well as the notion of truth itself, are not absolute but relative to circumstances and cultural values. In fact, some radical post-modernist approaches contend the positivist–empirical tenets that human actions are based on fixed roles and that ethical principles are universal and absolute. Instead, they espouse a world that can be known only through probability and not through certainty.

Post-modernism is a term developed in architecture to describe construction models that broke apart from classical styles, and was initially introduced in the humanities by the work of Jean-Francois Lyotard. It is contrasted to 'modernism', a term usually applied to the period from the end of the nineteenth century to World War II. That period was marked by various socio-cultural developments, most notably the development of capitalism, industrialism, the nuclear family and the tenets of individualism and private property that are connected with these factors. The social, cultural and political phenomena associated with modernism generally include:

- the emergence of capitalism as the dominant economic form based on private property, and national economies based primarily on free trade and market exchange;

- the development of industrial modes of production and an increasing reliance on science and technology;

- the growth of cities and the correlative development of increasingly complex transportation networks;

- trust in the ability of the scientific approach to provide solutions to many human and social problems, and a correlative adoption of this approach in discourses outside science;

- definitions of identity and agency based on individual characteristics, such as 'genetic make-up' and 'personality';

- the development of an ideological framework based on universalist values and rationality.

Modernist approaches to social conditions, such as Marxism and Freudian psychoanalysis, tend to look at how meaning is produced through conflict, usually between a hidden or deep layer of structures, whether in the mind or in society, and an apparent, surface layer of observable phenomena. The hidden layer is usually seen as a causal factor determining overt modes of behaviour.

Post-modern approaches tend to replace such depth models with a conception of practices (as opposed to objects), intertextual discourse (as opposed to individual consciousness) and textual play (as opposed to inherent meaning) (Jameson 1991). Depth is considered as an illusion and replaced with multiple surfaces, best illustrated by one of the master metaphors of post-modernism: the screen. The screen is a fortuitous metaphor, since it also brings into the picture the role of the media. In fact, the beginnings of post-modernism are characterized by the development of global media, the rapidly increasing role of technology in the representation and communication of knowledge, and the rise of media studies in universities.

Generally speaking, post-modernism includes the following phenomena:

- A conception of personal identity as fragmented or dispersed, mostly owing to our participation in many, and sometimes contradictory, contexts (simple examples being drastic career changes, drastic geographical relocations, the dissolution of the nuclear family and the proliferation of multiple marriages).

- An abandonment of the search for origins, the original, universal or transcendental cause. This includes the dissolution of the modernist–romantic notion of genius, the inspired creator of the new. The original work is replaced with intertextuality (cross-reference), parody and self-parody, an acceptance of contradiction as having no resolution, and a strong use of irony.

- A questioning of notions of linear reality and linear – causally based – narratives, opting for parallel universes or multiple realities. This questions modernist notions of subjectivity and stream-of-consciousness-type discourses, replacing them with a series of disconnected and/or fragmented images (collage), infinite regress-type techniques, ironic uses of sound or non-synchronized sound in multi-media texts, etc.

- Socio-cultural developments associated with the mass media, such as internationalization of information (people receive the same information through global channels around the world) and a dramatization of information that tends to blur distinctions between 'truth' and 'fiction'.

- Political practices based on group and cultural membership rather than on universalist and totalizing projects: for example, feminist, gay and other diversity-oriented groups form political unions that are increasingly replacing modernist ideological systems such as communism.

A major feature of the post-modern attitude is to question notions of objectivity and scientific legitimacy, as expressed by Jean-François Lyotard (1984: 29)

'How do you prove the proof?' or, more generally, 'Who decides the conditions of truth?' It is recognized that the conditions of truth, in other words, the rules of the game of science, are immanent in that game, that they can only be established within the bounds of a debate that is already scientific in nature, and that there is no other proof that the rules are good than the consensus extended to them by experts.

The concept of **subjectivity** is used in communication theory to understand the ways in which individuals form identities in particular social contexts by means of their personal experiences and the meanings that those contexts make available to them to interpret these experiences. This way, one's subjectivity is produced in the interface between personal desires and beliefs (an internal dimension), and socially constructed rules of interaction (an external dimension).

Another major theorist who has continued the questioning of objective truth is philosopher of science Paul Feyerabend. For example, in his caustic book *Against Method* (1976), he discusses the circumstances surrounding Galileo's theories about the sun-centred universe. Galileo is typically credited with carrying out the experiments needed to prove that the sun, and not the earth, as was believed till then, lay at the centre of our solar system. Yet, argues Feyerabend, when we look closely at what happened, we see that Galileo did not empirically disprove that the sun revolves around the earth. In fact, his opponents had empirical proof to support this: do we not see the sun rise and set while we, on earth, remain immobile? Actually the force of Galileo's arguments lay in his assumptions about the significance of evidence collected through the telescope. If one questioned the value of the telescope in providing verifiable data, one would automatically also doubt the 'truth' of Galileo's argument. So, to accept his argument, one actually had to be committed to the belief that telescopic data were valid, which made 'truth' and 'proof' closely dependent on a particular world-view: one first had to believe in order to know.

Besides those who focus on general claims about the nature of knowledge (such as Lyotard and Feyerabend), many who comment on contemporary social situations have also questioned notions of an objective reality. For example, according to influential post-modern theorist Jean Baudrillard, 'reality' cannot be known or accessed in an immediate fashion, through the senses or through the intellect. Instead, we know it through its representations, and especially through its media representations. Baudrillard uses the term 'simulacrum' to describe the various artificial environments that mediate our perception of the world. What we know about reality is influenced by the way we know it – the media through which our objects of knowledge are represented and communicated. In this conception, signs function as commodities and operate in a universal code that generates 'nothing but a gigantic simulation model of meaning' (Baudrillard 1988: 91).

To understand this statement, one only has to think of how television channels compete with each other by advertising their news as the most interesting, compelling, up-to-date or accurate. It is, therefore, more a case of who presents the 'best' news, rather than what the news actually is. Crisis situations, such as the London underground bombings on 7 July 2005 or the 11 September 2001 attacks on the World Trade Centre in New York, have been presented by the media in a highly dramatized way, using techniques created in film and the creative arts and thereby casting doubt on the distinction between reality and representation. Models of reality (images that stand in for 'the real thing') have taken over in the post-modern era, and produced a hyped-up and contrived form of reality, which Baudrillard calls 'hyper-reality'.

Of course, the question could be asked whether there ever was a more authentic version of reality or whether it is part of our psychological make-up to know the world by means of what we already know about it. If this is so, writings such as those of Baudrillard could reflect a misplaced nostalgia for a time that never was. This is not the place to engage in such a debate. Nevertheless, the possibility should be pointed out as an example of the kind of discussion that arises around issues of post-modernism.

The post-modern is also the post-human, in that the human-centred universe of capitalism and the Enlightenment has given way to the anonymous but highly influential and powerful consumer and to self-proclaimed group interests. The notion of community and of belonging is also different in post-modernism. Belonging to a group defined by race, blood ties, name or geographical proximity is superseded by belonging to a consumer group – a group of individuals with similar consumer tastes.

Cyberculture is a term designating all activities performed using the medium of computers. First coined by William Gibson in his novel *Neuromancer* (1984), the term **cyberspace** is now used to describe the space where cyberculture takes place – the digital world accessed through the computer interface. This world hosts many types of behaviours, from business transactions to the subversively creative activities known as **cyberpunk.**

Cyberculture has contributed to the development of new forms of identity that have replaced older versions based on sex, age and race. Electronic technologies have the power to produce virtual doubles of the body, as in virtual reality, or the textually created character descriptions, 'avatars', of multi-user computer games. Once again, the idea of a true self hidden in the depth of interiority is replaced with a decentred self acting out its many roles in public performance. In cyberculture, bodies are often conceived as changeable, disposable commodities, and stepping into a new body means adopting a new identity. In fact, officially classified as a disorder, 'multiple personalities' is championed by many prophets of cyberculture as a trendy mode of behaviour.

▊ Summary

◆ Foundational terms of communication theory include *text, model, method, medium, message, representation* and *code*.

◆ A great part of communication theory is based on models, many of which were developed in the period after World War II. Lasswell's model was designed to study public opinion in relation to political campaigns, and Shannon and Weaver's model was designed to study telecommunications processes. This places the origins of communication theory in the fields of politics and technology.

◆ Many early models of communication had a one-way orientation, from a sender to a receiver. This neglected the role of feedback or receiver-response in activating a piece of information and turning it into a message.

◆ Roman Jakobson's model of language functions, although still unilinear, introduced the element of purpose and context in the conceptualization of communication processes. This opened the way to allowing for the creative and the artistic in theorizing communication.

◆ Miscommunication is an important part of the study of communication. Miscommunication occurs when the message does not reach the receiver in the way it was intended by the sender. This often happens because there is 'noise' in the communication environment. 'Noise' is defined as any form of interference in the transmission of the message, including psychological elements, such as the receiver's lack of attention, ineffective message construction, such as information overload, technical glitches, such as the malfunctioning of equipment, and physical constraints, such as extremes of temperature in the setting where the communication takes place.

◆ Methods of data analysis fall into two broad categories: quantitative and qualitative. Quantitative methods favour measurement while qualitative methods favour interpretation.

◆ The group of approaches classified under the term 'post-modernism' resist traditional methods and even question the belief that we can know the world through any method as such. Instead of rational or systematic analysis, they propose a more fluid and playful orientation to knowledge.

■ Topics for discussion

▶ Brainstorm some cultural assumptions about identity that are typical of your culture. These could include assumptions and stereotypes about gender (for example, the belief that girls do not understand mathematics), about age (for example, the belief that those over the age of 50 do not enjoy wild parties), about sexuality (for example, the belief that gay men are effeminate), or combinations of these (for example, the belief that women over the age of 30 are mothers). Then read three issues of a popular magazine and watch three episodes of a popular television series. How are the stereotypes and assumptions that you brainstormed represented in these texts? You could extend this exercise by discussing the magazine articles and the shows with people you know who are consumers of these media objects. Did they notice the assumptions you noted? What was their reaction to them?

▶ Select a short story or an extract from a film. Analyse the language used in the dialogue according to Jakobson's model. How is this language used strategically to develop the story? If you are analysing a visual text, explain how visual signs, such as colours and the appearance of characters, reinforce the effect created by verbal signs.

▶ Find an article in an academic journal that presents quantitative research. Notice how facts and figures are used in combination with reasoning and interpretation in the writing of the article. How would the research findings be different if the writers had not used a quantitative method? Could the writers have used a qualitative method, or was only a quantitative approach suitable for this research topic? You may want to do this exercise in a small group and then describe your conclusions to the class.

■ References and further reading

Baudrillard, J. (1988) *Selected Writings*, ed. by M. Poster. Cambridge: Polity Press.

Berelson, B. (1952) *Content Analysis in Communication Research*. Glencoe, IL: Free Press.

Berger, A. A. (2000) *Media and Communication Research Methods: An Introduction to Qualitative and Quantitative Approaches*. Thousand Oaks, CA and London: Sage.

Burgelin, O. (1972) 'Structural Analysis and Mass Communication', in D. McQuail (ed.), *Sociology of Mass Communications*, pp. 313–28. Harmondsworth: Penguin.

Carey, J. (1992) *Communication as Culture.* New York: Routledge.

Cobley, P. (ed.) (1996) *The Communication Theory Reader.* London: Routledge.

Deacon, D. Pickering, P. and Murdock, G. (1999) *Researching Communications.* London: Arnold.

Eco, U. (1983) *The Name of the Rose,* London: Harvest Books.

Feyerabend, P. (1976) *Against Method: Outline of an Anarchistic Theory of Knowledge.* London: New Left Books.

Fiske, J. (1990) *Introduction to Communication Studies,* 2nd edn. London: Routledge.

Garfinkel, H. (1967) *Studies in Ethnomethodology.* Oxford: Blackwell.

Gerbner, G. (1956) 'Toward a General Model of Communication', *Audio-Visual Communication Review,* 4, pp. 171-99.

Gerbner, G. (1964) 'On Content Analysis and Critical Research in Mass Communication', in L. A. Dexter and D. M. White (eds) *People, Society and Mass Communications.* New York : The Free Press.

Gibson, W. (1984) *Neuromancer.* London: Penguin.

Hansen, A., Cottle, S., Negrinne, R. and Newbold, C. (eds) (1998) *Mass Communication Research Methods.* London: Palgrave Macmillan.

Hofstede, G. (1991) *Cultures and Organizations.* London: McGraw-Hill.

Jakobson, R. (1960) 'Linguistics and Poetics', in T. A. Sebeok (ed.) *Style and Language.* Cambridge, MA: MIT Press, pp. 34-45.

Jameson, F. (1991) *Postmodernism, or the Cultural Logic of Late Capitalism.* London: Verso.

Lasswell, H. D. (1948) 'The Structure and Function of Communication in Society', in Bryson (ed.), *The Communication of Ideas.* New York: Harper and Brothers.

Latour, B. and Woolgar, S. (1979) *Laboratory Life: The Construction of Scientific Facts.* Thousand Oaks, CA: Sage.

Lazarsfeld, P. F., Berelson, B. and Gaudet, H. (1968) [1944] *The People's Choice: How the Voter Makes up his Mind in a Presidential Election.* New York: Columbia University Press.

Lazarsfeld, P. F. and Merton, R. K. (1964) 'Friendship as a Social Process: A Substantive and Methodological Analysis', in M. Berger et al. (eds) *Freedom and Control in Modern Society.* New York: Octagon.

Lindlof, Thomas (1995) *Qualitative Communication Research Methods.* Thousand Oaks, CA: Sage.

Lyotard, F. (1984) [1979] *The Postmodern Condition: A Report on Knowledge.* Manchester: Manchester University Press.

McLuhan, M. (1964) *Understanding Media.* London: Routledge and Kegan Paul.

McQuail, D. and Windahl, S. (1993) *Communication Models for the Study of Mass Communication,* 2nd edn. London: Longman.

Saville-Troike, M. (2002) *The Ethnography of Communication.* Oxford: Blackwell.

Shannon, C. and Weaver, W. (1949) *The Mathematical Theory of Communication.* Urbana: University of Illinois Press.

Language and Rhetoric

This chapter looks at the fundamental ways in which humans communicate: words and physical behaviour.

3.1 Language

Human communication is multifaceted and multisensory. Visual signs, scents, sounds tactile signs and movement are all means by which people exchange information. However, words are the characteristically human and most complex form of communication. In fact, most forms of communication include language to some extent, and words very often accompany non-verbal sign systems, such as images. We begin this chapter, therefore, with a description of some important approaches to language.

Linguistics, the discipline that studies the form and function of language, divides its object of analysis into three main areas relevant to communication: *syntax*, *semantics* and *pragmatics*.

Syntax

This branch of linguistics studies the different possibilities that each language allows for words to be sequenced in a sentence. To produce a meaningful sentence, there are rules that specify how the words should be organized to establish who did what to whom, where, when and how. For example, the sentence 'George killed Jane.' would take on a completely different meaning if we switched the names and produced the sentence 'Jane killed George.': in the second sentence the subject (the active agent) of the first sentence has become the object (the passive agent). English is a subject-verb-object (S-V-O) language, which means that it takes the agent before the action, followed by the thing acted upon. Other languages have a different syntax: Japanese, for example, is a subject-object-verb (SOV) language and takes the verb after the object.

Groups of words get their grammatical classification from syntax. So, for example, a group of words such as /following his advice/ is a *phrase* because it does not contain both a subject and a verb. However, if we had the group of words /she followed his advice/, we would have a *clause* because the group includes a subject, /she/, and a verb that goes with this subject, /followed/. A clause can stand as an independent *sentence*, whereas a phrase cannot. Similarly the –ed *suffix* to the verb /follow/ indicates the past *tense*. Changes in voice also involve changes in syntax. English has two voices, the active and the passive. By saying /she followed his advice/ (SVO), we are using the active voice, which emphasizes the agent in relation to the action. However, if we say /his advice was followed/, /OV/, we would be using the passive voice, which emphasizes the action as a process that is carried out, often by an unspecified agent.

Semantics

This branch studies how it is possible for words and phrases to have meaning. In many cases, it looks at the components, or elemental units, of meaning within a word that allow it to generate meaning. For example, the word 'man' includes in its composition the semantic components male + adult, and 'woman' includes the semantic components female + adult.

However, meaning is a complicated factor. Many words do not have a fixed dictionary definition but acquire different meanings depending on the context in which they operate and on their form within the linguistic system. Consider, for example, the word /wrong/. This can mean 'incorrect' ('She took the wrong turn'), 'immoral' ('It is wrong to kill') or 'unsuitable' ('He wore the wrong clothes for the occasion'). Then consider the word /date/. Asking someone if they would like a date could mean asking them out or it could mean asking them if they wanted a piece of a certain kind of fruit. In such cases, the words are said to be 'polysemic' in that they have multiple meanings. Also, the word form (adjective, adverb, verb, noun, etc.) may affect the meaning. For instance, the noun /endure/ tends to have negative connotations of hardship: one endures pain, hardship and suffering. However, the adjective /enduring/ has positive connotations of popularity: one has an enduring reputation and enduring love.

Semantic questions underlie a great part of what is known as the philosophy of language. One reason for this is that we tend to use language to describe or refer to objects in the world. The question then becomes whether meaning is in language or in the world. As semanticist Nelson Francis said, 'words do not have meanings; people have meanings for words' (cited in Finch 2005: 137). Consider, for example, what happens when you try to explain to someone the meaning of the word 'cliff'. Describing it as a 'big rock with a declining sharp edge' would still assume that the person knows the natural object to which the word 'rock' refers. Much of our communication, therefore, depends on shared knowledge about the world and on conventional ways in which to talk about the world.

Although meaning, in order to be communicated, must be consensual (i.e. others must agree, more or less, on the meaning of a word), there is considerable leeway in accentuating certain elements in the semantic components of a word, while backgrounding others. So, even though Humpty Dumpty's statement that 'words mean what I say they mean' may be rather exaggerated, there is some truth in it, in that meaning is flexible to accommodate intentional and circumstantial influences. In cases where we study the meaning of a word or sentence, we are in the domain of semantics; where we study the meaning of a speaker, we are in the domain of pragmatics.

> The term **sentence** designates a grouping of words containing at least one subject and one verb. Sentences are studied by syntax and semantics in relation to their formal, or logical, properties. The term **utterance** designates a word, sentence or set of sentences in relation to a speaker's intention. 'Utterance', therefore, assumes an embodiment of language and a communicative context.

Pragmatics

This branch studies contextual and social factors in the creation of meaning. It examines how shared knowledge, or assumed shared knowledge, between communicating parties influences the way in which the discourse is structured, word choice, syntax, etc. Pragmatics is concerned not so much with what is explicitly stated as with the influence of what is said: that is, with what is communicated through manner and style of presentation. Whereas semantics studies the formal properties of *sentences*, pragmatics concentrates on the ways a speaker produces meaning through *utterances*. For instance, take the request 'please close the window'. A syntactic and semantic analysis would say that it is an imperative construction presupposing that there is a window and that it is open. Looking at it pragmatically, however, would introduce contextual considerations. If uttered from one patient to another sitting equidistantly from the window at a doctor's waiting room, the utterance 'please close the window' may not be as transparent. Why doesn't the person uttering it perform the action requested? Is this person unable to move because of illness? Is s/he just arrogant and bossy?

According to pragmatic approaches, in order to understand the implications of the utterance it is not enough to analyse its literal meaning; one needs to take into account the whole set of circumstances in which it was uttered. In a different scenario, 'please close the window' could be a code devised by two accomplices in a crime to communicate a hidden message. In this case, the utterance would not refer to the physical world at all (there is no window that needs to be closed), but to a constructed system of signs – a personal code.

In its origins, pragmatics was concerned with compensating for the perceived disadvantages of formal logic in dealing with natural language. Syntactic and, to a large extent, semantic analyses concentrate on the logical, or formal, properties of language. The way we use language in everyday life, however, often contradicts these logical properties by introducing a social element. Understanding how *language* works in reflecting human mental processes needs to be combined with understanding how *discourse* is used by social groups to negotiate their actions in the world.

> The term **language** designates the human capacity to articulate meanings through verbal signs. The term **discourse**, on the other hand, designates the instances of language as these are appropriated by a speaker (or writer) in a particular situation. This way, language is a formal category referring to a biological–cognitive phenomenon, while discourse refers to the social manifestations of this phenomenon.

Following the lead of sociolinguist Dell Hymes (1974), we can distinguish eight elements involved in a communicative interaction that involves discourse:

1   *Structure* is the form that the communicative interaction takes, such as a lecture, a public announcement, a quarrel, a love letter, etc. It is important to note here that this is the meaning attributed to the word 'structure' by Hymes. This same word has many other meanings in text theory and philosophy.

2   *Setting* is the spatiotemporal and physical aspect of the communicative interaction. A professor giving a lecture in a university auditorium interacts in a different setting than, say, if she were talking about the same topic at an informal gathering over drinks at a bar. The meaning attached to her words would be affected by the physical surroundings of the exchange. 'Setting' can also refer to the psychological investment of participants in an occasion: for example, a wedding tends to be associated with festive feelings whatever the actual physical surroundings – a wedding at a private home is as festive as one at a religious institution. Finally, 'setting' can refer to a forum of information exchange, such as a journal. In this sense, different settings can confer varying degrees of credibility and authority to the message communicated: for instance, a theory published in a respectable scientific journal would be received differently and given more credit than one published on a personal website.

3   *Participants* are the addressor and the addressee, the sender and receiver of the discourse. However, the category of participants also includes the more abstract agents of 'speaker' and 'audience', and their status in relation to each other. These are the roles, or subject positions, which the addressor and addressee take and which regulate the discursive techniques used. For example, Bill Gates, founder of Microsoft, may address a group of software developers on a personal level, but the dynamics created in the interaction would be greatly influenced by extra-personal, social factors. Bill Gates's discourse would not only reflect addressor individual traits but also his more abstract-speaker status as Chief Executive Officer (CEO) of a large corporation. Similarly, the developers' response would be coloured by the specific interests of individuals as well as by the attitudes and concerns of their discourse community as technical corporate employees.

4   *Purpose* is what brings the participants together and grounds the communicative act. For example, participants could be celebrating an event or discussing a policy change. Discourse analysis would study how the participants interpret their purpose through the words that they use. In cases where the discourse contradicts the purpose, we would have an instance of misunderstanding or miscommunication.

5   *Key* is the spirit or attitude with which the communicative act is conducted. This could be humorous, serious, hesitant, confident, authoritative, etc. The key is influenced by the structure, setting and purpose of the act.

6   *Topic* is the subject of the discourse. For example, we could have this scenario: in a company boardroom (setting), a team of company employees (participants) have come together for a business discussion (structure). They are attending their regular monthly meeting (purpose) and they are discussing the results of a certain marketing strategy (topic).

7   *Channel* is the choice of medium for the communicative act, such as speech, writing, song, dance, etc.

8   *Message form* is the strategies and techniques used by the speakers in presenting their message so that it will have an impact on the audience. Such techniques as being completely factual and objective or dramatizing an event so that it includes a personal element, etc. would constitute aspects of the message form.

3.2 Rhetoric

The simple definition of rhetoric is *a set of techniques aimed to persuade by using language.* If we take it that a large part, if not most, of our communication with others intends to some degree to sway opinion in our favour, then rhetoric is pervasive in all situations that use linguistic communication. The language used in a love letter to persuade the loved one of one's love is as rhetorical as the speech of a politician whose primary aim is to persuade the public to vote for him/her.

Rhetoric traces its roots to the work of the Greek philosopher Aristotle, who divided rhetoric into two general areas – public speaking and logical discussion. Aristotle (1991: 26) writes:

> Rhetoric may be defined as the faculty of observing in any given case the available means of persuasion. This is not a function of any other art. Every other art can instruct or persuade about its own particular subject-matter; for instance, medicine about what is healthy and unhealthy, geometry about the properties of magnitudes, arithmetic about numbers, and the same is true of the other arts and sciences. But rhetoric we look upon as the power of observing the means of persuasion on almost any subject presented to us; and that is why we say that, in its technical character, it is not concerned with any special or definite class of subjects.

Rhetorical text analysis looks at the situation that triggered the production of the text, the intended audience and the intended effect, and then traces the strategies of the enunciator (speaker or writer) in choosing sentence structures (syntax) and words (semantics).

Aristotle adds that speakers can use three modes of persuasion:

- *Ethos.* This mode of persuasion is based on reasoning that relies on ethical considerations of social justice and morality and on the moral character of the speaker-writer: that is, his/her credibility. It is very often the mode used in the discourse of lawyers and politicians.

- *Pathos.* This mode is based on reasoning that engages the audience's emotions and puts them in a certain frame of mind. This is the mode we associate with advertising and creative types of discourse where the aim is to appeal to the audience's needs and desires, or to elicit their empathy.

- *Logos.* This mode is based on objective proof or evidence. It is the mode mostly associated with logical argument that is devoid of emotion or subjectivity and, instead, relies on objectively testable statements. Persuasion based on logos tends to be universalist and rationalist, not allowing for contextual or individual differences or preferences.

In addition to these modes, Aristotle distinguished three types of public speaking according to the purpose of the speaker, the audience addressed and the situation concerned: *forensic, deliberative* and *epideictic*. Forensic speech is typified by legal discourse, where participants argue over the nature and cause of past events. Deliberative speech debates the best possible course of action in cases where there is some conflict or opposing viewpoints. Epideictic speech involves the values of the audience and generally presents a judgment over whether something deserves praise or blame. Although Aristotle's interest was in oral language, his categories are relevant for a variety of text types and discourses, in both written and oral codes.

Translating these categories into present-day text-types, we see that, in addition to legal texts, forensic discourse is used in many scientific texts which aim to persuade an audience about the causes and nature of certain observable phenomena. Deliberative discourse would be present in proposals to gain funding for projects, as well as in politicians' speeches on why a particular change in policy is needed. Epideictic discourse would be used in such situations as speeches made by corporate executives celebrating new company developments, in many public relations texts aiming to enhance the image of an institution, and in editorial articles that criticize authorities on the outcomes of their decisions.

A rhetorical analysis of texts can be used for any type of discourse, from poetic to formal, because, as noted above, entertainment involves techniques of persuasion as much as science or public debate do; both produce texts that have some effect or impact on society. As Martin Medhurst and Thomas Benson (1984: vii) point out,

> The study of how people choose what to say in a given situation, how to arrange or order their thoughts, select the specific terminology to employ, and decide precisely how they are going to deliver their message is the central focus of rhetorical studies.

Similarly, Robert Root (1987: 21) explains how he uses discourse in his text analysis:

> In every case I will attempt to apply rhetorical analysis to a specific aspect of popular culture and repeatedly ask the same questions about them: What is the mode of presentation? How does the mode affect the presentation? What is the purpose of the discourse? How is the discourse directed at the audience? What person is created, how is it created, and why is it created? What is the argument of the discourse? How is it arranged? Upon what is it based? Generally these are questions of rhetoric which can be asked of any discourse.

Rhetorical analysis approaches the text as a construction designed on the basis of an intention. An interesting study of the pervasive effect of rhetoric in the construction of arguments and theories is Stephen Pepper's *World Hypotheses* (1942). Briefly, Pepper classifies major scientific hypotheses into types by tracing their common elements. He then delineates the kinds of evidence needed for each type to be supported or disproved.

Pepper's rhetorical approach is to extract and analyse the main metaphorical structures with which scientific hypotheses are constructed – what he calls the 'root metaphors of world hypotheses'. This exercise guides him to trace four main categories into which these hypotheses can be classified: *formalism,* which includes the hypotheses based on the root metaphor of 'similarity'; *contextualism,* which includes the hypotheses based on the root metaphor of the 'historic event'; *mechanism,* which is based on the metaphor of the 'machine'; and *organicism,* which is based on the root metaphor of 'process as integration'.

Pepper then goes on to discuss the ways in which kinds of evidence are integrated within these hypotheses. His discussion shows how the common belief that science is based on 'real' or materially verifiable elements in the objective world is in fact misleading, since 'proof' can only be what is logically acceptable by the rhetorical construction of each model of knowledge. In other words, he proposes that the same root metaphors that generate theories also determine what forms of evidence will be used in each case. For example, physics and medical science require proof based on experimentation and repeated observation of the same phenomenon or causal chain. This kind of evidence Pepper calls 'multiplicative corroboration'. Most of the arguments used in various types of philosophy, on the other hand, rely on the logical connections among their constituent parts, or, in other words, on processes of reasoning and on drawing logical deductions from given premises. This he calls 'structural corroboration'.

There are many conventional devices that communicators use to present their messages in what they believe to be the most suitable and effective way to their target audiences. The next section outlines some major rhetorical devices. The list is organized from the most complex and pervasive to those which are simpler.

3.3 Main rhetorical devices

Metaphor

Metaphors use equivalence to produce an identification between two objects or terms. This is what happens, for example, when we say that the lion is the 'king of the jungle' or when we say that someone's look is 'icy'. Metaphors are short analogies and they make use of connotation, which makes them to a large extent culture-specific. Language itself is metaphoric because it uses one code (the linguistic sign) to represent another (the world as it consists of perceptual phenomena). In fact, writers such as George Lakoff and Mark Johnson (2003) have argued convincingly that most discourse is metaphoric in nature and that metaphors are not constricted to creative texts but play a much more prominent role in our everyday reasoning and communication. They distinguish three categories of metaphor:

- *Orientational* metaphors relate to spatial organization, such as up/down, in/out, front/back, on/off, near/far, deep/shallow and central/peripheral. Metaphorical expressions that use such spatial imagery would fall into this category; examples include 'she's down and out', 'he made several shallow remarks', and 'they bought some far-out furniture'.

- *Ontological* metaphors associate activities, emotions and ideas with entities and substances (most characteristically, metaphors involving personification). Metaphorical expressions that associate abstract elements with concrete objects would fall into this category: examples include 'it's the mother of all computer systems', 'to use an umbrella term' and 'to have a mercurial temperament'.

- *Structural* metaphors are overarching metaphors which allow the structuring of one concept in terms of another. These build on the other two types and create associations between two notions, which may be abstract or concrete: examples include 'time is money', 'he is a sly fox' and 'a heart-breaking story'.

Metonymy

Metonymy uses part of an object to signify the whole of the object. It differs from a metaphor in that the word or image used as a metonym is not equivalent to the object represented but is actually one of its constituents or attributes. For example, we say 'Parliament said' to indicate that members of parliament actually made a statement, and we may show the image of a limousine, a cigar or a stack of money to signify wealth. Hollywood is a metonym of glamour, a pair of running shoes is a metonym of athletics or sports, and a key can be a metonym of access.

Irony

Irony uses words and images to convey the opposite of what they literally mean. This is what happens, for example, when one exclaims 'what great weather' while it is freezing cold and raining cats and dogs. Together with metaphors and metonymy, irony is arguably one of the most widespread, effective and complicated rhetorical devices. For example, on the level of cultural analysis, irony is considered the master technique of post-modern texts, which want to emphasize the circularity and open-endedness of meaning (as described in Chapter 2). Post-modern writers and artists use irony to dramatize the idea that actual events can contradict one's intentions. When irony is used to criticize, ridicule or insult (that is, when it is used to attack another's intention), it becomes *sarcasm*. Exclaiming 'how graceful' when someone has just tripped over their own feet would be an example of sarcasm.

Paradox

A paradox is an extreme form of irony, a statement or image that seems, at face value, to contradict itself. Paradoxical statements point to a deeper truth by transgressing the limits imposed by physical reality and/or formal logic. Thus, we can say about someone that he lived only in death, or that she grew younger with time, or about a space that it was remarkably bright and exceptionally dark. Many structuralist and post-structuralist theorists elevate paradox to a very prominent position in discursive strategy, seeing it as characteristic of language in general. For example, the Saussurean–semiotic axiom that language means in terms of its opposite and contradictory (i.e. that we could have no notion of, say, 'cold', if we did not at the same time have a notion of 'hot'), which is described in the next chapter, embraces paradox as constitutive of meaning.

Cliché

A cliché is a word, phrase or image that, although deviating from standard or everyday discourse, has through extensive use become hackneyed, trite or unoriginal. Expressions with redundancies, such as 'first and foremost', 'at this point in time', 'one and the same', and 'each and every', are clichés, as are conventional metaphors such as 'food for thought' and 'to be wrapped up in your work'. In addition, some standardized combinations of adjectives and nouns (known as 'collocations') are clichés: 'utter destruction' 'positive outcome' 'intrinsic value' and 'absolute necessity' exemplify these.

Advertising and other forms of creative discourse often employ clichés in original contexts for effect. In this case, the cliché is redefined in literal terms. For example, the phrase 'no hard feelings', as a cliché, means 'I hold no grudges'. If used to promote a certain type of furniture, however, it becomes invested with a literal meaning (i.e. the furniture is soft and comfortable). The juxtaposition of the two meanings, that is, that we expect it to mean 'I hold no grudges' but in fact it does not, is what produces the creative effect. Generally, a cliché can be seen as an implied quotation, since it carries in its meaning the contexts in which it has been used and the voices of others who have used it – it is an 'as they say' construct.

Allusion

Allusion is an indirect or implicit reference to a well-known place, person, event or text. Functions of allusions in a text include illustrating a topic, creating an effect of irony, and making an association between two texts so as to produce a memorable impression (people tend to remember more what they recognize). For example, when IBM designed the chess-playing computer Deep Blue, they publicized it with the slogan 'That 1.4 ton 8-year-old sure plays a mean game of chess'. This was an allusion to The Who's song 'Pinball Wizard', which contains the refrain 'That deaf, dumb and blind kid sure plays a mean pinball'. Allusions are a widely used technique in intertextuality (described in Chapter 4).

The French poet **Stephane Mallarmé** described the power of allusion and suggestion in creative activities when he said that 'to define is to destroy; to suggest is to create'.

Definition

A definition sets the boundaries between one term and others by making explicit what meaning is given to the term. There are *lexical* definitions, which refer to the way in which words are conventionally used, there are *stipulative* definitions which are offered for the purposes of a particular argument and there are *operational* definitions, which offer a list of procedures to perform that will lead to an understanding of the thing that is defined. Defining is a common technique in discourse which needs to be clear (such as scientific or philosophical discourse) or discourse which sets rules (such as legal discourse). For example, the Scottish philosopher David Hume shows the importance of definition for argument construction in his *Treatise of Human Nature* (first published in 1740). This is what Hume (2000: 407) says:

I dare be positive no one will ever endeavour to refute these reasonings *otherwise than by altering my definitions, and assigning a different meaning* to the terms of cause and effect, and necessity and liberty, and chance. *According to my definitions,* necessity makes an essential part of causation; and consequently liberty, by removing necessity, removes also causes, and is the very same thing with chance. As chance is commonly thought to imply a contradiction, and is at least directly contrary to experience, there are always the same arguments against liberty or free-will. *If any one alters the definitions, I cannot pretend to argue with him,* 'till I know the meaning he assigns to these terms.

Definition, however, is not a very effective device in more creative forms of discourse, which use less specific or precise techniques in order to create subjective impressions. Advertising, for example, and creative art rarely define or explain their objects, but instead suggest or allude to their meanings.

Analogy

Analogy is a form of example where a story or element is described together with the thing exemplified in order to make it clearer. Analogies are often used to create parallels between one situation and another in order to highlight certain qualities of the thing explained. For example, this is the effect achieved by writer Flannery O'Connor when addressing a class in writing as follows (cited in Kane 1984: 64):

> I understand that this is a course called "How the Writer Writes", and that each week you are exposed to a different writer who holds forth on the subject. The only parallel I can think of to this is having the zoo come to you, one animal at a time; and I suspect that what you hear one week from the giraffe is contradicted next week by the baboon.

In this extract, O'Connor says that writing is a subjective process with no objective rules. The way she says this, however, is not by assertion but by analogy, and in this way she gives the idea a distinctive and memorable flavour.

Simile

A simile is a weaker form of metaphor where the resemblance between two things is signalled by the words 'like' or 'as'. In this way a simile explicitly states the relationship of similarity between two objects or terms, whereas a metaphor uses the two in a parallel way and therefore emphasizes their equivalence. Examples include 'soft like velvet', 'fast as a bird' 'sharp as a knife', etc. Similes can be serious or they can have humorous (or sarcastic) effects, as in the expression 'he is as useful as a broken leg', indicating that someone's assistance is more of a hindrance than a help.

Overstatement/understatement

An overstatement (called 'hyperbole' in literary studies) presents an opinion or fact in exaggerated form, usually either to dramatize a situation or to produce a comic effect. Overstatements often involve metaphors, as, for example, in the expression 'I'm drowning in work'; at other times, they can involve superlative expressions ('the –est in the world', 'this is the best film ever made') or simply statements whose meaning exaggerates the situation that it describes. The opposite of this is an understatement, where the object represented is portrayed as less than it actually merits; describing sub-zero conditions as 'chilly', for example, would be an understatement.

Oxymoron

Oxymoron is a form of contradiction in terms. It is used when a phrase contains words that are opposite or contradictory in meaning. It is mainly a poetic device used to create a striking image by combining elements that are not expected to be together, thereby producing contrast. For example, expressions like 'little giant', 'exquisite torture' and 'honest thief' are oxymorons.

Alliteration

Alliteration is a phonetic technique where a number of words begin with the same sound. This is often done to produce a slogan or phrase that is easily remembered so that it can come to represent the object it describes (often done in brand imaging and advertising), or to create a pleasant image because of harmonious sound (often done in poetry). Tongue-twisters, for example, rely on alliteration – 'she sells seashells at the sea shore' plays on the /s/, /sh/ sound.

Allegory

An allegory is a story that uses fictional characters and events to support abstract ethical tenets. Allegories are forms of extended metaphors that describe relations about the world through the development of their plots. In allegories, characters are usually personifications of abstract ideas, and their actions embody moral principles. Examples of allegories include the stories of Chaucer's Canterbury Tales and the stories told by Jesus in the New Testament.

As an example of a pragmatic and rhetorical analysis of a written text, consider the following article by horror writer Stephen King.

ANALYSIS OF AN ARTICLE

Stephen King: Why We Crave Horror Movies

I think that we're all mentally ill; those of us outside the asylums only hide it a little better – and maybe not all that much better, after all. We've all known people who talk to themselves, people who sometimes squinch their faces into horrible grimaces when they believe no one is watching, people who have some hysterical fear – of snakes, the dark, the tight place, the long drop . . . and, of course, those final worms and grubs that are waiting so patiently underground.

When we pay our four or five bucks and seat ourselves at tenth-row center in a theater showing a horror movie, we are daring the nightmare.

Why? Some of the reasons are simple and obvious. To show that we can, that we are not afraid, that we can ride this roller coaster. Which is not to say that a really good horror movie may not surprise a scream out of us at some point, the way we may scream when the roller coaster twists through a complete 360 or plows through a lake at the bottom of the drop. And horror movies, like roller coasters, have always been the special province of the young; by the time one turns 40 or 50 one's appetite for double twists or 360-degree loops may be considerably depleted.

We also go to re-establish our feelings of essential normality; the horror movie is innately conservative, even reactionary, Freda Jackson as the horrible melting woman in *Die, Monster, Die!* confirms for us that no matter how far we may be removed from the beauty of a Robert Redford or a Diana Ross, we are still light years from true ugliness.

And we go to have fun.

Ah, but this is where the ground starts to slope away, isn't it? Because this is a very peculiar sort of fun, indeed. The fun comes from seeing others menaced – sometimes killed. One critic has suggested that if pro football has become the voyeur's version of combat, then the horror film has become the modern version of the public lynching.

It is true that the mythic, 'fairy tale' horror film intends to take away the shades of gray . . . it urges us to put away our more civilized and adult penchant for analysis and to become children again, seeing things in pure black and whites. It may be that horror movies provide psychic relief on this level because this invitation to lapse into simplicity, irrationality, and even outright madness is extended so rarely. We are told we may allow our emotions a free rein . . . or no rein at all.

If we are all insane, then sanity becomes a matter of degree. If your insanity leads you to carve up women like Jack the Ripper or the Cleveland Torso Murderer, we clap you away in the funny farm (but neither of those two amateur-night surgeons was ever caught, heh-heh-heh); if, on the other hand, your insanity leads you only to talk to yourself when you're under stress   ⇨

or to pick your nose on your morning bus, then you are left alone to go about your business . . . though it is doubtful that you will ever be invited to the best parties.

The potential lyncher is in almost all of us (excluding saints, past and present; but then, most saints have been crazy in their own ways), and every now and then, he has to be let loose to scream and roll around in the grass. Our emotions and our fears form their own body and we recognize that it demands its own exercise to maintain proper muscle tone. Certain of these emotional muscles are accepted – even exalted in civilized society; they are, of course, the emotions that tend to maintain the status quo of civilization itself. Love, friendship, loyalty, kindness – these are all the emotions that we applaud, emotions that have been permanently immortalized in the couplets of hallmark cards and in the verses (I don't dare call it poetry) of Leonard Nimoy.

When we exhibit these emotions, society showers us with positive reinforcement; we learn this even before we get out of diapers. When, as children, we hug our rotten little puke of a sister and give her a kiss, all the aunts and uncles smile and twit and cry, "Isn't he the sweetest little thing?" Such coveted treats as chocolate-covered graham crackers often follow. But if we deliberately slam the rotten little puke of a sister's fingers in the door, sanctions follow – angry remonstrance from parents, aunts, and uncles; instead of a chocolate-covered graham, a spanking.

But anticivilization emotions don't go away, and they demand periodic exercise. We have such 'sick' jokes as "What's the difference between a truckload of bowling balls and a truckload of dead babies?" (You can't unload a truckload of bowling balls with a pitchfork . . . a joke, by the way, that I heard originally from a ten-year-old). Such a joke may surprise a laugh or a grin out of us even as we recoil, a possibility that confirms the thesis: If we share a brotherhood of man, then we also share an insanity of man. None of which is intended as a defense of either the sick joke or insanity but merely as an explanation of why the best horror films, like the best fairy tales, manage to be reactionary, anarchistic, and revolutionary all at the same time.

The mythic horror movie, like the sick joke, has a dirty job to do. It deliberately appeals to all that is worst in us. It is morbidly unchained, our most base instincts let free, our nastiest fantasies realized . . . and it all happens fittingly enough, in the dark. For those reasons, good liberals often shy away from horror films. For myself, I like to see the most aggressive of them – *Dawn of the Dead* for instance – as lifting a trap door in the civilized forebrain and throwing a basket of raw meat to the hungry alligators swimming around in the subterranean river beneath.

Why bother? Because it keeps them from getting out, man. It keeps them down there and me up here. It was Lennon and McCartney who said that all you need is love, and I would agree with that.

As long as you keep the gators fed.

Playboy Magazine, January 1981.

This text on the topic of horror films is transmitted through the channel of writing. The key is humorous and moderately provocative. Formatting and stylistic considerations show that the text is a journalistic article, as opposed to, say, an academic essay or business report. Consider some of these points in more detail:

- *Format.* Paragraphs are very short (paragraphs 5 and 13, for instance, are single phrases). This is consistent with journalistic writing conventions, but would be inappropriate for formal or academic texts. Also, the text does not contain any headings, as would, for example, a business report, and this contributes to its informal, 'chatty' tone.

- *Style.* The style is informal, with many colloquial expressions, giving the text the appearance of a spoken conversation. Phrases such as 'when we pay our four or five bucks', 'rotten little puke of a sister' and 'we clap you away in the funny farm' are just three examples of this. The extensive use of the personal pronouns 'you', 'we' and 'I' adds to the informality and conversational approach, giving the article a personalised tone. In addition, the text includes several transcriptions of oral, paralinguistic features, such as laughter ('heh-heh-heh') and hesitation (. . .).

- *Pragmatic Features.* We know that the writer is Stephen King and, since he has a reputation in the topic on which he is writing, we tend to read his words differently than if the writer were unknown. So, it is likely that readers will find the text more amusing knowing the reputation of the writer. When those who are famous in a field talk about this field, their authority tends to give them more freedom to experiment with ways of expression and to be provocative. As for the receivers of the communication, the stylistic features described above would suggest that it would be readers whom the writer considered to be peers.

There are also some indicators of assumed reader gender and age. The expressions 'if your insanity leads you to carve up women' and 'rotten little puke of a sister' would tend to construct the reader as male. The first expression poses women as 'other' (it does not say 'to carve up *other* women'), implying that the 'self' reading this would be male; the second expression conjures up the proverbial distaste that little boys are said to have of little girls. Although the readers' gender assumptions tend towards the male, we also have the expression 'no matter how far we may be removed from the beauty of a Robert Redford or a Diana Ross', which suggests that there is also a female readership, since males would not be expected to identify with the beauty of Diana Ross.

Regarding age, the expression 'horror movies, like roller coasters, have always been the special province of the young; by the time one turns 40 or 50 one's appetite for double twists or 360-degree loops may be considerably depleted' places the writer in the 40+ age range, since he is describing 'the young' as others. As the readers are constructed as peers, we could assume that they too would fall into that category. In addition, the term 'good liberals' also places the writer and readers in the 30+ age category, since it assumes a certain life experience that not many young adults would be expected to have or to express in such terms.

Textual features indicating the time at which the article was written would be the examples given to illustrate points. So, the references to Robert Redford and Diana Ross as examples of beauty would place the article in the 1970s or early 1980s, because these examples are not likely choices for a contemporary text. Also, the lack of film titles of the post-80s era would support this.

- *Rhetorical Devices.* The main rhetorical devices that the text uses are overstatements, metaphors and analogies. Examples include the title itself, which gives an overstatement in the word /crave/, chosen instead of a 'milder' term such as /appeal/. Also, the opening words, 'I think that we're all mentally ill', create a shock effect through the use of generalization and exaggeration (both elements of overstatement). The text uses metaphors and analogies to describe emotions, which play an important role in the writer's argument. So, emotions are described as forming a body with muscles that need to be exercised. These emotions are divided into two categories, those which are positive and those which are negative and anti-social, the latter being likened to alligators that eat raw meat. The alligators live in a subterranean river – a metaphor of the human subconscious. Finally, for the act of watching horror films, the writer uses the analogy of going on a rollercoaster ride, once again in order to foreground the importance of the emotions in the experience.

Interpretations of pragmatic features are influenced by the interpreter's assumptions and values as these are formed through personal experience and cultural norms. In cases where the interpreted text originates in a different culture or in a context whose conventions are alien to the interpreter, there is a higher risk of miscommunication. As regards the example of the Stephen King article, note that it was originally published in *Playboy* magazine (January 1981 issue), whose readership falls into the 'males aged 30–50' demographic. The leads we followed in the above discussion would therefore be correct.

3.4 Non-verbal communication

We end this chapter with a short discussion on non-verbal communication – communication that does not rely on words to convey meaning. Although human communication processes rely to a large extent on language, non-verbal communication, such as body language, and paralinguistic communication, such as intonation, also figure strongly in interactions with others. There is also general consensus among communication specialists that people tend to remember visual signs more than they remember verbal signs. Such considerations make paying attention to one's non-verbal signs vital for effective interpersonal communication. Non-verbal communication (NVC) takes place in different perceptual categories, including:

- facial expression
- gestures
- posture and movement (kinesics)
- physical contact or positioning (proxemics)
- clothes, hairstyles and general appearance
- non-verbal aspects of language, such as tone and pitch of voice.

Before discussing this any further, it should be emphasized that the meaning attached to non-verbal signals is to a very large extent culture-specific. Gestures, colours and proximity expectations differ from culture to culture. For example, the human face is capable of around 250,000 different expressions (Birdwhistell 1970: 8), and not all have conventional meanings in all cultures. Some facial expressions, however, are considered to have similar meanings internationally because they are associated with emotive responses that have evolved as part of the genetic make-up of the human species. These expressions reflect the 'universal emotions' of happiness, sadness, anger, fear, surprise and disgust.

Non-verbal communication, such as body language, can betray one's intentions and frame of mind more than can words, which are easier to manipulate and control. This is one reason why many personal and professional development courses train participants to become aware of the signs they emit through their bodies.

Other than these emotions, cultural diversity produces a whole range of non-verbal signs and their associations. For example, taking the Western cultural context, researchers have made the following general observations about non-verbal meanings:

- Clothing expectations often accompany the notion of professionalism. For example, research has shown that medical patients expect their doctors to dress formally in suits, or in white jackets if in a hospital situation. It appears that patients would not approve of or trust a doctor dressed in jeans or casual attire, regardless of the doctor's qualifications (Preston 2005). Also, in many corporate settings dress codes are part of performance, and an employee who does not follow these codes would get lower performance ratings, regardless of the quality of his/her work (Prachter 2002).

- Eye contact is an important sign of respect and attention. Looking at someone in the eyes gently (as opposed to staring) when they are talking generally displays willingness to listen and interest in what the person has to say.

- Eyebrows are expressive in conveying emotion: fully raised eyebrows indicate disbelief; half-raised eyebrows indicate surprise; half-lowered eyebrows indicate puzzle or worry; fully-lowered eyebrows indicate anger (Argyle 1983: 33).

- Giving affirmative head nods when one is listening tends to be a sign of empathy and understanding. Gentle nods also confirm that one is attentive.

- When listening to someone while sitting, the most effective position is sitting upright (not slumping on the chair) with a slightly forward bend. Similarly, when listening to someone standing up, a slight forward bend with the arms resting on the side indicate openness and attention to what the person is saying.

- Body movements and gestures that are commonly seen as blocking the flow of communication include keeping arms crossed (indicating a defensive attitude), putting arms to hips (indicating aggression), standing with a slight backward bend (indicating surprise or aloofness), and putting one's hands on one's chin while one's eyes wander around the room (indicating boredom).

- A low, well-modulated and relaxed voice inspires confidence. The opposite occurs if the voice is shrill, loud, too soft or monotone.

A technique for gaining more control over how one appears to others is to become conscious of one's facial expressions (maybe by practising different expressions in front of a mirror). Actors, for example, learn to project emotions on their face more strongly than they would in reality – sometimes what may feel in one's mind like an exaggerated grimace may not actually manifest itself outwardly this way.

Visiting Ko King

To understand how prevalent assumptions and beliefs are in physical behaviour and in the interpretations of this behaviour, consider this situation.

You are on a flight to another continent when, because of adverse weather conditions, your plane is forced to land in a small and virtually unknown country called Ko King. The Ko-Kingese government has sent a delegation to meet you at the airport and to entertain you while you wait for the weather to clear. The Ko-Kingese delegation takes you to a nearby temple where a traditional ritual that celebrates their cultural values is performed. You observe the ritual, which consists of a performance of stylized movements and actions accompanied by drum music, but no words or explanation.

The participants in the ceremony are divided into male and female. The men are seated on high stools in two rows facing each other. On the left row sit older men, while on the right row sit younger men. The older men sit on slightly more elevated stools than the younger men. All the men are dressed in what seem like heavy military costumes and they are holding spears. They wear many decorations and thick, golden sandals. In the middle of the temple, in front of the men, are several women of different ages: teenagers, young and elderly. They wear very little clothing and are barefoot. They are bowing low, their hands touching the ground.

After a few drum beats, the women stand up, go up to the men, remove their sandals and ceremoniously wipe their feet with their hands. They wipe the older men's feet first. They then take some cups from what looks like an altar situated in the centre of the temple and fill them with liquid, probably wine. They give them to the men, the older men first, who sip some wine before passing them back to the women to sip.

The women then perform a dance in the middle of the temple, in front of the men. Their gestures seem flirtatious and seductive and their twirling movements reveal considerable amounts of bare skin.

At the end of the dance, the women go back to the men and place the sandals back on their feet. They then go to the middle of the temple and resume their low-bowing positions, hands touching the ground. The older men stand up and ceremoniously walk out of the temple, followed by the row of young men. They walk in a single file. The women remain in their positions until all the men have left, and then get up and leave the temple in pairs.

By that time, the weather alert has passed and you board the plane for your original destination. What are your impressions of Ko-Kingese culture? In particular, which would you say is the dominant sex? What are some cultural values that you were able to decode by observing the ritual? Your interpretation of and reaction to the ritual would be influenced by your own values, beliefs and experiences, and these would depend on your own culture, sex, and personal life – the factors that form your identity. Here is one possible way that you might interpret the ritual.

You could think that men, and, in particular, older men, are the dominant sex in Ko-Kingese culture. Your reasoning could be that the men were seated in elevated positions, that they were dressed in a more substantial way than the women and that they did not have to go barefoot. They had the women serve them, as occurred when the women wiped the men's feet and when they served them the wine to sip first. Also, the men had priority in leaving the temple. Since the older men walked out first, they would be considered more important, and therefore more powerful. In addition, the men did not have to demean themselves by bowing or kneeling on the ground, but could sit comfortably on stools. Finally, the women were forced to entertain the men by reducing themselves to sex objects in the sexually provocative dance. The fact that all the women, regardless of age, acted in the same way indicates that, in Ko-Kingese culture, women are defined solely by their biology and are deprived of the civilizing signs of rank and status.

This interpretation would be based on certain assumptions, including the following:

• 'firstness' indicates power;

- 'highness' indicates superiority;
- 'lowness', as signified by feet, indicates inferiority;
- seniority is valued.

These assumptions are not mere subjective prejudices. In fact, they are built into the language systems of many cultures. In English, for example, we have metaphorical expressions, such as 'your highness' to indicate authority and prestige, 'on one's knees' to indicate submission and burden, and 'at one's feet' to indicate power over something, which verbalize the values and beliefs assumed in the above interpretation.

What if you now meet a Ko-Kingese student who explains the situation from a Ko-Kingese perspective as follows?

Ko-Kingese culture is earth-based and the women are considered guardians of the earth because of their association with birth and new life. Therefore, they are central to the culture (symbolized by their position in the middle of the temple), and the most powerful. Since, according to the Ko-Kingese, all laws are laws of life and come from the earth, women, being earth guardians, are the legislators.

In Ko-Kingese culture, men are hunters and warriors, and are therefore associated with the darker aspects of existence, such as killing and death. Therefore, in a sacred ground such as a temple, they are not allowed to come into direct contact with the earth. Accordingly, they are obliged to wear footwear to keep their feet off the ground and, when not walking, they must sit in an elevated position to avoid contact with the ground. The older men, having lived longer, are considered more 'impure' and so must sit higher. The act of wiping the men's feet is performed by women as a sign of ritual purification and as a symbolic reinforcement of their power.

Also, because of the brutal life that the men live, hierarchy and order is necessary for survival. Consequently, the men are forced to impose strict distinctions of rank and status on themselves, based mostly on age and vitality. Old men, therefore, who are less energetic and not as physically strong have less power among the male groups than young men. Women, on the other hand, have a more egalitarian structure and their behaviour is not dictated by age or status but by personal inclination. This explains why women of all ages were free to perform the same actions in the ritual.

In Ko-Kingese culture, women are the only ones who can touch the earth and, to celebrate the privilege, they were barefoot in the ritual and bowed low so as to signify their close ties with the earth. They are protected from harm, reflecting the way that the earth should be protected from harm. This was symbolized in the ritual by the men sipping the wine first to make sure it was not soiled or poisoned and by the men walking out of the temple first to make sure it was safe for the women to exit. The fact that it was the older men who sipped first and exited the temple first was due to their being more dispensable than the young men, and therefore less protected.

Also, women's sexuality is valued and their sexual desires are nurtured, while men's sexuality is channelled mostly into satisfying women's sexual needs. This was indicated by the women's dance, which symbolized free sexual movement, flexibility and variety, and the power to choose partners. During the dance the men were obliged to be passive spectators and, according to Ko Kingese culture, their immobile position signified submissiveness. Their heavy clothing, which contrasted so strongly with the women's light garments, signified modesty. Finally, all women, regardless of age or other distinctions, enjoy the same privileges in Ko-Kingese culture, and this was indicated by equal participation in the dance, and equal access to the pool of men for all women.

▊ Summary

◆ Language is central in communication and researchers have also used it as a model for conceptualizing and theorizing non-verbal forms of communication.

◆ Linguistics, the science of language, includes three main branches that have been influential in communication theory. These are *syntax*, the study of word order in a sentence, *semantics*, the study of word meaning, and *pragmatics*, the study of intentions and contextual factors in verbal exchange.

◆ Rhetoric looks at how language is used to persuade or create a favourable image of the speaker. Although it was first described by Aristotle as a political tool of public speaking, rhetoric is now recognised as a fundamental aspect of any discourse. Rhetoric describes the syntactic and semantic choices a speaker/writer makes, as an intentional strategy or as an unconscious act, to influence an audience.

◆ In all types of interpersonal communication, where the interacting parties have physical contact, non-verbal factors come into play. Gestures, posture, distance and clothing, most of which are culture-specific, convey messages that complement the verbal exchange.

▊ Topics for discussion

▶ Select a text aimed to persuade. This could be a politician's speech (famous speeches are transcribed in encyclopaedias and dictionaries of speeches), an editorial in a magazine, the web site of a corporation, etc. Analyse its rhetorical patterns, using the terminology described here. Who would you say the intended audience is? How well does the text target this audience?

▶ Describe a communicative interaction at your university or place of work. Analyse it using Hymes's model. Did the participants act the way they did because of the context and circumstances of the interaction? How would their behaviour and their discourse differ in other circumstances? How important was non-verbal communication in the interaction?

▶ Select an article from a magazine targeted at a specific audience. Analyse it in terms of its rhetorical strategies. Note its uses of cliché, metaphor and allusion. How effective are they? If there are visuals, such as pictures or photographs, discuss their impact. How do they relate to the written words? You can extend this activity by writing your own article for that magazine. Select a visual (picture or graphic) and explain how your words complement the visual.

■ References and further reading

Akmajian, A., Demers, R. A., Farmer, A. K. and Harnish, R. M. (2001) *Linguistics: An Introduction to Language and Communication*. Cambridge, MA: MIT Press.

Argyle, M. (1983) *The Psychology of Interpersonal Behaviour*, 4th edn. London: Penguin.

Aristotle (1991) *The Art of Rhetoric*, trans. by H. Lawson-Tancred. London: Penguin.

Aristotle (1996) *Poetics*, trans. by M. Heath. London: Penguin.

Axelrod, R. B. and Cooper, C. R. (2001) *The St Martin's Guide to Writing*, 6th edn. New York: Bedford St Martins.

Birdwhistell, R. (1970) *Kinesics and Context: Essays on Body Motion Communication*. Philadelphia, PA: University of Pennsylvania Press.

Booth, W. C. (2004) *The Rhetoric of Rhetoric: The Quest for Effective Communication*. Oxford: Blackwell.

Chomsky, N. (1972) *Language and Mind*. New York: Harcourt Brace Jovanovich.

Corbett, E. P. J. and Connors, R. J. (1999) *Classical Rhetoric for the Modern Student*, 4th edn. Oxford: Oxford University Press.

Finch, G. (2003) *How to Study Linguistics*, 2nd edn. Basingstoke: Palgrave Macmillan.

Finch, G. (2005) *Key Concepts in Language and Linguistics*, 2nd edn. Basingstoke: Palgrave Macmillan.

Hume, D. (2000) [1740] *A Treatise of Human Nature*. Oxford: Oxford University Press.

Hymes, D. (1974) *Foundations of Sociolinguistics: An Ethnographic Approach*. Philadelphia, PA: University of Pennsylvania Press.

Kane, T. (1984) *The New Oxford Guide to Writing*. Oxford: Oxford University Press.

King, S. (2001) *On Writing*. London: Hodder and Stoughton.

Knapp, M. (1995) *Essentials of Non Verbal Communication*. Orlando, FL: Harcourt.

Lakoff, G. (1987) *Women, Fire and Dangerous Things: What Categories Reveal about the Mind*. Chicago: University of Chicago Press.

Lakoff, G. and Johnson, M. (2003) *Metaphors We Live By*, 2nd edn. Chicago: University of Chicago Press.

Lanham, R. A. (1991) *A Handlist of Rhetorical Terms*, 2nd edn. Berkeley: University of California Press.

Levinson, S. (1983) *Pragmatics*. Cambridge: Cambridge University Press.

Medhurst, M. J. and Benson, T. W. (eds) (1984) *Rhetorical Dimensions in Media: A Critical Casebook*. Dubuque: Kendall-Hunt.

Pepper, S. (1942) *World Hypotheses: A Study in Evidence*. Berkeley, CA: University of California Press.

Prachter, B. (2002) *When the Little Things Count . . . and They Always Count: 601 Essential Things that Everyone in Business Needs to Know*. New York: Marlowe and Company.

Preston, P. (2005) 'Nonverbal Communication: Do You Really Say What You Mean?', *Journal of Healthcare Management*, Vol. 50, 2 pp. 83–8.

Root, R. L. Jr (1987) *The Rhetorics of Popular Culture: Advertising, Advocacy and Entertainment*. New York: Greenwood.

Yule, G. (1996) *Pragmatics*. Oxford: Oxford University Press.

Semiotics and Narrative

There is no binary division to be made between what one says and what one does not say; we must try to determine the different ways of not saying things.

Michel Foucault

This chapter extends the previous discussion on theoretical approaches to communication and on fundamental ways of human communication by focusing on the nature, role and different manifestations of signs.

4.1 Semiotics

In its brief definition, semiotics is an approach to text analysis that studies the nature of signs and their importance in the ways we make sense of the world. However, this is not to say that semiotics is interested in the meaning of particular signs in a text (i.e. what a text means), although some semiotic analyses may take this form. Instead, semioticians are more interested in how it is possible for signs to have meaning at all. In other words, semioticians look at what the components of meaning in general are in order for particular manifestations or instances of meaning to exist. In simpler terms, they look at how meaning works. Umberto Eco (1976: 7) has given one of the most creative definitions of semiotics:

> Semiotics is concerned with everything that can be taken as a sign. A sign is everything which can be taken as significantly substituting for something else. This something else does not necessarily have to exist or actually be somewhere at the moment in which a sign stands for it. Thus semiotics is in principle the discipline studying everything which can be used in order to lie. If something cannot be used to tell a lie, conversely it cannot be used 'to tell' at all.

What Eco means is that we communicate messages by representing ideas and emotions in some way. We use words, images, colours, scents, etc. to depict in a perceptible form something we sense or imagine. We also interpret others' messages through the way they use words, sounds, images or scents: that is, through the ways that they transmit the content of their messages. Signs never really tell the truth in a direct and objective form: they mediate reality by allowing us to select aspects of the perceptible world and create stories with them through which we communicate ideas about the world. With signs, we communicate our own perceptions of reality.

This probably sounds abstract and difficult to grasp, and there is a reason for this. Semiotics uses terms and concepts that are abstract and technical, and many semiotic analyses use models that analyse texts in terms of categories and typologies. This is motivated by the fact that semiotics looks at universal patterns of human communication as these are structured by mental processes. So, semiotics has no object of study as such (its object could be a literary text, a mode of behaviour, a trend of fashion, a set of culinary practices, etc.), but a methodology that can be applied to all types of conduct. Its tools, therefore, need to be abstract enough to allow for flexibility and generalization.

As a discipline, semiotics has only recently entered the field of the humanities. Although its main tenets were originally formulated in the late nineteenth century, it was only in the 1960s that semiotics became established as a legitimate approach to human activity and its meanings. However, this new approach is actually the result of preoccupations that have existed since ancient times. Inasmuch as it studies the common elements in all systems of signification that humans use to communicate (and often animals too, as in zoosemiotics), it forms part of the system of thought that led to the philosophy of language. In this respect it is, in many ways, an expansion of rhetoric and philosophy.

Interestingly, semiotics as an approach to text analysis started in two different parts of the world at about the same time – in Switzerland and in the United States at the end of the nineteenth century.

The term **semiotics** comes from the Greek word **semeion** meaning sign, and is defined as any object or word that can produce meaning. The branch of linguistics that studies the meaning of words and sentences, **semantics**, has exactly the same root.

Saussurean semiotics

The Swiss founder of semiotics was the linguist Ferdinand de Saussure (1857–1913), whose seminal book *Course in General Linguistics* (1969) is considered one of the founding texts of semiotics. This book was compiled and collated by Saussure's students at the University of Geneva, from their lecture notes, and was published after Saussure's death, in 1915. Saussure conceived of semiotics as a science that would study how signs function in society, especially through the use of language. His explanation of this is:

> A science that studies the life of signs within society is conceivable; it would be part of social psychology and consequently of general psychology; I shall call it semiology. . . . Semiology would show what constitutes signs, what laws govern them. Since the science does not yet exist, no one can say what it would be; but it has a right to existence, a place staked out in advance. Linguistics is only a part of the general science of semiology; the laws discovered by semiology will be applicable to linguistics, and the latter will circumscribe a well-defined area within the mass of anthropological facts.

Clearly this was an ambitious project that relied to a high degree on abstraction and generality. Saussure saw this as inevitable in a science whose aim was to investigate different institutions, such as language, religious rites, social customs, eating habits, costume, standards of physical appearance, etc., as actually being creations of the same system, that of the imagination (incidentally Saussure does not use the word 'imagination' because his intent was to attach the credibility of science to semiotics). Since those institutions are clearly not the same in any apparent way, in order to examine if they do have commonalities, the method used to analyse them would have to be based on abstract concepts.

Saussure divided the *sign* into two elements: the physical form that we perceive as the sign, and the concept, image or idea that this physical form designates. The first he called the *signifier* and the second the *signified*. For example, the word 'dog' is a signifier; the image of an animal that it evokes in our minds when we hear or see it is the signified. If we see a picture or drawing of a dog, then that image would be the signifier and, again, the animal that it depicts would be the signified. In many cases, signifiers can have different signifieds. So, for instance, we do not all have the same image of a dog when we hear the word 'dog'; For some it would be a curly little poodle, for others a sleek greyhound, etc. However, our image would have an essence of 'dogness', and that is what we mean when we say that we understand the word 'dog'.

In the words of Saussure,

> I call the combination of a concept and a sound-image a sign, but in current usage the term generally designates only a sound-image, a word, for example. . . . I propose to retain the word sign to designate the whole and to replace concept and sound-image respectively by signified and signifier; the last two terms have the advantage of indicating the opposition that separates them from each other and from the whole of which they are parts. As regards sign, if I am satisfied with it, this is simply because I do not know of any word to replace it, the ordinary language suggesting no other (1966: 67).

Figure 4.1 depicts Saussure's concept of the sign.

Sign = Signifier + Signified

Signifier (word)   Signified (image)

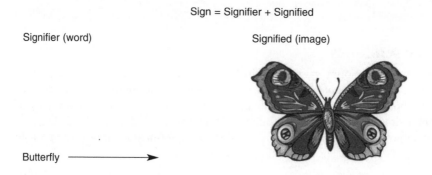

Butterfly ——————⟶

Figure 4.1 The Saussurean sign

Also, it is important to distinguish between a *signified*, the concept to which a sign refers, and a *referent*, the actual physical object that embodies the sign. So, for example, 'dog' could actually refer to a particular animal in the material world. However, even if it did not, the sign would still signify by evoking an image of the object it designates. Therefore, language signifies even if the signs it uses have no corresponding object in the world. There are, of course, many signs, such as 'love' or 'freedom', that do not have concrete referents. There are others, like 'dragon', 'unicorn' and 'angel', that signify objects in myths and stories and thus their referents would be in a *possible* world, as opposed to the *real* world.

A vital aspect of Saussure's concept of the sign is that the connection between its two parts is *arbitrary*. In other words, there is no reason why we designate a curly little poodle as 'dog'; there is nothing built into the word that makes it necessary for it to mean the animal we have in mind. The word has historical, etymological roots and is tied to conventions and choices made by speakers of Old English. Linguists oppose the term *arbitrary* with the term *motivated*: if a word is motivated it has some form of physical tie with the object it represents. This often happens in *onomatopoeic* expressions. For instance, the word 'buzz' is motivated; by saying it we make a sound that resembles the sound we are describing. Some signs, therefore, can be motivated, but most, according to Saussure, are arbitrary. It is important to remember also that even motivated signs have an arbitrary element to them. 'Buzz' is clearly an English word and, although it does resemble the sound of a bee, speakers of other languages have other words to describe precisely the same sound. 'Buzz' is, therefore, motivated within the limitations of the phonetic system (the system of sounds and pronunciations) of the English language.

Saussure also noted a subdivision of the sign, which he called a *symbol*. Being concerned mostly with linguistic signs, however, he did not pay too much attention to this. A symbol is a kind of image-sign that stands in a metaphorical relationship with the objects it represents: for example, a skull over two crossed bones, which stands for poison or piracy. According to Saussure,

> One characteristic of the symbol is that it is never wholly arbitrary; it is not empty, for there is the rudiment of a natural bond between the signifier and the signified. The symbol of justice, a pair of scales, could not be replaced by just any other symbol, such as a chariot (1966: 68).

Peircean semiotics

The American philosopher Charles Sanders Peirce approached semiotics from a more philosophical and psychological perspective than Saussure. Peirce was not as concerned with the linguistic sign as was Saussure, but focused, rather, on how people perceive the phenomenal world and then communicate it through their representations (which could be visual as well as verbal).

For Peirce (1931, vol. 2, para. 227):

> Logic, in its general sense, is, . . . only another name for semiotic, the quasi-necessary, or formal doctrine of signs. By describing the doctrine as 'quasi-necessary', or formal, I mean that we observe the characters of such signs as we know, and from such an observation, by a process which I will not object to naming Abstraction, we are led to statements, eminently fallible, and therefore in one sense by no means necessary, as to what must be the characters of all signs used by a 'scientific' intelligence capable of learning by experience.

Peirce's definition of the sign is 'something which stands to somebody for something in some respect or capacity'. In contrast to Saussure's dyadic model of the sign, Peirce proposed a tripartite model:

- *representamen*: the form which the sign takes;
- *object*: the thing or event to which the sign refers;
- *interpretant*: the sense made of the sign (not to be confused with 'interpreter').

For example, a fire alarm sounding would be a representamen; people fleeing the building and fire engines arriving would be the object; the sense made of the alarm, that there is a danger requiring expert action, would be the interpretant.

In addition to this basic model of *semiosis* (the process of signifying), Peirce distinguished three types of signs, *icons, symbols* and *indexes*. Put simply, icons signify by resemblance, symbols signify on the basis of convention and indexes signify by cause and effect. In his words,

> Every sign is determined by its objects, either first by partaking in the characters of the object, when I call a sign an Icon; secondly, by being really and in its individual existence connected with the individual object, when I call the sign an Index; thirdly, by more or less approximate certainty that it will be interpreted as denoting the object, in consequence of a habit (which term I use as including a natural disposition), when I call the sign a Symbol.

So, an icon is a sign that represents its object mainly by its similarity to it. An example of an icon would be a photograph, where the image portrayed resembles the object that it portrays, so that the resemblance and connection between the two can be seen. Icons can be further subdivided into classes: *images* and *diagrams*. In the case of images, 'simple qualities' are alike; in the case of diagrams, it is the 'relations between the parts' that are alike.

An index is a sign by virtue of an existential bond between itself and its object. The connection between an index and its object is one that can be deduced or figured out by some form of reasoning. Peirce gave several examples of this:

> I see a man with a rolling gait. This is a probable indication that he is a sailor. I see a bowlegged man in corduroys, gaiters and a jacket. These are probable indications that he is a jockey or something of the sort. A sundial or clock indicates the time of day.

Metonymical signs are also indices, such as smoke, which signifies that there is a fire, and medical symptoms, such as pulse rates, skin colour, etc., which signify that the patient has or does not have a particular disease.

Peirce's third category of sign, the symbol, is roughly equivalent to Saussure's arbitrary sign. Peirce also talks of the symbol as being based on a contract that eludes the individual will. In his words, 'you can write down the word "star", but that does not make you the creator of the word, nor if you erase it have you destroyed the word. The word lives in the minds of those who use it.' A symbol does not require the criterion of resemblance, as does the icon, nor the criterion of existential bond, as does the index. It is conventional and solidifies in culture through use over time. An example of a symbol would be the colour white symbolizing purity. In this case, we have to know that white = pure by learning the cultural conventions that associate the two – there is nothing intrinsic to white that makes it symbolize purity, nor does white symbolize purity in all cultures. However, because white does symbolize purity in Western European culture, it will do so for us unconsciously, even if the producer of the word or image 'white' has not intended it – the symbol has become part of our collective imagination.

It is important to note that Peirce's three categories of signs are not mutually exclusive and can sometimes overlap, especially depending on the context in which they are produced and the contexts in which they are interpreted. For example, here is what Peirce has to say about photographs, which, at face value, would tend to be classified as icons:

> Photographs, especially instantaneous photographs, are very instructive, because we know that in certain respects they are exactly like the objects they represent. But this resemblance is due to the

photographs having been produced under such circumstances that they were physically forced to correspond point by point to nature. In that aspect, then, they belong to the second class of signs, those by physical connection.

These are the basic concepts on which semiotics is founded. Although Saussure and Peirce founded two separate branches of semiotic analysis, it is not unreasonable or uncommon to combine concepts from both branches for a more eclectic approach. Above all, semiotics has helped to increase awareness of the fact that we know the world by means of signs, whether these are verbal or sensory. As well as having a material form, reality also has a semiotic existence. How we perceive objects, ideas or other people, and the meanings we attribute to them, are greatly influenced by the way these are represented and the medium through which they are represented.

In addition to the concepts described above, there are some other important distinctions and terms that semioticians use in text analysis. The next section overviews some of these.

As well as the fact that they were contemporaries, an interesting coincidence in the lives of **Saussure** and **Peirce** was that Peirce's work was also published after his death from student notes, between 1931 and 1935.

Denotation and connotation

These terms are associated with the work of Roland Barthes, developed in his influential books *Elements of Semiology* and *Mythologies*. Denotation refers to the literal, or *primary*, meaning of a sign, its exact definition. For example, 'fire' denotes a red, hot element that emits smoke and changes the shape of most things it comes into contact with. Connotation refers to the added, or *secondary*, meanings that have become attached to a sign through its repeated use in particular contexts. So, 'fire' connotes passion, heat, enthusiasm, energy, etc. Connotation reflects the artistic or creative aspects of language: the ways in which we use language to evoke images and sensations by showing analogies or similarities between different objects. In fact, in many ways connotations evoke the different contexts in which the term was used, and point to the phenomenon of meaning accumulation through usage.

Connotations often use rhetorical devices, such as metaphors and metonyms (described above). For example, the dollar sign is a metonym of money, but it also connotes wealth and associated ideas, such as greed, materialism, etc. that would be triggered by the juxtaposition of the sign with other signs within a context of use. Also, we can use a metaphor such as 'off the beaten track' to describe a remote location, but if we chose instead to describe this location as 'in the sticks', the remoteness that we were describing would have a different connotation, although both expressions are metaphorical. So, 'off the beaten track' would have more positive connotations of undiscovered tranquillity, whereas 'in the sticks' would have negative connotations of isolation. The same applies if we describe a person as an 'eccentric' (positive connotations of originality) or as a 'misfit' (negative connotations of maladjustment).

Connotation also reflects the social and political uses of language, and is very closely linked with context – signs assume different implicit meanings depending on the shared assumptions of those who use them in specific circumstances. We say, for example, that 'negro' has racist connotations because it tends to be associated with contexts where the word was used to segregate and discriminate against black people. At the same time, the term 'nigger', if uttered from one black person to another, can have connotations of comradeship or friendship (especially in the US social context).

Although connotations are sometimes considered 'attachments' to the denotative meaning of an utterance, this does not mean to say that they are less significant. In fact, many theorists would argue that most communication takes place on a connotative level, where beliefs, assumptions, contextual factors and idiomatic usage all play a role in the construction of meaning.

Theme and figure

These terms are associated with the work of semioticians of the Paris School, notably Algirdas-Julien Greimas and Joseph Courtes, as formulated, among other places, in their *Semiotics and Language: An Analytical Dictionary* (1982), and Greimas's collection of essays, *On Meaning: Selected Writings in Semiotic Theory* (1987). A theme is a sign that has a non-physical signified: that is, a signified that does not refer to a concrete object in the world. Signs such as /love/, /knowledge/, /serendipity/ are themes. Figures, on the other hand, are signs with material signifieds that refer to concrete objects in the real or in possible worlds. Examples of figures are /dog/, /girl/, /book/.

Figures can be used to explain themes, as themes can be used to explain figures. For example, a visitor in a foreign country observes gestures that s/he may not understand. These gestures are figural signs, signs with a concrete, physical manifestation. If the visitor were to ask what these gestures meant and were s/he to get a verbal explanation, this would be a case of themes (verbal signs) explaining figures (gestures). Similarly, figures can be used to explain themes, as often happens when someone explains technical or specialist terminology in layman's terms. For example, here is an extract from an article in *Scientific American* (Ashley 2004: 30). The writer begins with a story that describes physical action and is, therefore, figural. This story helps to explain the technical term 'radio-frequency identification tag', which is a thematic construct:

> Suppose you could go to the supermarket, fill the shopping cart with goods, and then just walk out the door without having to stand on a checkout line. Like an automated highway-toll collection system, an electronic reader at the store's exit would interrogate radio-based smart labels affixed to each item in the basket and ring up the purchases on a networked computer. Sometime later you would receive the grocery bill, perhaps by e-mail.

> Smart labels, or what engineers call radio-frequency identification (RFID) tags [the writer then continues by defining these tags].

Theoretical texts are mainly thematic because they are constructed with signs of abstract elements, such as concepts. Simple stories, on the other hand, such as fairy tales, are mainly figural because they are constructed with signs of concrete elements, such as human characters.

Type and token

This distinction was elaborated by Umberto Eco in his *Theory of Semiotics* (1976) from the semiotics of Peirce. Tokens are all the signs in a particular text, while types are all the signs in the text that belong to a specific category. Taking a written text as an example, tokens are all the words that compose the text; types are the different kinds of words that make up the tokens. Reproductions or imitations of an original text, such as a painting or a musical composition, would constitute tokens of the original type. In audience analysis, a researcher could select a token sample consisting of, say, female television viewers. From this token, the researcher could select a type, a particular kind of female television viewer. According to Eco's formulations, types and tokens are sign vehicles: that is, they represent the means by which signs are carried.

Intertextuality

This term originated in the work of Julia Kristeva (in her book *Semeiotiké*, 1966) and has become a very widely used concept in post-modern textual and cultural analysis. It describes the borrowing by a text of content or stylistic features that were present in a previously produced text. *Parody,* in which a text makes a humorous imitation of another text, is a common example of intertextuality. This is what occurs, for instance, in the post-80s trend of film spoofs, where one film explicitly uses characters, ideas and/or images from another film in a humorous manner.

Intertextuality underlines the fact that texts do not exist in isolation, nor are they creations of the totally independent mind of an artistic genius. Instead they are produced in a complex social context and enter into dialogue with one another. In fact, if we agree with Greimas's statement that 'there is nothing outside the text' (Floch 2001:1), meaning that the term 'text' does not have to refer to an object in the physical world but can include perceptual phenomena and subjective experiences inasmuch as they too are grasped cognitively as something that one can interpret and discuss, then the notion of intertextuality assumes another dimension. Much of our experience of the world is coloured by our knowledge, which comes from information sources such as books, newspapers, the mass media, etc. It could be said, therefore, that our knowledge of reality is intertextual, constructed through multiple links and cross-references between our individual preferences and dispositions, and the other texts with which we come into contact.

By including intertextual references in its composition, a text creates meaning by commenting on the meanings attributed to signs in other texts. This does not, of course, mean that texts are not also self-sufficient; even if a text makes intertextual references, it still functions as an independent entity. For example, Ken Loach's film *Sweet Sixteen* has many references to François Truffaut's classic film *The 400 Blows*. Both films are about a teenage boy's delinquent behaviour, both deal with the frustrations of intelligent and sensitive youth in an indifferent and coarse working-class community and both make implicit but sharp criticisms of the social situation that allows self-destructive behaviour to develop by neglecting or dismissing young people's problems and conflicts. *Sweet Sixteen* even ends in a parallel way to *The 400 Blows*, with the protagonist at the seashore, resignedly waiting to be arrested by the authorities after having committed a crime. Yet one does not need to have seen *The 400 Blows* to appreciate the meaning and subtlety of *Sweet Sixteen*, because it still stands as a self-contained text.

The concept of intertextuality has seen some revisions since its inception. For example, the French literary theorist Gerard Genette (1997) has proposed the term transtextuality to describe the influence and interrelationship between texts. Transtextuality includes five subcategories:

- *Intertextuality*: Genette takes this to include such devices as quotations, plagiarism and allusion.

- *Paratextuality*: the relations between text and paratext. Paratext denotes the techniques used to 'frame' the text, such as titles, prefaces, epigraphs, acknowledgements, footnotes, illustrations, etc.

- *Architextuality*: how a text designates itself as being part of a larger whole, such as a document type, genre, etc.

- *Metatextuality*: inclusion within the text of direct or indirect commentary on other texts. In as much as they discuss others' ideas and theories, textbooks are an example of metatextuality.

- *Hypertextuality*: the relations between a text and a preceding 'hypotext' – the text on which it is based but which it transforms in some way, by parodying it, translating it, creating a sequel to it, etc. In contemporary times, hypertextuality would also include computer-based texts which take the reader to other texts through a link. This kind of hypertextuality introduces multiple dimensions to the text, and challenges the traditional linear sequence.

4.2 Textual divisions: the syntagmatic and paradigmatic axes

The syntagm

Take the example of the sentence /I drink coffee/. Each word is related to each of the others, as part of the syntax of the English language. Looking at it grammatically, we would say it has a subject /I/, a verb /drink/ and an object /coffee/. From a more semiotic perspective, we would say that the relations between these words are syntagmatic: /I/ is altered by /drink/ which is further altered by /coffee/. Together these words have a different meaning than they would if each were seen separately. The syntagmatic axis of a text, therefore, comprises the links between consecutive units in the composition of a text (which could, of course, be made up of images as well as words). It looks at how meaning operates through the juxtaposition of a combination of elements, focusing on elements that constitute the text: in other words, elements that are present in the text.

Following this, a *syntagm* is defined as a system of interrelated, consecutive units. Examples of syntagms include the sequence of signs in a secret code; the sequence of notes in music; points and pauses in Morse code; the order of dishes in a meal, and any text where meaning is established by sequence and combination of units. A syntagm is a textual unit, but this unit can, in turn, be part of a more complex hierarchical organization, or, conversely, it can be subdivided into smaller units. So, the human body is a syntagm inasmuch as it is constituted of the elements of head, trunk, arms legs, etc., but a person can also enter into syntagmatic relations with others, as in a crowd, a couple, a team, etc.

The paradigm

Take again the example of the sentence /I drink coffee/. Now break it into three parts, /I/, /drink/ and /coffee/, and substitute a different word for each of these words. Looking just at

/coffee/, we probably could not have /table/ or /hair/ in its place, but we could well have /water/, /lemonade/, /wine/, amongst others. At the point in the syntagm /I drink coffee/, where we have /coffee/, the English language dictates we need a word that denotes liquidity and drinkability but is not 'coffee'. The relations between /coffee/ and the chosen substitute would be associative, or paradigmatic. Importantly, the chosen substitutes are not present in the syntagm, but need to be able to replace the selected element. The relationship between the selected element and its substitutes is a relationship of potentiality and selectivity. The paradigmatic axis of a text, therefore, looks at how meaning is constructed through a relationship of absence between elements.

Following this, a paradigm can be defined as a class of elements that are semantically homogeneous. This homogeneity, moreover, is established by what is known as the 'commutation test'. The commutation test involves substituting a unit for another in the same syntagmatic position and thereby changing the meaning but still maintaining a similar grammatical form. For example, consider the algebraic syntagm $(x + y)(x - y)$. If I substitute x for y, the result $(x + x)$ remains grammatical because x and y constitute part of the same paradigm. However, I cannot substitute − for y, because the result $(x + -)$ is absurd, i.e. meaningless, since y and − are not part of the same paradigm and therefore are not substitutable. Similarly, in the above example /I drink coffee/, I can substitute /wine/ and /water/ for /coffee/, because all three words belong to the same paradigm. However if I said /I wine coffee/, I would produce an absurd statement because /wine/ and /drink/ belong to different paradigms.

As an illustration of the above discussion on semiotics, we will use the T-mobile advertisement (Illustration 4.1). This will demonstrate a method of analysing, as well as creating, graphic advertisements.

Analysis of an advertisement

Print advertising works according to the combination of *illustration* and *copy*. By comparing these three elements from a semiotic perspective, we can trace the semantic categories, or basic units of meaning, that connect them into a coherent whole. In this advertisement, we distinguish the categories:

- contrast
- mobility
- abundance.

Using these semantic categories, the elements in the construction of the advertisement create an overall image that evokes diversity of experience, activation of potential and progress. This is how it is achieved.

Contrast. The actions described in the first half of the text – checking e-mail after finishing a conference call – imply a business context and a controlled space. The conjunction 'and' expresses addition or compounding. The additive element is further reinforced by the image, which shows two riders (rather than just one). However, the actions described in the second half of the text – adjusting sunglasses and starting a motorbike – suggest a different context, one evoking dynamic movement and open spaces. Therefore, the conjunction 'and' connects contrastive settings. Contrast, of course, also entails signs of change, and this leads smoothly to the next category – mobility.

I checked my e-mail after
I finished the conference
call. I replied to all

AND

I adjusted my sunglasses.
I took aim at the asphalt
as I popped the clutch,
ignoring the view in my
rearview mirror.

Who says you can't have both work AND life? Get the new BlackBerry 7105t™ from
T-Mobile, now with the easiest way to use Yahoo!® Mail. Plus, you get unlimited
BlackBerry® service with e-mail, instant messaging, Web browsing, and the most
WHENEVER Minutes.® All this, for as little as $59.99 per month on the world's
largest all-GSM network. A small price to pay for something that could change your life.

Find out more at www.t-mobile.com or call 1.800.TMOBILE.

T‑ ‑Mobile‑®
Get more from life®

⁙ BlackBerry.

Illustration 4.1 T-Mobile advertisement

Mobility. The image, depicting motorcycle riders in motion, represents fast movement. The fact that the picture is taken from behind the cyclists emphasizes this element of movement – the cyclists have left their departing point and are moving forward. Mobility also evokes change, and the advertisement includes several signs of change too. For example, the question in the subtext, 'who says you can't have both work AND life?' is followed by the introduction of the Blackberry with the words 'new' and 'now', implying that the Blackberry brings about a situation that changes the previous one indicated by the question. In other words, now the Blackberry can help you to resolve the contrast between work and life. Also, the tilting position of the riders implies a turning point – a change in direction. The phrase 'ignoring the view in my rearview mirror' suggests a strong commitment to moving forward and leaving the past behind. Finally, the text explicitly brings in the sign of change in the phrase, 'that could change your life.'

Abundance. The conjuncting aspects of the advertisement described in the contrast section above indicate a multiplication or increase of elements, and, therefore, activate also the semantic category of abundance. The advertisement suggests that the Blackberry makes it possible for you to succeed in more than one aspect of life – in fact, to manage both business *and* adventure. This concept is further reinforced through the use of the superlative and absolute expressions in the subtext: 'easiest way', 'unlimited service', 'the most minutes', and 'largest network'. Finally, the company's slogan 'Get more from life' evokes abundance in the word 'more'.

4.3 Formalist aesthetics

It is reported that the painter Degas once asked the poet Stephane Mallarmé why none of his interesting ideas could be found in his poetry. To this, Mallarmé replied that you write poetry not with ideas but with words. This remark is often cited to support the notion that artistic creation, like any other type of creation, is technique and construction rather than inspiration or vague sentiment. This is the notion that underpins the formalist movement in aesthetics.

Formalist approaches to the text and art trace their origins to a Russian intellectual movement that developed in the early twentieth century (roughly between 1915 and 1930). This movement was created around a group of linguists, literary critics and folklorists (who included Viktor Shklovsky, Roman Jakobson, Vladimir Propp and Boris Eichenbaum), and its mission was to trace and understand the techniques used in the creative use of language that distinguish artistic texts from their everyday counterparts (Lemon and Reis 1965; Erlich 1981; Steiner 1984). The main objective of formalist critics was to identify universal structures and linguistic devices that made the artistic text effective in eliciting an aesthetic response from audiences. Their guiding question was 'what makes a text art?' or, more precisely, 'what are the techniques used to turn simple language into art?' Formalists decided that such factors as 'emotive arousal' relied too heavily on the vague notions of intuition and subjective impression to be of much use to a rigorous approach to textual analysis. They aimed to free the study of art from sociological, biological and psychological considerations, and were some of the first scholars to approach it systematically as an autonomous and self-determining, universal form of human activity.

According to Viktor Shklovsky, the essential function of art was to make familiar things 'strange' and thereby liberate us from habitual ways of perceiving the world. This concept of 'making strange' or *defamiliarization* was central to the formalist approach to text analysis. By positioning an object with objects with which it is not usually associated, or by constructing a word differently from its normally accepted form, the artist presents the world in a novel way, introduces in it a sense of wonder and thereby encourages the reader or viewer to grow out of habitual modes of perception and notice things anew. Art produces a heightened awareness of reality by changing the light in which it is seen, so to speak.

In an experiment to show the contrived nature of gender roles, in 1989 a group of activists aptly named the Barbie Liberation Organization (BLO) switched the voice-boxes of GI Joe and Barbie dolls. This way, the Barbie dolls made such gender inappropriate comments as 'blow their brains out', while GI Joe dolls exclaimed 'I love shopping'. The surprise with which the dolls were received shows how entrenched our assumptions and beliefs about gender behaviour are. The experiment itself was a political statement making use of defamiliarization and distancing techniques in order to raise awareness of social prejudices.

A related concept is *distancing*, described by Boris Eichenbaum. This refers to the process through which an artist perceives an object in a detached manner in order to be able to depict it more vividly. This allows for the object (which can be physical, such as a person, or abstract, such as an idea) to be seen in detail but with no emotional investment. Of course, distancing is not the physical process of removing oneself from the vicinity of the object; rather, it entails an emotive separation from an object that makes the observer aware that what s/he is observing is a representation instead of a physical thing. The object can then be assimilated in the artist's perceptive framework (it becomes something one can take away while still leaving it in its place) and creatively reproduced in the work of art.

By seeing things differently and from a psychological distance, we become aware that what we take for granted has a constructed nature and is more than just 'there' – it has been set up in some way. Thus we come really to *see* the objects that make up the world in which we live and not just to *recognize* them. The way in which we have learnt to see things, therefore, becomes unveiled as one possible way to see them. Inevitably, such a conception of art has a strong revolutionary element that encourages people to be critical of inherited social conventions. It was this revolutionary element, furthermore, that caused the demise of the formalist movement in Russia by the Stalinist regime in 1930, scattering its participants to different countries.

Since the time of the Russian formalists, the idea of artistic distancing has been developed further by other theorists and artists. A notable example is the German playwright and social theorist Bertold Brecht, who developed an approach to theatrical staging that has come to be known as the 'theatre of alienation' or 'acting as alienation'. According to Brecht, spectators were more likely to become aware of social injustices and problems and to become active in various causes if the play were presented to them in an exaggerated or overly dramatic form that did not aim to be realistic or to hide its 'fakeness'; actors should not embody their roles or impersonate their characters, but should actually comment on these roles by acting them dispassionately. According to Brecht, art often presents a mellow or sentimental view of reality, which prevents it from fulfilling its role as a consciousness-raising field. In one of the plays he directed, Brecht even set up a banner for the audience with the words 'Don't be so romantic'.

4.4 Narrative

French film theorist Christian Metz (1974: 17) noted that 'a narrative has a beginning and an ending, a fact that simultaneously distinguishes it from the rest of the world'. Stories are central in the process of communication. They exist in all cultures and permeate all types of discourse, from entertainment to science. Children compose simple stories shortly after they acquire language (at around the age of two), which supports the claim that language tends to organize itself in narrative form almost automatically. Our perception of the world has a narrative basis in that we learn about the functions of different objects through stories.

In a famous article called 'The Structural Analysis of Narrative' first published in 1966, theorist Roland Barthes pointed out that life itself is in fact a story.

This ubiquity and universality of narrative induced language and culture scholars to create a discipline that studied specifically the form and functions of narrative. The two branches into which this discipline has evolved are *narrative semiotics* and *narratology*.

Russian folklorist and member of the formalist school Vladimir Propp is generally credited as the founder of the systematic study of narrative. Working in the early part of the twentieth century, Propp undertook an extensive comparison of Russian folk-tales with the aim of tracing common patterns. Motivated by the formalist ideal of finding out what was unique in creative texts, Propp used an approach that broke away from tradition, where stories were seen in terms of characters. Instead he studied the folk-tales in terms of the characters' actions (or 'functions' as he called them): that is, he looked at what characters did, not who they were.

From his analysis, Propp distinguished a common pattern in all folk-tales that ran roughly as follows: a king sends the hero on a quest that will solve a problem or bring back something for the king. The hero performs certain acts that usually involve breaking a rule, being punished, being deceived by someone, meeting someone who helps him and finally returning to the king, having accomplished the aim. His reward tends to be the hand of a princess and/or ascension to the throne. Propp found 31 functions that were present in all stories. These are shown in Table 4.1.

The kinds of character that Propp's typology recognizes are:

- villain
- donor
- helper

Table 4.1   Propp's functions

	Function	Description
	Initial situation	Members of family are introduced; hero is introduced
1.	Absentation	One of the family members absents himself/herself
2.	Interdiction	Interdiction is addressed to hero (can be reversed)
3.	Violation	Interdiction is violated
4.	Reconnaissance	Villain makes attempt to get information
5.	Delivery	Villain gets information about victim
6.	Trickery	Villain tries to deceive a victim
7.	Complicity	Victim is deceived
8.	Villainy	Villain causes harm to a family member; or
	Lack	Family member lacks something, desires something
9.	Mediation	Misfortune is made known; hero is dispatched
10.	Counteraction	Hero (seeker) agrees to counteraction
11.	Departure	Hero leaves home
12.	First donor function	Hero is tested, receives magical agent or helper
13.	Hero's reaction	Hero reacts to agent or donor
14.	Receipt of agent	Hero acquires use of magical agent
15.	Spatial change	Hero led to object of search
16.	Struggle	Hero and villain join in direct combat
17.	Branding	Hero is branded
18.	Victory	Villain is defeated
19.	Liquidation	Initial misfortune or lack is liquidated
20.	Return	Hero returns
21.	Pursuit, chase	Hero is pursued
22.	Rescue	Hero is rescued from pursuit
23.	Unrecognized arrival	Hero, unrecognized, arrives home or elsewhere
24.	Unfounded claims	False hero presents unfounded claims
25.	Difficult task	Difficult task is proposed to the hero
26.	Solution	Task is resolved
27.	Recognition	Hero is recognized
28.	Exposure	False hero or villain is exposed
29.	Transfiguration	Hero is given a new appearance
30.	Punishment	Villain is punished
31.	Wedding	Hero is married, ascends to the throne

- princess (and father)
- dispatcher
- hero
- false hero.

After listing and discussing the 31 functions, Propp makes a number of general inferences, which can be summarized as follows:

- There are only 31 functions.
- One function develops out of another logically (i.e. there is a causal sequence of functions).
- Functions can often be classified in pairs (struggle/victory) or in groups (villainy, dispatch, decision for counteraction, departure from home).

Propp (1968: 89) also suggests that it is possible to identify 'one tale with respect to which all fairy tales will appear as variants', and that at the core of fairy tales are certain abstract representations, which he identifies as myths. These ideas underline Propp's position as a major influence on structuralist text analysis because they highlight two tenets of this type of analysis: first, that the discourse level of the text (the level that is most apparent) is generated by an underlying structural level of a simpler and more abstract nature; secondly, that the elements making up the deeper level are to be found in a variety of texts with different discourse levels and can be used for typology formation. So, for example, we all recognise the story of Cinderella, regardless of the way in which it is told, the period in which it is set, what the characters are called, etc. 'Cinderella' does not denote a particular story but a prototypical story structure that brings into play a specific set of relationships and situations which can be told in many different ways and improvisations.

Narrative semiotics

Since its original formulation, Propp's model has been extensively adapted and improvised in order to make it appropriate for the study of more complex and innovative narrative constructions than the folk-tales from which it originally developed. A major reworking of Propp's model to universalize its application was undertaken by Algirdas-Julien Greimas in his *Structural Semantics* (1966). Greimas's formulations now form the basis of contemporary French semiotics, also known as *literary semiotics* and *narrative semiotics*. Two main models that Greimas extrapolated from his revision of Propp's work were:

- the performers of actions (the actantial model)
- the transformational stages of development (the model of the quest).

The actantial model

The actantial model is based on this prototypical scenario:

> Someone (the sender) sends another (the subject) to perform a series of actions in order to obtain something of value (the object). The subject will be helped by someone (the helper) and obstructed by someone (the opponent). From the acquisition of the object someone will benefit (the receiver).

The actantial model is presented graphically in Figure 4.2.

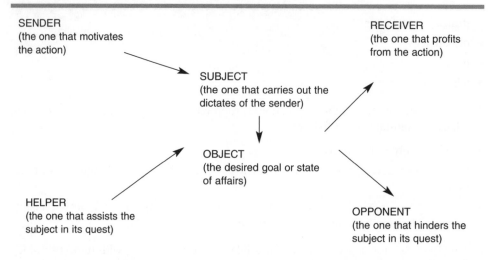

Figure 4.2 The actantial model

In addition, the actions that position the elements of the story in these categories are regulated by certain relations. So, the relation between the sender and the subject is a *contract*; the relation between the subject and the object is a *struggle*; and the relation between the sender and the receiver is a *communication*.

Note that this model's elements do not denote the identity of specific agents. Actually, they designate the main positions that agents take in the performance of their acts and the unfolding of events. The actions performed by a particular agent in a sequence of the story place this agent in one of the actantial categories. For instance, the position of sender, which includes the motivations or reasons for an action, need not designate just one agent, nor need this agent be human. In fact, the position of sender may be occupied by any agent that is the motivating force behind a series of actions leading to a result: a king, the mind, love or gravity are equally suitable senders. Similarly, if the one who performs the actions is the same as the one who motivates them, the positions of subject and of sender are occupied by the same agent – and the same is true of the other positions.

The actantial model represents the basic narrative. It is not based on how a story is told, but on the relative positioning of elements making up the story. As an example of how this would work, consider the well-known film *The Matrix* (A. and L. Wachowski 1999). Briefly, the story is as follows: Neo (Keanu Reeves) is a software developer and hacker recruited by a group of rebels, led by Morpheus (Laurence Fishburne), who have discovered that reality is an illusion created by a supercomputer. The rebels believe that Neo will be their saviour and will restore reality and re-empower the human race. The actions of Neo and the other rebels are opposed by the agents, who are computer clones. In the set of adventures that compose the narrative, Neo is especially helped by a female member of the rebel group, Trinity (Carrie-Anne Moss), and by a woman who can forecast the future in enigmatic ways, the oracle (Gloria Foster). Figure 4.3 shows an actantial model of this.

Neo is motivated to undertake the quest to restore reality and save humanity by Morpheus (figural sign with anthropomorphic signified), as well as by his own dissatisfaction with life and his suspicion that something is not quite right (thematic signs with

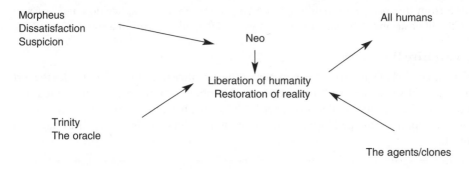

Figure 4.3 Actantial model of *The Matrix*

abstract signifieds signifying emotion). If he wins, all humans will benefit. In the quest he is helped by some (e.g. Trinity and the oracle) and opposed by others (notably the agents). The way in which this story is presented, for example in the language used, the costumes, and the episodes that compose the narrative sequence, is not shown in the actantial model. Its aim is to trace the minimal narrative (the bird's eye view of the story, so to speak) on which the presentational process is based.

Because of its simplified and abstract nature, the actantial model can be extracted from most texts, except perhaps the very simple – a fact that narrative semioticians use to support the claim that narrative underlies most forms of discourse, even the ones that are not presented as stories. In fact, for narrative semioticians, narrative forms the deep level of texts, and is common to many textual constructions, regardless of the discourses in which they are presented. For example, consider the definition of the 'greater happiness principle' from the *Dictionary of Philosophy* (Flew 1979: 135):

> The basic tenet of utilitarianism holds that the supreme good is the greatest happiness of the greatest number of people. Happiness is construed as the maximization of pleasure and minimization of pain; it is contended that only in terms of this programme do concepts like 'good', 'duty', and 'right' have meaning and application.

According to this utterance, utilitarianism teaches that society should seek the happiness of the majority as opposed to the happiness of a minority or the pain of the majority. Pain is the villain to be overcome and concepts such as 'good', 'duty' and 'right' are helpers or opponents according to whether they accept the dictates of the sender. Using the actantial model, this narrative is represented diagrammatically in Figure 4.4.

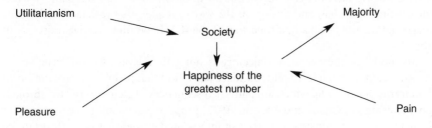

Figure 4.4 Actantial model of utilitarianism

Seen from this perspective, although the text is written as an explanation and not as a story, it still positions elements in roles that we understand in terms of a story.

The narrative trajectory

The second model of basic narrative structure is the narrative trajectory. This divides the text into a chain of sequences, with each sequence describing actions that are positioned in a causal order. This is the model that describes what happens in a story, as a sequence of events. This model is divided into four stages, each including a series of events as shown in Figure 4.5.

Initial situation → Qualifying test → Decisive test → Glorifying test

Figure 4.5 Narrative trajectory

The initial situation begins the narrative and sets the scene for the actions that will be performed. The qualifying test introduces a complication, problem or lack that sets the subject on its quest to solve the problem. The decisive test includes the actions that will be performed to fill the lack or solve the problem. And, finally, the glorifying test includes the actions that confirm that the problem has been solved (or not). Each sequence can include a set of subsequences with a list of actions, depending on the complexity and length of the narrative.

Taking the example of *The Matrix* described above, we would have the following narrative trajectory. In the initial situation we would place Neo's life activities as a corporate programmer by day and dissatisfied hacker by night, and the overall social setting that humans perceive as reality. The qualifying test would include the sequence where Neo finds the cryptic message from Morpheus on his computer and the dictate to 'follow the rabbit', as well as the sequences where Neo is initiated into the world of Zion, becomes aware of the human condition, learns to act as a virtual reality agent, and is asked if he wants to remain aware or re-enter the world of illusion.

Continuing the trajectory, the decisive test would include the sequences where Neo and his friends struggle against the computer clones in order to regain control of the world. The glorifying test would include the sequences where Neo is established as being 'the one' who will save the world, attains skills equivalent to those of the clones, returns from the dead and takes up his position as leader of Zion. The problem of subservience to computers and existence in a virtual world has not been solved, but the question about who is capable of overturning the existing order has, and this opens the way to sequels that re-establish elements of the initial situation and begin a new trajectory. Table 4.2 shows the narrative trajectory of *The Matrix*.

Again, this model of the narrative trajectory is not only relevant for the structure of stories. In fact, recent research in cognitive science has found that people perceive the world and think in terms of *schemata*, which are patterned sequences of elements related through association. For example, Schank and Abelson (1977) propose that people place information on a topic in a system that consists of a series of interrelated elements. Taking the example of a topic such as job-seeking, we would get these associated elements:

Table 4.2 Narrative trajectory of *The Matrix*

Initial situation	*Qualifying test*	*Decisive test*	*Glorifying test*
• Neo is a dissatis-fied programmer and hacker with many existential questions	• Neo finds a message on his computer telling him to 'follow the rabbit'	• Neo and his friends undertake a series of adventures fighting against the clones	• Neo's powers equal those of the clones
	• Neo is transported to Zion and meets Morpheus	• Neo meets the Oracle	• Neo manages to save Morpheus from the clones
	• Morpheus shows Neo what he can do in the virtual world and asks him if he wants the 'red pill or the blue pill'		• Neo is killed and resurrected
			• Neo is proclaimed as 'The One'

- a generic theme (such as 'applying for a job');
- assumed conditions (such as 'the candidate has the necessary qualifications and needs a job');
- a series of sequential stages (such as 'preparing a résumé, writing a résumé, writing a cover letter, sending it', etc.);
- a series of actions within each stage (such as 'typing the résumé and the letter, putting them in an envelope', etc.).

This implies that, even if these elements are not directly stated in the communicated information ('job-seeking'), they are assumed, in that interpreters will access them in the stored knowledge of their mental frames, or mental schemata, through association and inference.

The narrative structure of a mental schema is clearly evident. Taking the above example of job-seeking, we would get the model of the narrative trajectory shown in Figure 4.6.

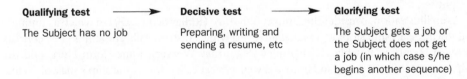

Qualifying test $\longrightarrow$	**Decisive test** $\longrightarrow$	**Glorifying test**
The Subject has no job	Preparing, writing and sending a resume, etc	The Subject gets a job or the Subject does not get a job (in which case s/he begins another sequence)

Figure 4.6 Narrative trajectory of job-seeking scheme

The semiotic square

Following the lead of Saussurean structuralist linguistics, semiotics shows that the meaning of a word is formed in terms of its opposite. For example, we cannot have a notion of 'cold' if we do not at the same time have a notion of 'hot' with which to contrast it. This supports a binary division of meaning construction which can lead to some problems. Would saying that something is not cold mean that it is hot? Or would telling someone that you don't love them mean that you hate them? Clearly this binary dichotomy of the sign needs to be looked at more closely. These issues led narrative semioticians to formulate the analytical tool of the semiotic square. The semiotic square introduces two other poles to the basic oppositional structure of the sign: the sign's complementary aspect and its contradictory. So, returning to the example of 'cold–hot', this pair would also contain the implicit aspects 'not cold–not hot'. We then get the semiotic square shown in Figure 4.7.

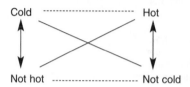

Figure 4.7 The semiotic square of cold–hot

In this semiotic square, 'not cold' contradicts 'cold' and complements 'hot'; 'not hot' contradicts 'hot' and complements 'cold'.

We can analyse a narrative with the semiotic square by following a set of steps. First, we trace a major semantic category on which most important actions are based– the main kernel of meaning that centres the story. For example, a story may revolve around the notion of guilt, of liberation or of power – to name just three of an infinite number of possibilities. Secondly, we decide what notion would be the opposite of this central sign: for guilt you may have righteousness, for liberation you may have restriction and for power you may have weakness. You can then design a semiotic square, including the contraries and complementaries of each pole. You now have a tool that can help you understand how the story develops by 'playing around' with the signs that make up the four corners of the semiotic square.

As it is when first formed, the semiotic square is empty. The next step is to 'fill it in' by identifying and isolating actions and characters that represent the categories of the square. This will show how seemingly different elements are connected in a logical network, and will shed new light on how the story works on a fundamental level, and what beliefs and values it espouses.

As an illustration, consider the famous film *Alien* (Ridley Scott 1979) in which a commercial towing spaceship stops at a planet after receiving a distress call. The ship's crew consists of seven members, notably Helen Ripley (Sigourney Weaver), Kane (John Hurt) and the ship's science officer, Ash (Ian Holm), as well as a cat called Jones, the ship's mascot. While investigating the distress call, Kane is attacked by an unidentified form which eventually turns out to have invaded his system and reproduced in his body. After killing him, the 'offspring', an alien, animal-like creature, threatens to invade the other crew members as well. Although the ship's company orders the crew to bring the creature back to Earth for research, they resist and attempt to destroy the creature. In this they are opposed by Ash, who urges them to obey the company's commands. In an altercation with Ripley, Ash is revealed to be an artificial humanoid hostile to the interests of the crew, who destroy him.

Finally, after a series of clashes between the crew and the alien creature, the only survivors are Ripley and the cat.

The main semantic category which pervades the narrative action is *life*. In a semiotic analysis, we arrive at this conclusion by identifying common elements in what motivates the actions that make up the story:

- The ship responds to an SOS call → attempt to save life.
- The crew waive the quarantine policy and transport the infected Kane into the ship → attempt to save life.
- The alien creature is born through Kane → reproduction of life.
- The crew try to kill the creature so as to survive → survival.
- Ash tries to save the creature and the creature tries to survive → attempt to save life and survival respectively.

However, life is not the only element at play here. The story revolves around conflict about *whose* life is worth saving, and clearly specifies two camps – the humans and the aliens. Our initial semantic category, life, needs to be modified, therefore, into humanness and alienness. Including also contradictories and complementaries of these two signs, we get the semiotic square shown in Figure 4.8.

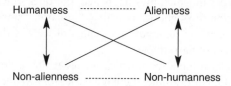

Figure 4.8 First semiotic square of *Alien*

Looking at the characters and their interrelationships in terms of these signs, we see some interesting correspondences. Ripley and most of the crew would fall into the category of humanness. The creature is clearly a hostile being that opposes the interests of the humans, while fighting for its own, so it would go into alienness. Ash has the appearance of a human but is actually a robot, so he is a representative of non-humanness (not quite alien but not quite human either). Interestingly, the cat is not a human but it is friendly to humans and provides comfort to Ripley in her dangers, the two being the only survivors at the end of the film. It would therefore typify non-alienness (different but not quite alien, as it does not threaten human life). We now have the 'filled' square shown in Figure 4.9.

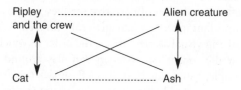

Figure 4.9 Second semiotic square of *Alien*

If we now re-examine the actions that make up the narrative, we see that they reflect the tensions captured by the semiotic square. Ripley and the cat are complementary in that their interests do not conflict, while at the same time they are different enough not to be substitutable (we could not include the cat in the category of human life, for instance). Similarly, the alien creature and Ash are complementary in that their interests coincide while their narrative positions are different (one could not play the role of the other).

Ripley's contrary is the alien creature, as this is the character that diametrically opposes human life and its values, and threatens to destroy everything that represents this category. However, her contradictory would be Ash because he has enough elements to enable him to be classified as human but his actions reject this classification. In a similar vein, the cat's actions contradict the alien creature's actions because, although both creatures are not human, the cat plays a supportive role, rather than a threatening one (in a couple of instances, for example, the cat's presence is mistaken for the alien's, only to provide relief when its identity is revealed). This analysis also brings to light the importance of the cat as a character in *Alien*. It shows that the cat is not an ornamental extra providing relief, but actually fills a logical position and provides narrative coherence.

Narratology

French film director Jean-Luc Godard once said that he liked a film to have a beginning, a middle and an end, but not necessarily in that order. A story-teller does not have to tell the events of a story in the order in which they happened, nor does s/he have to keep the same identity or the same location throughout the telling. Similarly, a story can be told from the narrator's point of view or it can juxtapose the points of view of different characters. All these factors are the domain of narratology.

Narrative semiotics looks at the ways in which stories exhibit a similar structure, regardless of the way they are told. For example, there is a basic story we recognize as built around the prototype of the seducer Don Juan or of the split personality Dr Jekyll and Mr Hyde, even though each version may be told in different ways and may be embellished, reduced or improvised. Narratology, on the other hand, takes a somewhat different approach. Instead of looking at the ways in which narrative elements are positioned in relation to each other to produce universal underlying patterns, it focuses on the ways in which stories are told, and on the relations between the content of the stories and the process by which they are presented. Narratology looks at the discourse used to present a story, the relationship between the narrator and the narrative (i.e. between the one who tells and what is told) and the organization of the different voices in the text (i.e. what is presented as a description in the narrator's voice and what is presented as the speech and/or point of view of a character) (Genette 1980; Bal 1985; Chatman 1978; Prince 1982; Stanzel 1984; Gibson 1996).

Time, an element downplayed in semiotics, assumes prominence in narratological approaches. In fact, a cause-and-effect linear order, linking one event to another in a chain sequence, becomes a defining criterion of narrative for these approaches. In verbal stories, therefore, the tense is important to show when an event occurred. Also, the juxtaposition of sequences, in both verbal and visual stories, affects the order in which events occur and the order in which we know they occur. Story-tellers can play around considerably with the concept of time. For example, a story can be told as a flashback (*analepsis* in Genette's terminology), it can be seen or predicted before it actually occurs (*prolepsis* in Genette's terminology) or it can be repeated at different stages (*iteration* in Genette's terminology).

Writers and film-makers often use narratorial switches and inconsistencies to create an effect. For example, Italo Calvino's novel *The Non-Existent Knight* is a bizarre story filled with references to unconventional sexual behaviour and graphic bodily functions. At the end of the story the narrator is revealed to be a nun. This is intended to surprise the reader and make him/her re-evaluate what s/he has just read. Similarly, Bryan Singer's film *The Usual Suspects* has a crippled and socially insignificant narrator telling the story of a notorious and powerful criminal. At the end of the story, the narrator is revealed to be the hero of his own story, his modest appearance having been a deceptive façade. Once again, the spectator is led to redefine the events s/he has just seen. If we were to read *The Non-Existent Knight* or see *The Usual Suspects* again, we would react to the recounted events differently, knowing who the source of information is. This shows that we respond to the identity of the messenger even more than we do to the content of the message. Narrative is a powerful code in showing this.

The identity and location of the teller of the story, or narrator, are also important for the meaning of the story – a story told by an idiot is not quite the same as one told by a judge because of the different credibility we attach to each identity. Also, a story told by one of the characters has certain constraints and liberties, while a story told by someone external to the action has certain other constraints and liberties. A story can be told by a narrator who is external to the location and action of the events, in which case s/he would be extradiegetic (according to Genette's definitions). A narrator who is a character in the story would be intradiegetic. In a parallel way, a narrator who tells someone else's story is heterodiegetic, while one who tells his/her own story is homodiegetic.

Consider this extract from William Gibson's novel *All Tomorrow's Parties* (1999: 94) as an illustration of these concepts:

Fontaine has two wives.

Not, he will tell you, a condition to aspire to.

They live, these two wives, in uneasy truce, in a single establishment, nearer the Oakland side. Fontaine has for some time now been opting to sleep here, in his shop.

The younger wife (at forty-eight, by some five years) is a Jamaican originally from Brixton, tall and light-skinned, whom Fontaine has come to regard as punishment for all his former sins.

Her name is Clarisse. Incensed, she reverts to the dialect of her childhood: 'You tek de prize Fonten.'

Fontaine has been taking the prize for some ten years now, and he's taking it again today. Clarisse standing angrily before him with a shopping bag full of what appear to be catatonic Japanese babies.

These are in fact life-sized dolls, manufactured in the closing years of the previous century for the solace of distant grandparents, each one made to resemble photographs of an actual infant. Produced by a firm in Meguro called Another One, they are increasingly collectible, each example being to some degree unique.

The narrator in this extract is intradiegetic, since he places himself within the narrative, in the location where events take place: this is indicated by the word /here/ in line 4, and by the word /today/ in line 8, which shows that the narrator's time coincides with that of the narrative. He is heterodiegetic since the events recounted do not involve him in the action: he tells the story of another agent, Fontaine. The tense chosen to recount the events is the present, making the action immediate and urgent. The speech includes *indirect discourse* (most of the extract), *direct discourse* ('You tek de prize Fonten' – the exact words of Clarisse), and *free indirect discourse* (not, he will tell you, a condition to aspire to – the point of view of Fontaine presented in the words of the narrator, a technique that is between direct and indirect discourse). The juxtaposition of these three types of discourse produces rhythm and a dynamic orientation to the story – a jump-cut approach to the narration, similar to rapid editing in film.

The point of view is mostly that of Fontaine, except for the last paragraph, which describes the origins of the dolls. There is no information in this extract which tells us whether Fontaine knows the facts presented in this paragraph, or whether it is the extradiegetic narrator who is filling the gaps and giving the reader more information than the characters actually know.

This extract recounts one event: Clarisse standing in front of Fontaine with the dolls. The rest of the information acts as background to this event, building up the characters, and is constructed on a different temporal level from the event. It describes a situation that existed before the event took place.

▌Summary

◆ Semiotics is the science of signs, what they are and how they work in creating a text. The theoretical origins of semiotics lie in linguistics and philosophy, while semiotics as a method of analysis can be applied to anything that is considered a text, from literary novels to dance movements.

◆ Narrative, or story structure, pervades most forms of communication. Semioticians recognise the ubiquity of narrative in text construction, and have developed various tools to study it, for example the *actantial model* and the *semiotic square*. In addition, literary and cultural theory has developed an approach especially for the study of narrative, known as *narratology*.

▌Topics for discussion

▶ Brainstorm some words and signs that have different connotations from their denotative meanings. List the common uses of these words and signs and discuss some contexts where they appear in popular culture.

▶ Using the actantial model, the narrative trajectory and the semiotic square, analyse the narrative structures of a popular film. Did this analysis make you aware of aspects of the film that you had not observed before?

▶ Read a short story. Note who the narrator is, how you know him/her and what effect this has on the way you respond to the recounted events. A useful way to understand the significance of the narrator is to substitute the existing narrator with another character (for example, by changing from a first-person to a third-person narration). Then note how the narrator's choice influences the order in which events are recounted (as in prolepsis, analepsis, etc.). What changes would you need to make to the story if you changed this order?

▋References and further reading

Ashley, S. (2004) Penny Wise Smart Labels. *Scientific American* August.

Bal, M. (1985) [1977] *Narratology: Introduction to the Theory of Narrative*, trans. by C. Van Boheemen. Toronto: Toronto University Press.

Bal, M. (1991) *On Story-telling: Essays in Narratology.* Sonoma, CA: Polebridge Press.

Barthes, R. (1968) *Elements of Semiology.* London: Cape.

Barthes, R. (1984) [1957] *Mythologies.* New York: Hill and Wang.

Barthes, R. (1990) [1966] 'The Structural Analysis of Narrative', in S. Sontag (ed.), *A Barthes Reader.* New York: Farrar, Straus and Giroux.

Berger, A. A. (1999) *Signs in Contemporary Culture: An Introduction to Semiotics*, 2nd edn. Salem, WI: Sheffield.

Booth, W. C. (1961) *The Rhetoric of Fiction.* Chicago: Chicago University Press.

Chandler, D. (1999) *Semiotics: The Basics.* London: Routledge.

Chatman, S. (1978) *Story and Discourse: Narrative Structure in Fiction and Film.* Ithaca, NY: Cornell University Press.

Danesi, M. (1995) *Interpreting Advertisements: A Semiotic Guide.* Toronto: Legas.

Eco, U. (1976) *A Theory of Semiotics.* Bloomington: Indiana University Press.

Eco, U. (1984) *The Role of the Reader: Explorations in the Semiotics of Texts.* Bloomington: Indiana University Press.

Chatman, S. (1980) *Story and Discourse: Narrative Structure in Fiction and Film.* Ithaca, NY: Cornell University Press.

Chatman, S. (1990) *Coming to Terms: The Rhetoric of Narrative in Fiction and Film.* Ithaca: Cornell University Press.

Coste, D. (1989) *Narrative as Communication.* Minneapolis: University of Minnesota Press.

Currie, M. (1998). *Postmodern Narrative Theory.* New York, NY: St Martin's Press.

Danesi, M. (ed.) (2000) *Encyclopedic Dictionary of Semiotics, Media and Communications.* Toronto: University of Toronto Press.

Eco, U. (1976) *A Theory of Semiotics.* Bloomington: Indiana University Press.

Erlich, V. (1981) *Russian Formalism: History and Doctrine*, 3rd edn. New Haven, CT: Yale University Press.

Flew, A. (ed.) (1979) *A Dictionary of Philosophy.* London: Pan.

Floch, J-M. (2001). *Semiotics, Marketing and Communication*, trans. by R. Orr Bodkin. Basingstoke: Palgrave Macmillan.

Genette, G. (1980) [1972] *Narrative Discourse: An Essay in Method*, trans. by J. E. Lewin. Ithaca: Cornell University Press.

Genette, G. (1997) [1987] *Paratexts.* Lincoln: University of Nebraska Press.

Gibson, A. (1996) *Towards a Postmodern Theory of Narrative*. Edinburgh: Edinburgh University Press.

Gibson, W. (1999) *All Tomorrow's Parties*. London: Penguin.

Greimas, A. J. (1966) *Sémantique structurale*. Paris: Larousse.

Greimas, A. J. (1987) *On Meaning: Selected Writings in Semiotic Theory*, trans. by P. Perron and F. Collins. Minneapolis: University of Minnesota Press.

Greimas, A. J. and Courtes, J. (1982) *Semiotics and Language: An Analytical Dictionary*, trans. by L. Crist et al. Bloomington: Indiana University Press.

Kristeva, J. (1969) *Semeiotiké*. Paris: Seuil.

Lemon, L. T. and Reis, M. J. (1965) *Russian Formalist Criticism: Four Essays*. Lincoln: University of Nebraska Press.

Metz, C. (1974) *Film Language: A Semiotics of the Cinema*, trans. by M. Taylor. New York: Oxford University Press.

Nadin, M. and Zakia, R. (1994) *Creating Effective Advertising Using Semiotics*. New York: Consultant Press.

Peirce, C. S. (1931). *Collected Papers of Charles Sanders Peirce*. Cambridge, MA: Harvard University Press.

Prince, G. (1982) *Narratology: The Form and Functioning of Narrative*. Berlin: Mouton.

Prince, G. (1987) *A Dictionary of Narratology*. Lincoln : University of Nebraska Press.

Propp, V. (1968) [1928] *Morphology of the Folktale*. Austin, TX: University of Texas Press.

Saussure, F. de (1966) *Course in General Linguistics*. New York: McGraw Hill (original published in 1916).

Schank, R. and Abelson, R. (1977) *Scripts, Plans, Goals and Understanding: An Inquiry into Human Knowledge Structures*. Hillsdale, NJ: Lawrence Erlbaum.

Stanzel, F. K. (1984) *A Theory of Narrative*, trans. by C. Goedsche. Cambridge: Cambridge University Press.

Steiner, P. (1984) *Russian Formalism: A Metapoetics*. Ithaca: Cornell University Press.

Professional Communication

CHAPTER 5

They'll negotiate; they're corporate.

Johnny in *Johnny Mnemonic*

This chapter looks at interpersonal communication and group communication, especially as they relate to professional settings. Interpersonal communication refers to one-on-one or small-group interactions. Research generally suggests that this type of communication is influential in changing opinions, dealing with resistance and apathy to issues, and generally maintaining harmony in social situations – more so than its opposite, mass communication. The main features of interpersonal media are:

- They provide a two-way exchange of information. Individual participants can obtain clarification, explanation and negotiation. This characteristic of interpersonal networks often allows them to overcome problems of message distortion caused by excessive noise (as described in Chapter 2).

- They generally have a significant effect in persuading an individual to form or to change a strongly held attitude.

- In many situations, they can help to resolve conflict because they provide a means of airing personal feelings and dealing with misunderstandings or grudges.

Here we discuss interpersonal communication in business and management contexts, by focusing on *cultural influence, team interaction, conflict, information management* and *project management*.

5.1 Culture

Individuals interact in networks or groups which carry expectations, rules, norms and ideals. These regulative practices are based on assumptions about the order of things, values, ethical beliefs, and attitudes towards status and authority – all characteristics of the misleadingly transparent concept of 'culture'. Meanings about the world and its objects are constructed in social interactions within or between cultural groups and then serve to identify the group both socially and globally.

So what is culture? For the purpose of this discussion, I define it as *a system of activities and discourses, which have been codified and crystallized by usage, and which reflect the conventional practices of a group.* All collectivities develop a culture over time – a nation has a culture, as does an organization, a fan club or a gang. Complex societies have a diversity of cultures, including those of minority groups, such as ethnic cultures and gay cultures. The more complicated a culture becomes, the greater the chance that groups will break apart to form subcultures, which may be *alternative* (different from the mainstream but not challenging it), or *oppositional* (different from the mainstream and attempting to change it) (Williams 1980; De Certeau 2002).

As regards the culture of business or government organizations, this is manifest in such factors as the organization's objectives and 'mission', the hierarchy (allocation of roles in order of seniority), the internal and external patterns of negotiation, and the management of conflict. The organization's public image is also significant in making cultural values apparent and known to others. This is achieved through various community-oriented projects and ecological initiatives, encompassed under the umbrella term of Corporate Social Responsibility (CSR).

The culture of an organized group of individuals, such as in a corporation, designates the beliefs, values, norms and attitudes that directly affect behaviour. The organizational culture can be seen in action in company strategies, the company mission, public relations ventures, and employee relations.

Researchers in business communication have offered several models and taxonomies of features that help to define the culture of an organization. Robbins and Barnwell (2002), for example, distinguish the following as key elements in analysing business culture:

- *Individual initiative*: how much and what kind of responsibility, freedom and independence do individuals have?

- *Risk tolerance*: are employees encouraged to take initiatives and engage in risk-taking behaviour?

- *Direction*: are the organization's objectives and performance expectations clearly communicated and implemented?

- *Integration*: is it easy for groups within the organization to operate in a coordinated manner and are they motivated to do so?

- *Management contact*: are managers accessible, supportive and helpful to their subordinates?

- *Control*: what is the extent and nature of the rules and supervision regulations which the organization employs to oversee employee performance?

- *Identity*: does the organization encourage employees to identify with the company and the company's public image?

- *Reward system*: how and to what degree are employees rewarded for their performance (i.e. through promotion, salary increases, bonus schemes, etc.)?
- *Conflict tolerance*: is there a mechanism and/or procedure that allows employees to communicate conflicts and criticisms?
- *Communication patterns*: are communication channels restricted to the formal hierarchy of command, or are they diverse (i.e. do junior employees have easy access to senior managers; can members of one section co-operate with members of another)?

Answers to these questions would come from surveys of company employees, an examination of formal company procedures, and case studies involving particular situations where action and decision-making reflect the company's structure and value system, i.e. its culture.

Two influential models in the analysis of organizational culture that we will consider here in more detail are Geert Hofstede's (2001) practice dimensions and House's (1998; House et al. 2004) GLOBE model.

Hofstede's work spans approximately a 20-year-period (from the late 1960s to the late 1980s) and is based on two surveys, one conducted of 116,000 IBM employees scattered over 72 countries, and another conducted of 1150 male and 1150 female students from 23 countries. From this research, Hofstede distinguished five practice dimensions which he used to classify cultures. These are:

1 *Power distance*: the different attitudes to inequality between people. High-power distance cultures tend to value the following elements: hierarchy, fixed roles, authoritarian decision-making styles, and conformity. In addition, in such cultures subordinates are not often consulted in decision-making, and, in situations that involve negotiation, individuals tend to prefer to work with high-status negotiators rather than lower-level representatives (exemplified by the 'I want to talk to your manager' syndrome). Low-power distance cultures, on the other hand, tend to value these elements: low hierarchical structure, independence, individual initiative, freedom (which could manifest itself in anything from the ability to voice dissent to being allowed to dress eccentrically) and consultative decision-making styles. In such cultures, subordinates tend to be consulted and there is more emphasis on rewards and negotiation.

2 *Uncertainty avoidance*: the level of acceptance of an unknown future. High-uncertainty-avoidance cultures tend to exhibit the following characteristics: a preference for engaging in risky behaviour (such as initiating legal action), rather than waiting to see how a situation will unfold; security through predictability and routine; adherence to rules, regulations and operating procedures; traditional gender roles; controlled presence of innovators; and belief in specialists and experts. Low-uncertainty-avoidance cultures tend to exhibit these characteristics: patience in taking action; belief in the importance of emotive or intuitive responses to situations; freedom in gender roles; support for innovation and experimentation; and belief in generalists.

3 *Individualism versus collectivism*: the manner in which individuals are integrated in groups. Individualist cultures generally define identity according to personal and separate values. They tend to exhibit these characteristics: appreciation of an individual 'voice' or opinion; guiltless pursuit of self-interest and material gain; calculative rela-

tionships (exemplified by the 'what's in it for me?' syndrome); and individual incentive. On the other hand, collectivist cultures generally define identity according to group positioning and communal values. They tend to exhibit these characteristics: decision-making in groups; focus on the pursuit of the public good; emotional commitment to group membership; collaborative incentive.

Personal identity is influenced by one's professional culture. In many organizations there are fixed rules about conduct, such as what one may or may not wear, the language one may or may not use, and even whether one may or may not flirt with or date co-workers.

4   *Masculine versus feminine*: the manner in which roles and emotive responses are divided according to gender. This practice dimension reflects traditional gender roles that associate males with assertiveness and females with nurturance, and extends these into the organizational domain. Typical characteristics of masculine cultures include: the importance of challenge and recognition; performance or results orientation; a division of individuals into 'losers' and 'winners'; more men in top management positions; a competitive advantage in manufacturing industries and price competition. Typical characteristics of feminine cultures include: co-operative orientation; process orientation and reflexive practice; more sympathy for the disadvantaged; greater facility for women to reach top management positions; a competitive advantage in the service industries and consulting.

5   *Long-term versus short-term orientation*: the different values attached to future as opposed to immediate results. Long-term-oriented cultures tend to value savings and investments, while short-term-oriented cultures may be more entrepreneurial and focus on immediate gains. Long-term-oriented cultures tend to exhibit these traits: persistence; deferral of gratification; a strong market position and relationship marketing; equality; and provision for old age (which is not seen as a negative factor). Short-term-oriented cultures tend to exhibit these characteristics: schemes that produce fast results; appreciation of leisure time; grasping opportunities in business affairs; and deferral of concerns regarding old age.

Hofstede's practice dimensions do not represent exclusive or rigid categories, but rather a continuum of degrees between the two extremes of each dimension. Thus, for example, some cultures would probably fall somewhere in between the long-term- and short-term-oriented categories or individualist and collectivist categories. Also, a temporal element would come into play, with some cultures changing their positioning over time and in different circumstances.

For all its success as a research tool, Hofstede's model carries certain dangers typical of attempts to construct an abstract modelling of human behaviour. First, as happens in research based on surveys, the findings tend to be influenced by the wording of the questions and the circumstances in which the surveys were administered. It cannot be certain that the results would have remained the same if different wording had been used and the surveys had been repeated in different contexts. Secondly, even if the populations chosen to be surveyed constituted a representative sample and a substantial number of respondents were interviewed, the results would still be abstracted from the general attitudes of a majority. Exceptions that would actually contest the findings or that would highlight the circumstantial nature of responses would be overshadowed. Finally, even though the results can be used for taxonomies and classifications of cultures, the evaluative or interpretative dimension is absent. For example, what does being an individualist or a collectivist actually mean to particular members of an organization, and how does it play out in the social arena?

Bearing these reservations in mind, as anyone who has worked in different organizations or who has lived in different countries knows, culture is indeed a very influential factor in behaviour and attitudes, in what one can and cannot do, and even in what one can or cannot *imagine* doing. In fact, structures and mental frames that determine our patterns of thinking are deeply embedded in social institutions and in language. To take one example, the Japanese language has different forms reserved for men and for women, and for degrees of respect based on levels of seniority. In this case, unless a speaker actually impersonates another, s/he cannot express an identity that his/her social role is not culturally associated with. Identity is already inscribed in the status system of the culture and reflected in linguistic form. As Harry Irwin (1996: 79) points out with regard to gender equality in Japan, '[t]his begs the question of whether a Japanese female manager could ever succeed in giving a direct order to a male, and presents a long-term and deeply rooted difficulty for Japanese women seeking workplace equality'.

The second approach to organizational culture that we consider here is based on Robert House's Global Leadership and Organisational Behaviour Effectiveness (GLOBE) model (House 1998; Javidan and House 2001; House et al. 2004). The GLOBE model was based on surveys that asked participants to describe cultural situations both as they experienced them in their organizations and as they thought they should ideally be. The GLOBE survey drew on data from around 17,000 questionnaires completed by middle managers from approximately 825 companies in 62 countries. The GLOBE project divided the countries surveyed into ten clusters based on geography, common language, religion and historical factors. The ten GLOBE clusters were:

- Anglo
- Latin Europe
- Nordic Europe
- Germanic Europe
- Eastern Europe
- Latin America
- Sub-Saharan Africa
- Arab
- Southern Asia
- Confucian Asia

Building on the work of Hofstede and others on cultural influences on behaviour, the GLOBE study distinguished nine cultural dimensions, as set out in Table 5.1.

Table 5.1 The GLOBE dimensions

GLOBE dimension	Description	Examples
Assertiveness	The degree to which a culture encourages individuals to be confrontational and competitive as opposed to modest and accommodating	High-scoring cultures (e.g. USA, Austria) value competition and show sympathy for strong people. Low-scoring cultures (e.g. Sweden, New Zealand) value co-operation and solidarity. They show sympathy for the underprivileged.
Future orientation	The degree to which a culture encourages such future-oriented practices as investing, planning and delaying gratification	High-scoring cultures (e.g. Singapore, the Netherlands) have a greater tendency to save and plan for the future. Low-scoring cultures (e.g. Italy, Russia) tend to make shorter-term plans and to value immediate gratification.
Gender differentiation	The degree to which a culture emphasizes gender roles	High-scoring cultures (e.g. South Korea, China) favour traditional gender dichotomies. They tend to accord males higher social status than females. Low-scoring cultures (e.g. Poland, Denmark) do not favour strict gender dichotomies and tend to give females a stronger 'voice' in decision-making.
Uncertainty avoidance	The degree to which a culture uses rules and procedures to counteract unpredictability	High-scoring cultures (e.g. Sweden, Germany) favour predictability and consistency, and have clear specifications of social expectations. Low-scoring cultures (e.g. Russia, Greece) tolerate ambiguity and uncertainty more, and have less-structured social expectations.
Power distance	The degree to which a culture distributes power unequally	High-scoring cultures (e.g. Thailand, Spain) clearly distinguish between those with and those without power, and expect obedience towards superiors. Low-scoring cultures (e.g. Denmark, the Netherlands) favour stronger participation in decision-making and expect a more equal distribution of power.

⇨

Table 5.1 The GLOBE dimensions (continued)

GLOBE dimension	Description	Examples
Collectivism versus individualism	The degree to which a culture expects individuals into be integrated into groups and categories	High-individualism-scoring cultures (e.g. Italy, Greece) value self-interest, and reward individual performance. High-collectivism-scoring cultures (e.g. Japan, South Korea) value similarity rather than difference, and are more likely to classify and group individuals, They tend to favour the collective good and co-operation more than individual autonomy.
In-group collectivism	The degree to which a culture expects individuals to belong to non-organizational groups, such as family units and circles of friends	High-scoring cultures (e.g. India, China) favour belonging to an in-group of family or friends. Nepotism (favouring one's relatives and friends in work situations) is common in such cultures, as is foregoing work commitments for family or personal reasons. Low-scoring cultures (e.g. Denmark, New Zealand) do not favour in-groups, and individuals are not pressured to ignore work commitments for family or personal reasons.
Performance orientation	The degree to which a culture rewards individuals for performance improvement and excellence	High-scoring cultures (e.g. Singapore, USA) value initiative and a 'can-do' attitude. They favour a direct style of communication. Low-scoring cultures (e.g. Russia, Italy) tend to value loyalty and belonging, emphasizing tradition and an individual's background rather than performance. These cultures tend to see feedback as negative and to associate competition with defeat.
Humane orientation	The degree to which a culture rewards altruism, generosity and a caring attitude	High-scoring cultures (e.g. Malaysia, Ireland) value human relations, sympathy and support for the weak or underprivileged. Low-scoring cultures (e.g. France, Germany) value power and material possessions as motivators. They tend to prefer assertive styles of conflict resolution and expect individuals to solve their own problems.

Source: Adapted from Javidan and House 2001: 293–302.

Probably the first impression one would get from this classification is that it is based largely on stereotype. In fact, in many ways it is reminiscent of such generalizations as 'Southern Europeans are emotional', 'Scandinavians are well-organized', etc. In addition, as we discussed earlier regarding survey-based research, answers to questionnaires carry the risk that respondents may not have been truthful or that what they understood by particular terms may not be what the researcher intended. Also, the clustering itself may be based on assumptions that are quite arbitrary or at least not self-evident. For example, the GLOBE model classifies Japan as Confucian Asia – but how Confucian is Japan in reality? Latin Europe includes Israel – but does Israel really have enough similarities with France, Italy and Spain to justify its inclusion in this cluster?

On the other hand, there is little doubt that such research is useful in bringing to light possible group reactions to situations, and in indicating the similarities and differences among these reactions. Classifying individual attitudes also plays an instrumental role in being able to talk about and understand these attitudes. In fact, the process of categorizing is part of the human mental and cognitive make-up and is vital for reflecting upon the objective world. The popularity of cultural models in business consulting and executive professional development courses shows that they are perceived as relevant and useful by industry practitioners. As cognitive scientists Glass and Holyoak (1989: 149) point out, 'If each experience were given a unique mental representation, we would be quickly overwhelmed . . . . By encoding experiences into an organized system of categories, we are able to recognize significant commonalities in different experiences.'

What do these considerations imply for cultural influence on professional communication? Allowing for the fact that cultural models are general and therefore approximate, and also that the dichotomies they distinguish are two ends of a continuum and not disconnected polar opposites, such models are useful in analysing how different organizational structures and policies are often influenced by cultural values and expectations. Therefore, if they are used as analytical tools as opposed to vehicles for negative stereotyping, they do have a role to play in helping to prevent cultural misunderstandings, to acknowledge diversity and to enhance international collaboration.

Collaboration and misunderstandings, however, do not occur only between different cultures; they occur as part of any interpersonal act of communication. How these social phenomena play out among team members is the topic of the next section.

5.2 Groups and teams

This section looks at the ways in which humans communicate in a group situation. Research in group interaction has shown that, when formed, a group attains its own identity which exists irrespective of the identities or personal characteristics of each individual member. A group has a 'personality' of its own, so to speak. At the same time, the group with which one identifies or is a member of has a great effect on one's identity and social potential. As Abrams and Hogg (1988: 20) point out, 'the groups to which people belong will be massively significant in determining their life experience'.

Teams are also groups, but it is important to distinguish between a group and a team. As defined by Abrams and Hogg (1988: 7), a group comprises a number of individuals who 'perceive themselves to be members of the same social category'. So, groups include those who share the same ethnicity, those who share the same gender, those who share the same music tastes, those who share the same sexual orientation and those who share the same hobby – to name just a few possibilities. Teams, on the other hand, are groups that have been formed for a specific purpose or task. The groups formed in work situations to carry out a project and those formed to play a game are examples of teams. A team may include members of different groups; people of different races, genders, sexual preferences and leisure tastes can come together to form a team for a purpose. Teams tend to have clear objectives and more or less specified roles and duties, usually related to professional concerns. Since the aim of this chapter is to discuss interpersonal communication in business contexts, teams will be our main focus.

Team dynamics

Those working in collaborative projects or in situations that require negotiation skills often use reasoning techniques to manage conflict and to sway others' opinions. The problem with this is that, in reality, issues of power play a major role in interpersonal communication, which means that many decisions are not made rationally. In fact, people are much more likely to respond positively to someone who, they believe, is 'on their side', protects their interests, and shares their ideals than to someone who can produce a perfectly reasoned argument.

At their best, teams can produce excellent results by combining the specialized skills that individual team members bring. At their worst, teams produce delays, misunderstandings and conflicts. For this reason, the ability to deal productively with other people, peers, juniors and superiors, is a highly valued skill that contributes greatly to the smooth and successful management of an organization (Marsen 2003).

> The success of a team project is largely due to such skilled procedures as effective negotiation, duty allocation and conflict management.

Teams can be effective problem-solvers for many reasons, including the following:

- More extensive information is available in a team than an individual may have alone.
- Individuals bring different approaches to a problem within the team. This allows for a wide range of options to be considered.
- Improved understanding of the problem and possible solutions is possible, because team members are aware of the reasoning used in problem analysis.
- It is more likely that consensus will be achieved if a decision was made in consultation with members of the team; no one is likely to feel 'left out' and therefore oppose a decision.
- Risks can often be managed more effectively in teams. What can be a high-risk decision for an individual could actually be a moderate-risk decision for a team, because different

team members bring new knowledge to the issue and because risk is often a function of knowledge.

- Motivation and confidence are likely to increase in decisions made in team situations because individual team members feel supported by others.

Major disadvantages of reaching important decisions as part of a team include the following:

- Decisions can be made too soon: teams that feel uncomfortable with conflict may decide on the first option which meets with some support from the team members, regardless of whether this would be the best option.
- On the other hand, decisions can take too long if the team cannot agree on a topic.
- If the team structure is too democratic, there may be a lack of initiative and responsibility.
- Teams may be influenced by one person, whose charismatic or persuasive strengths may induce members to overlook pertinent factors in the problem involved.
- If there is too much conflict in a team, the team may become inoperable or ineffective.
- Teams may displace responsibility so that it may be difficult to hold a team or an individual member accountable for a negative outcome.

Good team dynamics are generally achieved in three main ways:

- members are attracted to the team's purpose;
- members share similar values, needs and interests;
- members fulfil for each other important interpersonal needs, such as affection (acknowledging each other's point of view), inclusion (allowing each member to play a role in activities) and control (allowing each member to determine certain actions pertinent to the member's role).

Individuals participate in teams through the roles they play in them. Researchers have formulated different classifications of the role structure of teams. Two commonly used models are the *Task-Maintenance Classification* and the *Belbin Inventory of Team Roles*.

The Task-Maintenance Classification divides team roles into two main categories: *task roles* and *maintenance roles*. Task roles represent the actions members must take to accomplish specific goals, and include the roles of 'information giver', 'information seeker', 'expediter' and 'analyser'. Maintenance roles represent the types of behaviour that each member must exhibit to keep the group functioning smoothly, and include the positive roles of 'supporter', 'harmonizer' and 'gatekeeper' and the negative roles of 'aggressor', 'joker', 'withdrawer' and 'monopolizer' (Verderber and Verderber 1992).

It should be emphasized that all these roles are inclusive in the sense that each member can play one or more roles within one team. The roles are defined in terms of what the team members do in response to situations that arise in the team interaction, not in terms of who the team members are, as in personality characteristics. Consider each role in more detail.

Task Roles

Information givers provide content for discussion. Because the function of a team is most often to discuss or analyse and work with information, they are the foundation of the team; usually all members play this role, unless one member is specifically assigned to present information from sources that s/he has researched. Information givers need to be well-prepared by having consulted various sources and having thought about the issue carefully before participating in a meeting. In business settings, the more objective and evidence-supported a team member's opinion is, the more this member's information-giving role is appreciated and effective in influencing the team.

Information seekers ask for more information or clarification on an issue. They protect the team from reaching a decision before all sides have been considered, by eliciting more details and explanations on the issue. Again, in many teams, more than one person may assume the role of information seeker.

Expediters keep the team on track. Although digressions are sometimes useful in enlarging the scope of an issue or brainstorming alternative viewpoints, they are just as often a hindrance to the smooth functioning of team dynamics. The expediters help the group stick to the agenda, by asking for relevance.

Analysers consider the issue in depth by probing both information content and line of reasoning. Analysers point out that the group has skipped a point, passed over a point too lightly or not considered pertinent information. They are important in acknowledging and addressing the complexity of an issue. Methods used by analysers include asking questions that test the data presented, and asking for definitions and alternative viewpoints.

Maintenance roles

Supporters recognize the contribution of team members and show appreciation for their input. Supporters' methods are usually encouraging comments, or non-verbal cues, such as a smile or a nod.

Harmonizers attempt to resolve conflict by reducing tension and straightening out misunderstandings and disagreements. They try to cool down high emotions by introducing objectivity into the discussion and mediating between hostile or opposing sides.

Gatekeepers generally have a bad reputation – from the point of view of the consumer or client – as those who prevent access to a desired location, person or object. For example, the secretary through whom we have to pass to reach the managing director is a gatekeeper. In broadcasting, programming managers are gatekeepers in selecting the programmes we watch or listen to, thereby channelling and restricting our options. From the point of view of management or team dynamics, however, gatekeepers are significant in monitoring that all eligible parties have equal access to a decision-making process, and in keeping communication channels between different parties open. In meetings, for instance, gatekeepers keep in check those who tend to dominate, and encourage those who are reluctant to contribute to be more forthcoming.

Aggressors produce conflict in a group by constantly or inordinately criticizing others' opinions or behaviour and by making personal attacks when they do not agree on a point. One way to counteract aggressors is to take them aside and describe to them what they are doing and the effect it is having on team dynamics.

Jokers produce conflict by ridiculing or playing down others' opinions or behaviour, or

'Big Brother' issues, on the whole, involve gate-keepers and their actions. In formal discussions or conference presentations, the session chairperson would act as a gatekeeper or an expediter, depending on the context.

by making complex topics look light-hearted when in fact they need to be taken seriously. Humour is a positive factor in team dynamics, helping members to keep their spirits up and see the optimistic side of things. However, if humour is inappropriate, inconsiderate or offensive, it needs to be kept in check to avoid irritation or resentment. As with aggressors, the best way to deal with jokers is to make them aware of what they are doing.

Withdrawers refuse to contribute to the team, usually out of lack of interest, lack of confidence or inadequate preparation. Some ways to deal with withdrawers include asking them questions, finding out what they are good at and making sure that they are given the opportunity to contribute in that area, acknowledging their positive contributions.

Monopolizers dominate discussions by voicing an opinion about everything said, and interrupting or not allowing others to make a contribution. In some cases monopolizers try to impress the team with their skills or knowledge; in other cases, they try to compensate for a lack of confidence by asking too many (often irrelevant) questions or trying to answer every question to prove their competence. When they are genuinely knowledgeable, monopolizers can be beneficial because they help to direct the group. When they become disruptive or intimidating, however, they should be interrupted and others should be drawn into the discussion.

The second model we examine here is the one formulated by communication researcher Meredith Belbin (2000). Belbin constructed a typology of roles of participants in team interactions – the Belbin Inventory. In this, he distinguished nine team roles:

- *Plants* are 'ideas people', innovators and inventors, who provide the foundations from which major developments emerge. They are often eccentric, working alone and approaching problems in an unconventional way. Although clever and competent, they are not good at social communication. As their function is often to generate proposals and solve complex problems, they are needed in the initial stages of a project and/or when a project is failing to progress. One plant in a team is usually enough, since plants tend not to be co-operative but focus more on reinforcing their own ideas and challenging each other.

- *Resource investigators* are good at communicating, both within and outside the group, negotiating and exploring links with different contacts. They are generally not a source of original ideas, but are adept at picking up and exploiting other people's ideas. They have a practical inclination, which gives them the skill to find out what is available and how it can be used. Resource investigators are inquisitive and ready to see new possibilities, but they need to remain stimulated and part of an approving team. Their function in a team is to explore and report back on ideas, developments and resources outside their group.

- *Monitor evaluators* are the 'down to earth' contributors, whose main function is to analyse and evaluate information. They tend to have a high critical-thinking ability and capacity for shrewd judgments. They also need a good eye for objectively evaluating the advantages and disadvantages of a situation. A team with a plant and a resource investigator but no monitor evaluator would be at a serious disadvantage, because it is the monitor evaluator who steers the group in practical ways, and helps the members reach difficult decisions.

| Co-ordinators are better at working with equals rather than directing junior subordinates, | because their style is more consultative than directive. |

- *Coordinators* are distinguished by their ability to encourage others to work towards shared goals. Coordinators need to be trusting and confident, since they have to delegate duties. They need to detect individual talents and use them productively in the pursuit of shared goals. They should have the ability to manage people and command respect. In teams that have diverse skills and characteristics, coordinators are very important because they can bring together the team's different features for more harmonious and effective co-operation.

- *Shapers* have a directive function and perform the duties of leaders in the team. They tend to be highly motivated, with a strong sense of achievement and energy drive. They have a winner's mentality and, although they are resourceful in overcoming obstacles, they can also exhibit strong emotional reactions to disappointment and frustration. They do not delve into the maintenance tasks of the group, aiming instead to achieve their objectives and those of the group. They generate action and thrive under pressure, so they can enthuse the members of a team and can be useful in teams where political complications tend to slow the pace. They are well-suited to change and do not hesitate to take unpopular decisions. As their name suggests, they forge a shape on group discussions and activities and are the most effective members in guaranteeing positive action.

- *Team workers* are the most supportive members of a team. Their skills include flexibility, tact, intuition and sensitivity. They are good listeners and are generally popular in the team. The major problem of team workers is indecisiveness: they tend to leave important decisions to others. Their role is to prevent interpersonal conflict within the team and thus allow members to function effectively. They complement shapers, who are not inclined to consider the team cohesion. The presence of team workers in a team improves morale and co-operation.

- *Implementers* are disciplined and practical. Although they can be inflexible, they are systematic, which makes them work for the group's interests. They tend to be reliable and apply themselves to the problem at hand. Implementers tend to do what needs to be done, and they have an eye for relevance.

- *Completer–finishers* are able to follow projects through, and tend to start only what they can finish. Typically, they do not require external stimuli but are self-sufficient and self-motivated. They tend to be intolerant of those who lack perseverance or exhibit a casual attitude to the project. They tend not to delegate, preferring to complete tasks by themselves, and they generally complete projects by set deadlines.

- *Specialists* have expert knowledge and technical skills in a specific area. They tend to be self-sufficient, lacking interest in others' work. They maintain professional standards and are keen to further knowledge in their field. In a team, specialists provide the knowledge base and command support because they know more about their field than other members, so they are often called upon to make decisions based on their experience. In some teams, every member is a specialist in his/her own field. In this case, each member combines this role with another role to maintain cohesion.

As was noted with the previous model, these roles are not always exclusive, and an individual can play more than one role in a single group, depending on the situation. Individual characteristics, such as 'personality traits', do play a part in the allocation of roles. However, it is mostly the demands of the project, and contextual factors, such as the hierarchy of the organization, its values, etc., as well as practical concerns, such as time and money, which have the final say in who plays what role.

5.3 Leadership

Leadership is a complicated topic that deserves more attention than we can give it in this chapter. Here we look at some pertinent issues related to leadership, especially as they underlie the functioning and effectiveness of a team.

The distinction between maintenance focus and task focus is pertinent also when it comes to leadership of a team. Maintenance-focused leaders tend to pay attention to the cohesion of the group, ensuring that it remains harmonious while working towards team objectives. They are good at resolving conflict and can delegate and supervise effectively. Such leaders, however, may be ineffective in some situations, such as when there is strong opposition within the group. Task-focused leaders, on the other hand, are focused on achieving objectives, whatever the cost, and they can drive change through resistance. They are not too concerned about cohesion or harmonious co-operation, focusing, instead, on achieving results. Their directive skills work best with subordinates rather than equals, and leading self-motivated people is not generally their strong point.

Regardless of whether their focus is to maintain cohesion or to initiate tasks, effective team leaders share certain characteristics. According to Qubein (1986), these common characteristics are:

- They value people: they acknowledge the importance and contribution of others.
- They listen actively: they make an effort to understand the needs and desires of others.
- They are tactful: they criticize sparingly, constructively and diplomatically.
- They give credit: they praise others and their contributions publicly.
- They are consistent: they control their personal moods, and are fair in their exchanges with others.
- They admit mistakes: they take the blame for errors they have committed.
- They have a sense of humour: they maintain a pleasant disposition and pleasant manner.
- They set a good example: they follow their own regulations.

Effective leaders are not only personally ambitious and well-organized, but should also be people-oriented, willing to assist and direct subordinates, and able to improvise and innovate in their field within ethical parameters.

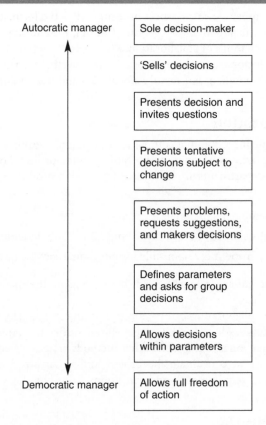

Autocratic manager — Sole decision-maker

'Sells' decisions

Presents decision and invites questions

Presents tentative decisions subject to change

Presents problems, requests suggestions, and makers decisions

Defines parameters and asks for group decisions

Allows decisions within parameters

Democratic manager — Allows full freedom of action

Figure 5.1 Leadership continuum
Source: Sutherland and Canwell 2004: 175

Like other managers, team leaders can exhibit styles of direction with varying degrees of dominance or control. These styles vary from contexts where the leader enforces his/her decision on team members, to the opposite extreme where the leader listens to all parties and allows for unlimited individual initiative. In many cases the leader's powers and responsibilities are inscribed in the organization's management structure, but, as in most facets of human behaviour, they also depend on the individual leader's interpretation of this structure. According to the leadership continuum model first proposed by R Tannebaum and W. H. Schmidt (1973), leadership strategies range from autocratic to laissez-faire, and comprise several steps in between. The leadership continuum is shown in Figure 5.1.

5.4 Collaboration

Apart from the leader's role, which is usually assigned, the above-described team roles typify individual practices that take place in meetings and discussions. They describe forms of behaviour, reflected usually in language but also in non-verbal communication, that can be exhibited by any team member. Another aspect of teamwork is the formally implemented system for duty allocation, negotiation, delegation of duties, monitoring of progress and feedback: in other words, methods of collaboration.

Three methods of collaboration that are commonly used in business and industry contexts are *sequential collaboration, functional collaboration* and *mix-and-match collaboration* (Marsen 2003).

Sequential collaboration

In this type, each department/section in a company, or person in a group for smaller projects, is assigned a specific, non-overlapping responsibility in the project. For example, in a software company, three departments are sometimes involved in producing the user documentation:

- software specialists assemble the material;
- communication specialists are in charge of word processing and designing;
- the art and printing department is responsible for publishing the documentation.

In this case, each department must finish its job before passing the material to another department for the next stage.

The sequential type of collaboration can be effective at times, especially when the work of each segment is specialized and each stage is self-sufficient. However, projects completed sequentially take longer than when other methods are employed, and a project manager is often necessary to coordinate the project and to ensure that deadlines are kept, all parties understand requirements, and transitions from one stage to the next are smooth.

Functional collaboration

This type is organized according to the skills or job function of the members. All stages of a project are undertaken concurrently, and all parties can monitor procedures at each stage. For example, a four-person team carrying out a user documentation project for software might be organized as follows:

- A manager schedules and conducts meetings, assists team members, issues progress reports to management, solves problems by proposing alternatives, and generally coordinates efforts to keep the project on schedule.
- A researcher collects data, conducts interviews, searches the literature, administers tests, gathers and classifies information, and then prepares notes on the work.
- A writer/editor receives the researcher's notes, prepares outlines and drafts, and circulates them for corrections and revisions.
- A graphics expert obtains and prepares all visuals, specifying why, how and where visuals should be placed and designing the document layout. (S)he might even suggest that visuals replace certain sections of text.

All parties work on the project at the same time and interact regularly through meetings and e-mail communication.

Mix-and match collaboration

In this type of collaboration, team members agree on shared objectives and then work independently on separate sections of the project by undertaking all tasks. The team members meet at specified times to compare their work and choose the best samples from each other's work. This approach is constructive in smaller-scale projects when team members have similar skills but cannot meet regularly.

A different version of this approach occurs when all members share the same interactive software and can work on the same project concurrently, each contributing according to his or her own skills which may or may not overlap. Continuing our software documentation example, a mix-and match type of collaboration could mean that members from the engineering, communication and art departments have the same software installed in their computers and work on the same documentation project at the same time, without waiting for one department to finish their tasks before passing the project to another department. This would most likely cut costs and reduce time, compared with the sequential model, but it would require all members to work co-operatively and project milestones and outcomes to be very clearly set out and agreed by all in advance (to reduce the risk of the 'you're treading on my toes' syndrome).

5.5 Conflict

Conflict is embedded in human relationships. It arises when there is incompatibility of orientation between individuals or groups, and it can occur in such situations as when people form incompatible goals and behaviours, when resources have to be allocated and when decisions have to be made. Conflict is associated with:

- *Values*: underlying values are different. This is arguably the most important and serious type of conflict because values are entrenched in social interaction and behaviour, and are very difficult to change.

- *Interests*: what promotes one person's self-interest opposes that of another. For example, when two colleagues compete for the same promotion, inevitably some degree of conflict will arise.

- *Policy*: existing regulations do not reflect current needs. This often manifests itself in cases where conflict leads to employees' strikes or group protests. This is what happens, for example, when prices increase but salaries remain static, leading to a strike, or when women have achieved breakthroughs in social equality but legislation regulating gender issues remains at a primitive level, leading to demonstrations or ground-breaking legal proceedings. Policy is very closely aligned with value.

- *Goals*: there is controversy or disagreement about where a project is going. In a project, for example, some members may think the goal is to produce routine results, whereas others may want to produce a radical breakthrough.

- *Method*: there is controversy or disagreement about how to arrive at the desired outcome. Such conflict may arise when one side has low uncertainty avoidance, and is therefore more optimistic about the future, while the other side has high uncertainty avoidance and wants more control over a situation, leading them to choose high-risk methods (such as war over negotiation, for instance).

Managed properly, conflict can result in growth because it allows for different points of view to be aired and considered. Managed badly, it can be destructive and costly – in resources and relationships. Groups can suffer from two opposite evils: too little conflict and too much conflict. A little conflict can be a good thing for change and rejuvenation of outmoded structures and beliefs. A lot of conflict, however, can destroy a project and, in serious cases, even lead to costly lawsuits and official investigations.

Avoiding conflict: the groupthink syndrome

Sometimes people think that avoiding conflict at all costs is the best course of action in order to maintain harmony within a group or organization. This attitude can often lead to a 'sweeping things under the carpet' approach, where serious differences in policy or values are politely ignored until they burst out violently and destructively. Yale sociologist Irving Janis (1982) studied such cases where wrong decisions were made about important matters because the interested parties did not consider options that were outside their established framework. He referred to misplaced conformity or agreement within a group as 'group-think' (a 'group' being for him a collectivity of individuals working together as decision-makers in a large organization).

Janis examined a number of 'fiascos', historical cases where groups made ineffective decisions because they strived to reach consensus without taking into account possible risks or alternatives. In these cases he observed certain common features pointing to three categories and eight symptoms of group behaviour. These constitute the groupthink syndrome, described in Figure 5.2:

Janis's findings supported his hypothesis that 'whenever a policy-making group displays most of the symptoms of groupthink, we can expect to find that the group also displays symptoms of defective decision-making' (Janis 1982: 175). Major signals indicating that a faulty decision-making process is at play include the following:

- The group has not fully considered alternatives.
- The group has not clearly examined objectives.
- The group has not taken into account the possible risks of their decision.
- The group has not re-evaluated alternatives that it rejected at a previous stage of the process.
- The group has not conducted a comprehensive information search and may therefore be ignorant of important issues.
- The group has shown prejudice or bias in evaluating the information at hand.
- The group has not worked out what to do in an emergency or if their decision proves ineffective.

Type I: Overestimations of the group

1 *Belief in being invincible*
   The group believes it is invincible, which may lead to excessive optimism and unnecessary risk-taking.

2 *Belief in inherent morality*
   Group members believe that their decisions are inherently moral and they brush away thoughts of unethical behaviour by assuming that they cannot do anything wrong.

Type II: Closed-mindedness

3 *Attempts to rationalise about all issues*
   Group members explain away warnings or threats.

4 *Stereotyping*
   The group stereotypes opponents as being too evil, stupid or weak to take seriously.

Type III: Pressures towards uniformity

5 *Self-censorship*
   Group members with doubts censor themselves to preserve the appearance of consent.

6 *Belief in unanimity*
   The group believes there is unanimity on an issue because nobody raises an objection.

7 *Direct pressure*
   Group members apply direct pressure to conform on anyone who tries to question the status quo within the group.

8 *Imposing mind-guards*
   Just as bodyguards protect from physical harm, so some group members set themselves up as censors or gatekeepers in order to prevent challenging or threatening information available outside the group from appearing before the group.

Figure 5.2 Groupthink
Source: Adapted from Janis 1982: 174–5

Assessing conflict: the Thomas-Kilman conflict mode instrument

Individuals react differently to conflict. In fact, different reactions are necessary to deal with different forms of conflict, different contexts, etc. An influential method of assessing these reactions to conflict was formulated by Kenneth Thomas and Ralph Kilmann, and is known as the Thomas-Kilmann conflict mode instrument.

Thomas and Kilmann examined individual reactions in situations involving conflict and described their behaviour using two axes: (1) assertiveness, the extent to which the individual attempts to satisfy his/her interests, and (2) co-operativeness, the extent to which the individual attempts to satisfy the other person's interests. They then used these axes to define five modes, or methods, of dealing with conflicts: *competing, collaborating, compromising, avoiding* and *accommodating*. No mode is better or worse than another per se; rather, each mode is appropriate in certain situations but inappropriate in others, and successful conflict management depends on knowing which to choose and when. Here are some more details on each mode.

- *Competing*. This mode is assertive and unco-operative. The person pursues his/her own concerns, usually at the other person's expense and, using whatever power seems appropriate for this end. Competing may mean standing up for one's rights, defending a position one believes is correct, or simply trying to win. Cases where competing would be appropriate include:

  - emergency situations where decisive action is required;
  - when unpopular courses of action need to be implemented;
  - as a safeguard when non-competitive behaviour is exploited.

- *Accommodating*. This is the opposite of competing – unassertive and co-operative. The person sacrifices his/her own concerns to satisfy the concerns of the other person. This includes selfless generosity or charity, obeying a command when one would prefer not to, or yielding to another's point of view. Cases where accommodating would be appropriate include:

  - when one realizes one is wrong;
  - when the issue is not important to one person but is important to the other;
  - when continued competition would damage one's cause, for example when one's opinion is outnumbered by the opposite view;
  - when preserving harmony is especially important.

- *Avoiding*. This mode is unassertive and unco-operative. The person does not pursue his/her concerns directly nor does s/he yield to the other person. Rather s/he does not address the conflict. This might take the form of diplomatically sidestepping an issue, postponing an issue until a better time or simply withdrawing from a threatening situation. Cases where avoiding would be appropriate include:

  - when an issue is not as important as others at one time;
  - when there is no chance to satisfy one's concerns, for example in cases of low power or when confronted by a situation where one's sphere of influence is diminished;
  - when the costs of confronting a conflict outweigh the benefits of resolving it;
  - when the situation involves high risk, and more information is important in assessing the advantages of a decision;
  - when the issue is symptomatic of a more fundamental issue.

- *Collaborating*. This is the opposite of avoiding – assertive and co-operative. The person attempts to work with another person to find a solution that satisfies the concerns of both. It attempts to identify the underlying concerns of both parties and to find an alternative that meets both sets of concerns. This includes exploring a disagreement to learn from each other's insights, resolving some condition that would otherwise have the two parties competing for resources or confronting each other and trying to find a solution to a problem. Cases where collaborating would be appropriate include:

  - when the concerns of both parties are too important to be compromised;

- when the objective is to learn by understanding the views of others;
- when trying to gain commitment from others by incorporating their concerns in a decision.

- *Compromising*. This is intermediate to assertiveness and co-operativeness. The person attempts to find an expedient, mutually acceptable solution that satisfies both parties. It includes addressing an issue more directly than avoiding it, but not exploring this issue in as much depth as when collaborating. It could mean exchanging concessions or seeking a middle ground. Cases where compromising is appropriate include:

- when the goals are not worth the effort of the potential disruption involved in being more assertive;
- when two opponents are equally committed and equally strong;
- when there is time pressure and an expedient solution must be reached.

Conflict in teams

Some teams are highly effective, while others never seem to get off the ground. When teams are not working well, it can be a very serious matter, costing the organization time and money. While the reasons that make a team unproductive are not fixed or universal, there are some guidelines regarding what may be wrong that can be used to clarify the situation:

- The team may be lacking the required specialist skills to tackle a project expertly and confidently.
- The team may be lacking one or more vital roles (from the roles described earlier in this chapter).
- Members may feel their personal skills are not appreciated and they may lose motivation (often the result of weak leadership or bad management).
- The team may feel that their efforts will not be supported by authorities and funding agencies, especially if they are working under budget constraints and/or on obscure or unpopular projects.
- A conflict of values or expectations may exist where some team members may expect different results from the project, or the team may be expecting different results from the management.
- The brief describing the objectives and scope of a project may be unclear, leading to confusion.
- Personal conflicts may hinder the achievement of goals. This is especially true of competitive environments where people are not accustomed to working co-operatively.

Managing conflict in teams

As has probably become clear from the preceding discussion, managing conflict is no easy matter. In most aspects of interpersonal communication, contextual factors, such as the setting of the interaction, the background of the participants and the nature of the interaction, are important in pointing to the most appropriate reactions, and conflict management is no exception to this. However, as regards teamwork, which has been our main focus in the last two sections, a general process for managing conflict involves five steps:

1. *Define the problem.* The definition of the problem is the most important step in finding a solution. In many cases there is low morale and a lack of commitment by team members because there is a problem that has not been voiced or made conscious within the group dynamics. An effective method of discussing the problem that caused this conflict is to describe it in writing. Each conflicting side should describe their perspective on the matter as clearly and as objectively as possible, avoiding 'I said/he said'-type criticism. It is also important to avoid generalizations, such as 'they', 'always' and 'never', and to determine if the reaction is proportional to the situation. In describing the issue, consider if it had objective grounds for escalating into conflict, or if it is likely to have been caused by misunderstanding. Also examine the history of the situation and the participants: are there left-over emotions or grudges from a previous event?

2. *Analyse the problem.* Once the group agrees on the nature of the problem, the next step is to analyse it in terms of size, causes and criteria of evaluation. At this stage, it is important not to succumb to the temptation of listing possible solutions before having analysed the problem thoroughly. Before answering the question of what can be done to solve the conflict, team members should decide why this is a conflict and for whom it is a conflict.

3. *Generate possible solutions.* Brainstorming is usually an effective way to generate ideas that could lead to the resolution of the conflict. At this stage, evaluation or nitpicking criticism of ideas should be avoided, and team members should produce as many possible solutions as they can.

4. *Evaluate and test the various solutions.* After the brainstorming stage, each possible resolution should be examined to ascertain its merits and drawbacks. Factors to consider carefully include whether the solutions are likely to work, if they are fair to all, and whether they can be implemented easily. This should eliminate the solutions that are not worthwhile and leave a reduced number of options.

5. *Choose a mutually acceptable solution.* From the reduced number of possible solutions, the one that seems to be the most effective can be chosen for a trial period. The best way to articulate this would be, once again, in writing. Choosing an option is at times a risky act, with no guarantees that the selected solution will work. However, if the decision was reached by (relative) consensus (while avoiding the traps of groupthink), all the parties involved will be responsible for testing it and providing feedback.

Effective listening

Effective listening contributes enormously to group dynamics and conflict resolution. In interpersonal communication, poor listening skills are at fault in many, if not most, cases of misunderstanding.

When working with others, much of the communication that takes place when suggesting, instructing, requesting, criticizing, praising and negotiating is non-verbal. Listening actively by making a physical and mental effort to understand what someone else is saying engages the whole body, not just the ears. It is a way of communicating that signifies:

- I hear what you are feeling;
- I understand how you see things now;
- I am interested and concerned;
- I understand where you are;
- I do not wish to judge you or change you.

Here are seven tips for active listening:

1 *Stop talking.* Many people talk too much because they feel uncomfortable with silence. However, you cannot listen if you are talking.

2 *Remove noise as much possible.* 'Noise' is used in the communications sense of distractions to the unhindered transmission of the message. Therefore, it refers not only to external factors such as street noise but also to other factors, such as distracting mannerisms and excessive heat or cold. Common distracting mannerisms include clicking pens, shuffling papers, checking clothing or fingernails, and gazing around the room (see the section on non-verbal communication for more on this). If you need to talk to a team member or colleague about something serious, it is advisable to arrange a meeting in pleasant and relaxed surroundings.

3 *Ask open questions which begin with the 5 Ws and 1 H: what, when, why, where, who and how.* This helps to keep the conversation on the topic and to obtain as much information as possible on it. When people answer W and H questions, they have to reply in full sentences and so their replies are more factual than they would be if the questions were of the 'do you . . . ' type, which elicit, simpler 'yes–no' answers.

4 *Be supportive.* Let the other person know that you want to know what he or she is talking about. It is well-attested that most people will talk if they receive attention and interest from the listener. Sensing indifference or impatience discourages a constructive response.

5 *Respond to feelings.* If the situation at hand has an emotional investment by one or all of the participants, it is best to acknowledge this. Hidden or 'bottled' feelings may cloud or sabotage the information you require.

7 *Summarize to check mutual understanding.* A summary ensures that both parties have the same understanding of what has been said, and helps to create closure to an issue or topic of discussion. In business, for example, a summary is formalized in a memorandum of understanding listing the points that have been agreed upon in a previous discussion.

From a top-down perspective, conflict can come in two main forms: *structural conflict*, where it is the actual structure of an organization or government agency that creates the conflict, and *substantive conflict*, where the conflict exists in the issues associated with particular problems or situations. Generally, a conflict situation has three stages: the stage when conflict is *latent*, that is, when something happens that begins a conflict; the stage when conflict is *apparent*, that is, when conflict behaviour is observable; and the *aftermath*, when the particular conflict episode ends.

5.6 Information management

Information management refers broadly to the systematic and deliberate accessing and organizing of the knowledge that the members of a company possess. The concept behind information management is that tapping into available (but sometimes hidden) mental resources and skills can reap substantial benefits. The value of information management practices has been aptly captured by an often-quoted remark by Lew Platt, former Chief Executive Officer of Hewlett-Packard: 'If Hewlett-Packard knew what it knows, we'd be three times as profitable' (cited in Dearlove 2000: 152).

> Although technology is a pivotal player in the rise of initiatives to manage information, it is not the only factor. Information management also involves an attitudinal orientation towards people and their skills, and is intrinsically linked with the culture of an organization.

Several examples have been documented to support the positive effect of information-management initiatives. For example, in May 2001 IBM held a brainstorming session called WorldJam with all its employees. This produced about six thousand ideas suggested by approximately fifty-two thousand employees. The ideas were recorded in an online archive that could be accessed by staff (Figallo and Rhine 2002: 56–7). Also, a British company set up an interactive voicemail system called 'what's hot and what's not'. Employees contributed short news items about customers, technology and products, and these could be accessed on cellphones by all company staff (Cook 1999: 103). Finally, Xerox employees who encounter a problem that is not mentioned in product documentation can enter a description and analysis of this problem in a database called Eureka. This database can be accessed by Xerox representatives worldwide and provides valuable assistance in dealing swiftly with product glitches (Kermally 2002: 162–3).

Such initiatives have fuelled an interest in the general nature of information and knowledge, and in how knowledge is communicated in business settings (Davenport and Prusak 2000; Asslani and Luthans 2003). A useful model for analysing the processes involved in knowledge acquisition was formulated by Takeuchi and Nonaka (2004). This model is based on a distinction between *explicit* knowledge that exists in the public domain or the external world, and *tacit* knowledge that belongs to particular specialist groups or individuals. It has a spiral pattern, going through four sequences: socialization, externalization, combination and internalization (SECI):

- *Socialization* (tacit-to-tacit). This is what happens when those involved in a project do not have enough insider or specialist knowledge to accomplish the task and need training to acquire this knowledge. An example would be software engineers designing a new program aimed to monitor the heart and general health condition of mountain climbers. Unless the engineers were mountain climbers themselves, they would not be aware of such vital information as the clothing, occupational habits and body movements of climbers, and lack of such knowledge would hinder them from designing effective equipment that would be portable and able to record accurate data on the health of the climbers. What the engineers would have to do, therefore, would be to obtain information from climbers through interviews, observations, etc. This would be a case of socialization: a systematic transfer of knowledge by means of interviewing, observation, on-the-job-training, coaching and mentoring.

- *Externalization* (tacit-to-explicit). In this second phase, what starts off as peripheral data becomes central in solving a problem or dealing with an issue. Continuing the above example, having obtained the necessary information from mountain climbers, the engineers would be faced with the problem of what material to use for containing their software. They would need something light enough to be carried around unobtrusively while at the same time strong enough to withstand extreme changes in temperature (when climbing mountains in very hot or freezing climates). To solve the problem they would build virtual simulations and experiment with different materials, they would brainstorm ideas, they would connect with colleagues in a different department of the company who had worked on similar projects in the past, and they would form hypotheses, which they would then test. All this activity represents the externalization phase of the acquisition of knowledge. From the data they would gather during this process, the engineers would be able to determine the appropriate material needed to encase their software.

- *Combination* (explicit-to-explicit). In this stage, the knowledge acquired during the previous phases would be put into practice, tried out and publicized to allow for revision and integration. The software engineers in our example would now have created their software and would be combining the new knowledge they had created with the knowledge that already existed. They would write an article for a specialist journal and present a paper at a conference, describing what they had accomplished and how this differed from or was similar to other software in related areas. More importantly, they would present their product to the mountain climbers who would be using it and would carry out a trial experiment. They would take on board suggestions and criticisms for consideration. This activity represents the combination phase of the acquisition of knowledge.

- *Internalization* (explicit-to-tacit). This final phase of the SECI sequence completes the cycle. The knowledge gained in the previous phases through interaction with others becomes specialist knowledge. The engineers would have established an evaluation plan, which would help them to get feedback from the practical applications of their product (this could take the form, say, of meeting twice-yearly with the group of mountain climbers over the following two years). Since the product would now be on the market, the marketing section of the company would also have established an interactive database to obtain feedback from users and retailers. This activity represents the internalization stage of the acquisition of knowledge.

The SECI model of knowledge acquisition is represented graphically in Figure 5.3.

Information management has evolved since the mid-90s in line with technological developments, mainly because computer technology has allowed new developments in information retrieval, allocation and storage. Databases that store information from across an organization at a central place, intranet sites and blogs to which a large number of individuals can contribute are all examples of information-management schemes.

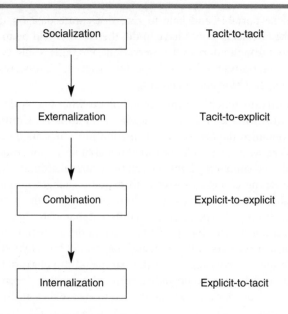

Figure 5.3 SECI model of knowledge

Quality indicators of information

The functioning and effectiveness of information management, is also dependent on the quality of information collected. Gathering and classifying a large amount of information is not enough, or even appropriate, to make this information effective, usable or credible. Evaluating the quality of information, therefore, becomes key. Organizational analyst Harold Wilensky (1967) proposed a useful model for evaluating information that has been constructively used by researchers since its formulation. In this model, Wilenski distinguished six criteria for high-quality information:

1   *Clarity*. Information must be easily understandable by its intended receivers, and enough information must be given to allow receivers to interpret it within a meaningful context. Clarity is defined from the point of view of the receiver, so audience analysis assumes an important role.

2   *Timeliness*. Information must be available when needed and must be kept up to date. For example, in areas afflicted by earthquakes, the government must have enough information about how to handle such a natural disaster before an earthquake actually occurs and must receive updates of this information as new scientific findings become available.

3   *Reliability*. Information must be accurate, unambiguous and consistent so that those who use it to take action will not be faced with contradictory or vague directives and regulations. Recording sources, double-checking and revising data are important tasks for ensuring reliability.

4   *Validity.* Information must be unbiased and closely reflect existing conditions. For example, when statistical analyses are conducted, it is important to ensure that the sample population was not selected deliberately to favour particular conclusions that represent the interests of certain groups. Recording sources (e.g. stating where the statistics came from) and justifying hypotheses and conclusions are important tasks in ensuring validity.

5   *Depth.* Information must be comprehensive, taking into account all relevant facts, issues and/or options with regard to the situation. Although this is of course very important in making the information effective, at the same time care must be taken not to include too much information, as this may result in overload. The challenge here is to gather comprehensive information while maintaining time limits, so that the information is not outdated by the time it is communicated.

6   *Diversity.* Information must come from a variety of sources and include different viewpoints and angles. This indicator must also be used with care, keeping in mind that not all sources of information are equally credible or valid. Trying to gather as much information as possible about a topic can often lead to scope creep, where a project becomes expanded out of proportion to its initial objectives. Therefore, a balanced approach to information collection should be sought.

5.7 Project management

A project in business and industry consists of a series of activities leading to one major goal or purpose. Project management refers to the planning necessary to complete a major project on time, within budget, according to specifications, and with the consultation and consent of all relevant parties. Projects tend to be undertaken by a project team, a group of people responsible for managing a project. Projects usually begin with a proposal and end with a completed outcome, together with a final report showing how the initial goals were reached or not. During the progress of a project, the team is generally required to submit progress reports at specified times (such as monthly or bi-monthly) in order to keep management informed of what has been achieved and what still remains to be done.

The components of effective project management are *definition, planning* and *direction*.

A project portfolio is a collection of projects that a team or company department is undertaking. The projects will be at different stages of completion, and the portfolio ensures that attention be given where it is needed for each project. A portfolio also helps to maintain consistency in the management of all projects, provides a point of reference for newcomers to the project management process, and facilitates the writing of progress reports.

Briefly, project definition involves describing the envisaged final product and its place in the market; planning involves identifying and prioritizing the tasks necessary for the completion of the product; and direction involves allocating roles to team members and setting a timeline for the execution of tasks. Consider each component more carefully.

Definition

As the first step, a project is carefully defined. Aspects of project definition include:

- *Project overview.* Is the project attempting to solve a problem? If so, for whom is this a problem? How is the problem defined? Is the project creating a new product? What are the characteristics of this product? What types of markets will it target?

- *Scope.* What issues, topics or features will the project cover? How much detail will it provide? What are the parameters that project team members have to work within?

- *Outcome.* What will the result of the project be? For example, if a computer system is being developed, what functions should it perform and to what standard?

Planning

Each step in the process is planned before further action is taken. The following tasks (activities representing one step towards the completion of a project) should be undertaken in the planning stage:

- Identify the steps required to complete the project.

- List the priorities. What should be done first, second, third?

- Identify dependent and independent tasks. Which tasks need to be put aside while other tasks are being completed? Which tasks are urgent, and which may be delayed without damaging the project? Project managers usually divide tasks into three categories:

  1 A critical task must be completed on time for the entire project to be completed on time.

  2 A milestone is an event that signifies the accomplishment of a series of tasks during a project. A milestone often signals the ending of a stage or section in the development of the project.

  3 A deliverable is a concrete object produced at a specific stage in the project (and usually delivered to a manager or client). Deliverables are used in some types of project management: in software design and engineering, for example, the systems requirements report, produced near the beginning of the project and describing what the projected software will achieve, is a deliverable.

- Create a timeline for task completion and allocate roles to project team members.

Direction

Each project is directed according to a line of responsibility. Project managers are responsible for monitoring and controlling progress and activities. Members of the project team report to managers, who in turn report to upper-level management and clients. Team members who are able to meet all the requirements of the project at a minimum cost and on time are highly valued.

The direction of a project also involves issues of *resources*, *constraints* and *risks*, which may propel the project forward or inhibit its development:

- *Resources.* What advantages do the team have in undertaking the project? Are they highly skilled? Do they have a large budget? Do they have adequate time to complete all the tasks? Is up-to-date technology available to them?

- *Constraints.* Is the budget modest? Is the staff limited, in numbers or in knowledge? Are there tight deadlines? Is there a lack of appropriate technology?

- *Risks.* What are the possible dangers of the project and what can be done to minimize them?

Two particular dangers that often arise in project management are known as *scope creep* and *feature creep*. Both of these can lead to delays, incomplete projects and conflicts within the project team.

Scope creep is exemplified by the tendency of stakeholders and project participants to expect more and more from the outcome of the project as it progresses. For example, businesses and users might expect increasing functionality and performance from a computer system as the process of developing the system unfolds.

Feature creep refers to the tendency to add more and more features and details to the expected product of the project without bearing in mind that the incorporation of these features will take extra time and money. The type of project determines what kind of feature creep may exist. In software design, for example, feature creep leads to the uncontrolled addition of technical features to the software under development. In a personal project, such as writing a university assignment, feature creep might refer to the tendency obsessively to perfect the details rather than to focus on the major requirements of the assignment.

One way to keep the project under control and to monitor progress is to have a clear plan at the beginning, agreed upon by all members, to implement a feedback process where any conflicts or miscommunication can be aired and resolved, and to discuss progress at regularly organized meetings. A simple model to help define and record the stages of the project is shown in Table 5.2.

Feedback in project management

In professional organizations, feedback regulating employee relations and client satisfaction is usually built into professional processes through customer checks, appraisals and performance reviews.

Team projects need to be monitored to ensure they are progressing satisfactorily. Communication among team members is essential in appraising the development of the allocated tasks, solving disputes and coming up with alternative courses of action when necessary. Unfortunately, feedback is not an easy matter. Personal concerns often cloud the objective assessment of a situation, and projects are obstructed because of communication breakdowns and the individual idiosyncrasies of team members. Communication experts tend to concur on some general guidelines for giving and receiving feedback:

- Feedback should not be personal. All critical comments should be focused on behaviour within a professional context, not on personal aspects.

Table 5.2   Project stages

Stage 1: Defining the project

Product definition	
Market and significance	

Stage 2: Planning the tasks

Milestones	1. 2. 3.
Deliverables	1. 2. 3.
Critical tasks	1. 2. 3.
Other tasks	1. 2. 3.

Stage 3: Directing the project

Resources	1. 2. 3.
Constraints	1. 2. 3.
Member roles	1. 2. 3.
Time management	Major deadlines: 1. 2. Meeting times: 1. 2. 3.

- Positive remarks should be included, and specific examples that are relevant to the project aims should be given.

- Feedback should be given soon after the particular situation, but at a time when it is likely to be received well. In many cases, if a problematic situation is allowed to continue for a long period, it might be very difficult to correct it later.

- Feedback should be given in small doses and should focus on the main points. Commenting on everything that may be unacceptable in a situation can be counterproductive and may be perceived as hostile.

- In oral feedback, body language and tone of voice should be consistent with verbal comments. For example, praise should be accompanied by appropriate eye contact and tone of voice.

When receiving feedback:

- Time should be allowed between the feedback and the response. Impulsive responses are often not well thought out and, therefore, inappropriate. Care should also be taken to avoid defensive responses:

  - *Diverting*: 'I think that many would say . . . '
  - *Explaining*: 'That's because . . . '
  - *Rejecting*: 'Yes, but . . . '
  - *Discounting*: 'I didn't think you'd take this so seriously'.
  - *Intellectualizing*: 'The premises of your argument are conditional on . . . '
  - *Attacking*: 'Who are you to make such comments?'
  - *Whining*: 'If only I had more time, I'd . . . '.

- It is important to understand clearly what the feedback is about and to ask for explanations when the feedback is unclear.

- It is also important, in cases where criticism is excessive and expectations unfairly demanding, to indicate that the point has been taken and that no further comment is necessary ('enough is enough').

Summary

◆ The communication that takes place within and between groups in organizations is strongly influenced by cultural factors. The term 'culture' refers to the conventional set of activities and expectations characteristic of a group, which give this group its identity and distinguish it from outsiders.

◆ Organizational culture has been studied by various communication theorists. Major studies include Geert Hofstede's *practice dimensions* and Robert House's *GLOBE model*.

◆ In professional settings, a number of individuals come together to form a team working towards the completion of a project. In order for teams to function effectively, members must share fundamental values and develop a sense of belonging and allegiance.

◆ Researchers have studied the composition of teams and the functions that each member has within the team. Well-known examples of team role definitions include the *task-maintenance classification* and the *Belbin inventory*.

◆ Leadership or good management is vital to the success of a team project. Leaders can be in charge of particular tasks and/or of maintaining harmony. Their approach varies from authoritarian to liberal.

◆ In team projects, collaboration can take different forms. These include the *sequential* form, where each member completes a stage of the work before passing the project on to other members, the *functional* form, where all members work at the same time on their individual area of expertise, and the *mix-and-match* form, where all members work together on all areas of the project concurrently.

◆ Team projects involve various degrees of conflict. The conflict may be constructive, allowing for new ideas to develop, or it may be destructive, preventing collaboration. If the team attempts to avoid conflict at all costs, the phenomenon of *groupthink* may arise. A more productive method for acknowledging conflict and making it work to the advantage of the project is to distinguish situations where a competitive style would be appropriate from situations where an accommodating style would be more suitable. The model known as the *Thomas-Kilman conflict mode instrument* is an effective and popular tool for achieving this.

◆ In addition to effective collaboration between individuals and between departments, the success of an organization depends on its method of capitalizing on the knowledge and expertise of its members. This is known as information management, and involves constructive ways of using information that originates from external sources in combination with information that originates from within the organization.

◆ Much of the work carried out in organizations and corporations is project-based. A project is a set of tasks leading to a specific result, such as the development of a product. A project is managed in several stages, including the definition and delimitation of the project, its planning and its direction. Setting milestones and providing feedback are important factors in successful project management.

■ Topics for discussion

▶ From your reading of this chapter, what would you say are the organizational problems suggested by the following statements? Some statements may indicate more than one communication problem.

- 'Our team could tell you how to achieve this in half the time and cost, but if this became public, they'd probably dismantle the team.'

- 'I could have told management this would happen, but I didn't think they would listen, and I wasn't asked anyway.'
- 'There's a better way to do this, but I doubt the project manager would want to learn about it.'
- 'The design team originally made this suggestion, and it eventually made millions for the company. But the design team got nothing out of it.'
- 'I didn't know this was the correct procedure.'

▶ Conceptualize a team project in your area of expertise or interest. Then, taking the point of view of the project leader, describe the skills and abilities you would want your team members to have. After doing this, take the point of view of a team member and describe the skills and abilities you would expect from your leader.

▶ Describe from experience or from research a situation where conflict was beneficial to growth, and a situation where it was detrimental. Discuss the differences between the situations, and outline some measures that could have been taken in the negative situation.

■ References and further reading

Abrams, D. and Hogg, M. A. (1988) 'Comments on the Motivational Status of Self-Esteem in Social Identity and Intergroup Discrimination', *European Journal of Social Psycholology*, 18, pp. 317–34.

Argyle, M. (1983) *The Psychology of Interpersonal Behaviour*, 4th edn. London: Penguin.

Asllani, A. and Luthans, F. (2003) 'What Knowledge Managers Really Do: An Empirical and Comparative Analysis', *Journal of Knowledge Management*, vol. 7, no. 3, pp. 53–66.

Bazerman, C. and Paradis, J. (eds) (1991) *Textual Dynamics of the Professions*. Madison, WI: University of Wisconsin Press.

Belbin, R. M. (2000) *Beyond the Team*. London: Butterworth Heinemann.

Cook, P. (1999) 'I Heard it through the Grapevine: Making Knowledge Management Work by Learning to Share Knowledge, Skill and Experience', *Industrial and Commercial Training*, vol. 31, no. 3, pp. 101–5.

Davenport, T. H. and Prusak, L. (2000) *Working Knowledge: How Organizations Manage What They Know*. Boston, MA: Harvard Business School Press.

De Certeau, M. (2002) *The Practice of Everyday Life* trans. by S. F. Rendall. Los Angeles, CA: University of California Press.

Dearlove, D. (2000) *The Ultimate Book of Business Thinking*. Oxford: Capstone.

Dunnette, M. (ed) (1976) *The Handbook of Industrial and Organizational Psychology*. Chicago: Rand McNally.

Figallo, C. and Rhine, N. (2002) *Building the Knowledge Management Network*. New York: John Wiley.

Gardner, H. (2004) *Changing Minds: The Art and Science of Changing Our Own and Other People's Minds*. Boston, MA: Harvard Business School Press.

Glass, A. L. and Holyoak, K. J. (1989) *Cognition*, 2nd edn. New York: McGraw Hill.

Hofstede, G. (2001) *Culture's Consequences: Company Values, Behaviours, Institutions and Organizations across Nations.* Thousand Oaks, CA: Sage.

House, R. J. (1998) 'A Brief History of GLOBE', *Journal of Managerial Psychology*, vol. 13, 3–4: pp. 230–40.

House, R. J., Hanges, P. J., Javidan, M., Dorfman, P. W. and Gupta, V. (2004) *Culture, Leadership and Organizations: The GLOBE Study of 62 Societies.* Thousand Oaks, CA: Sage.

Irwin, H. (1996) *Communicating with Asia: Understanding People and Customs.* St Leonards, NSW: Allen and Unwin.

Janis, I. L. (1982) *Groupthink: Psychological Studies of Policy Decisions and Fiascoes*, 2nd edn. Boston: Houghton Mifflin.

Javidan, M. and House, R. (2001) 'Cultural Acumen for the Global Manager: Lessons from Project GLOBE', *Organizational Dynamics*, Vol. 29, 4, pp. 289–305.

Kermally, S. (2002) *Effective Knowledge Management: A Best Practice Blueprint.* London: John Wiley.

Lester, A. (2003) *Project Planning and Control.* Oxford: Butterworth Heinemann.

Marsen, S. (2003) *Professional Writing: The Complete Guide for Business, Industry and IT.* Basingstoke: Palgrave Macmillan.

Pettinger, R. (2002) *Introduction to Management.* Basingstoke: Palgrave Macmillan.

Qubein, N. R. (1986) *Get the Best from Yourself.* New York: Berkley.

Robbins, S. and Barnwell, N. (2002) *Organisation Theory: Concepts and Cases.* Sydney: Prentice-Hall.

Sutherland, J. and Canwell, D. (2004) *Key Concepts in Management.* Basingstoke: Palgrave Macmillan.

Takeuchi, H. and Nonaka, I. (2004) *Hitotsubashi on Knowledge Management.* New York: John Wiley.

Tannebaum, R. and Schmidt, W. H. (1973) How to Choose a Leadership Pattern. *Harvard Business Review.*

Verderber, R. and Verderber S. (1992). *Inter-Act: Using Interpersonal Communication Skills*, 6th edn. Los Angeles, CA: Wadsworth.

Wilenski, H. (1967). *Organizational Intelligence.* New York: Basic Books.

Williams, R. (1980) *Problems in Materialism and Culture.* London: Verso.

Audience Analysis and Mass Communication

CHAPTER 6

I know how I can get the public to like me
– I'll buy every media outlet in town

Mr Burns in *The Simpsons*

This chapter looks at issues of communicating to a large and often anonymous public through various technological media that facilitate the process. It discusses definitions and approaches to the audience, and describes some ways in which communication researchers approach the relationship between the audience and the media text.

6.1 The audience

As Ernest Dichter (1985: 49) aptly remarks in his book *The Strategy of Desire*, 'an object and its representation are turned into a semiotically interpretable entity – a sign – only if there is a subject to interpret it as a sign'. Audience research looks at the role of the audience in interpreting the messages transmitted by the media.

Throughout the history of audience research, audiences have carried different definitions, including: a) a group of people (for example, 'young males'), b) a locality or community (for example, 'metropolitan residents'), c) a type of medium (for example 'TV viewers'), d) a genre or style (for example, 'science-fiction fans') or e) time (for example, 'prime-time audiences').

Descriptions of the audience as a factor regulating performance have existed since ancient times. It was in the twentieth century, however, that the audience started to be systematically defined as a sociological concept. Sociologist Herbert Blumer (1951) recognized that the audience needed to be redefined to take into account its changing nature in the economic and technological circumstances of modern society. Blumer distinguished four segments in the composition of the audience:

- *The group* is a collectivity where members know each other and interact within given parameters. The allocation of roles is more or less clear to all members, and a sharing of values and common interests binds the group together and enables it to persist over time. Communication among group members is interpersonal.

- *The crowd* is larger than the group but still located in the same place. It is temporary and when it breaks up it is unlikely that it will re-form in the same way. It tends to have a degree of commonality of rhythm or mood but not in a systematic or ideological manner like the group. In fact, the crowd's behaviour is basically irrational and impulsive. The value composition of its members is dissimilar and ethical standards do not therefore apply to the actions of a crowd.

- *The public* is an audience defined in terms of its civil practices and rights within a sociopolitical context. As such, it is the product of modern democratic politics. Members of the public are located in the visible and open level of society, the public arena, where they can engage in debate on issues and policies that affect society as a whole.

- *The mass* is the largest of all audiences and, like the public, it is dispersed over a wide geographical area. It is characterized by anonymity and a lack of group cohesion or organization. The mass audience converges on an object of interest usually produced methodically by a specialist industry over which the mass audience has no direct control. It is similar to the crowd in its lack of structure, but different in that it has no fixed location or physical proximity with other members.

Blumer's definition of the mass audience is admittedly rather bleak. It is probably true that there is a large-scale, global audience that is impersonal and relatively passive in relation to the powerful media companies which produce and transmit the messages that it receives. However, researchers have increasingly been observing two phenomena that question this definition.

First, they have observed that the audience's experience of the media text is personal and integrated in meaningful everyday activities and social life. Groups and individuals interpret the same media text differently. Most notably, the 'uses and gratifications' approach developed in the 1980s has been influential in documenting this phenomenon (Ang 1991; Barker and Brooks 1998). In this respect, an audience is 'mass' only in so far as it is seen from a distant perspective and defined in very general terms. Also, much research has found evidence that what is seemingly a mass audience actually consists of many overlapping networks of common-interest or local-community individuals, who incorporate the information they receive in the social framework that orients their group. The work carried out by political campaign researchers such as Katz and Lazarsfeld (1955) and Merton (1949) was instrumental in showing this and helping to restore the social and communal face of the 'mass' audience.

Secondly, approaches to the mass audience have also had to take into account evidence produced by persuasion theorists who showed that individuals are influenced much more strongly by their social networks and personal relations than by the media. In fact, much of the contact individuals have with media texts is mediated by interpersonal relationships that filter the information and guide the response. For example, a person who has an opinion about, say, a political party is much less likely to change this opinion because of a media-transmitted message than because of influence from someone s/he respects – an 'opinion leader'. The media tend to have an informative function, but actually there is little evidence that they have the final say in changing public, or even individual, opinion about important matters.

Recently, developments in computer-based 'new media', and in particular the internet,

Spotlight on the history of the audience

A general definition of an audience is a group of people assembled voluntarily at a particular place and time to view and listen to a public performance of a secular nature. The origins of audiences as an observable and classifiable category lie in the ancient Greco-Roman world where people congregated as spectators for public theatrical and musical performances and sporting events, as well as political gatherings. This function of the audience still exists today in theatres and stadiums, as well as 'live' public events of all kinds.

The audience as a mass-media phenomenon arose with the emergence of the printed book, in the mid-fifteenth century. For the first time, communication could take place at a distance, and the audience could receive messages in private. This led to the development of a collection of individuals, dispersed geographically, who could buy copies of the same book for instruction or entertainment purposes. Literacy was, of course, a prerequisite, as was a certain income level, which meant that the first reading publics were composed of city dwellers or educated churchmen of a relatively high social status. These publics often turned patrons of publishers and authors, thereby supporting the industry that informed and entertained them (Febvre and Martin 1984; Kaufer and Carley 1993).

By the early eighteenth century, magazines and newspapers had entered the market and created a subpublic of print media. The increasing industrialization and the move to cities that this entailed, as well as developments in technology, transportation and the rise in living standards and education, led to the print media becoming large-scale industries by the end of the nineteenth century. By the beginning of the twentieth century, advertising had become a major source of income for magazines and newspapers, reflecting the rise of free market enterprises and the production of more and more consumer products. With these developments came a more sophisticated differentiation and segmentation of audiences, who were now seen clearly as consumers. Manufacturers started to use the media to compete for consumer attention and, therefore, a larger market share.

The invention of film at the turn of the twentieth century redefined the audience of print media, which was essentially a group of individuals consuming media objects in their own time and space, into a 'mass' audience, in the sense of large-scale receptions of the same text. In addition, in parallel to theatrical performances and public speaking, it reinstated the 'public' and 'local' nature of audience reception by gathering audiences in established locations, cinemas, where they participated in the media production as a collectivity.

Starting in the 1920s, broadcasting constituted another turning point in the history of the audience. Because broadcasting is essentially a technology of distribution with roots in radiotelephony, its communicative function depended largely on hardware. Receiving a message depended on having access to the technical equipment through which the message was transmitted. This defined the audience as a group who possessed the appropriate tools for the communicative exchange to take place (Williams 1974; McQuail 1997).

Television is easily the most popular and widespread broadcast medium, overshadowing both print and other broadcast media in its impact. Television has played a significant role in the globalization of the media, with national audiences world-wide being influenced by programmes produced by the major US-based media companies, such as Warner and Fox. Television remains a controversial issue in media research with regard to its influence on audiences. By many, traditionally, the television audience has been considered passive and easily influenced. Media-effects theorists, in particular, often cite television as inciting audiences to inertia or violence. In contrast, more radical television theorists see the medium as a means for minorities to voice their world-views, as a check on authorities and the privileged, preventing them from keeping information from public scrutiny, and as a pathway to social tolerance and public debate (McKee 2003).

Convergence, the interactive use of various media based on digital applications, is the most recent tool of transformation of the concept of the audience. In convergence, media users can acquire control of the information environment by selecting and combining the texts they wish to view or interact with. Convergence has two aspects: first, computer-based applications allow optimal resolution of screen image (TV and broadband), and wide-reach transmission of data through cable and satellite. This aspect has been received positively by mass audiences because of the ease of accessibility that it entails and the high quality of the reception. Secondly, convergence allows for interactivity and customization, which makes audiences less passive in receiving media objects, and dissolves the notion of a mass audience in favour of groups or individual users. However, much research suggests that users/viewers do not generally want to be interactive, but prefer a more passive reception of the text. This would imply that the changed concept of the audience that the new media hail has not quite 'latched on'.

In the future, definitions of the audience will change consistently with the rise of new media and their global distribution. What form this will take cannot be predicted with certainty. It could be that the new media will perfect three-dimensional image projection, maybe through holographic laser displays. In that case, performances could take place in a staging space that would be similar to the ancient proscenium arch, but where the performers, or indeed the audience, would not need to be physically present.

have added another challenge to the notion of a mass audience. The interactivity embedded in such media makes them amenable to customization according to personal needs and tastes, giving audiences (or, in this case, 'users'), more autonomy in selecting what services to use and how to use them. Modern policy-makers, whether government, business or community, use surveys and trials to test new media developments, in the absence of a unified theory that can predict what new media the public will use. Examples of such needs-identifying experiments include the French government giving away thousands of special terminals in the project *Minitel* to see how French citizens would use a computer-like screen to access simple data like the telephone directory. More recently in the US, Time Warner undertook a major trial involving 4000 households in Orlando to see how people would use a full network service. Other trials on delivery of broadband services have included Bell Atlantic in Alexandria and Arlington USA (Oracle Media Server), Viacom and AT&T in Castro Valley USA (video on demand to 1000 homes), US West in Omaha (2500 households with full network services), Videotron in Montreal (interactive television) and British Telecom in Colchester and Ipswich (2500 households with interactive television).

6.2 The public sphere and media values

Notions of a mass audience are also often aligned with ideas about the relationship between the state and society. One of the most famous and influential theories of the state and society in relation to people as a mass is Jürgen Habermas's theory of the public sphere (Habermas 1979; McKee 2005). According to Habermas, the public sphere is a condition that emerged in a specific phase of the history of bourgeois society: the period that saw the rise of literary clubs, newspapers, political journals and institutions of political debate in the eighteenth century. This is when a realm of debate was formed that mediated between society and the state and gave rise to 'public opinion'. This public sphere was partially protected from both the Church and the State by the efforts and resources of private individuals and was, in theory although not in practice, open to all.

According to Habermas, the strengthening of the state under capitalism since the eighteenth century and the development of corporations that commodified (i.e. turned into consumer objects that can be bought and sold) more and more aspects of life also transformed individuals from citizens to consumers. Through their advertising and public relations functions, the mass media have also played a significant role in eroding the public sphere by promoting corporate interests as opposed to free debate. At the same time, the state itself has been increasingly organized as a corporation, taking power in both the economic realm, as corporate manager, and the private realm, as welfare and education provider.

In formulating his concept of the public sphere, Habermas followed a Marxist approach that favoured concepts of rationality and determinism. This approach sees power as being connected to ownership of the means of production. Therefore, the opportunity to voice an opinion in a sphere that is not dependent on such ownership would enable individuals to engage in discussions of issues that affected the welfare of the collectivity without coercion or control from 'authority'. This is what happened when public forums were not owned by global megacorporations. In contemporary society, however, such independent but still accessible venues for debate are scarce, and what was once the domain of literary clubs and intellectual circles is being taken over by television chat shows and 'reality TV', where serious issues tend to be trivialized and where viewpoints that pose a serious challenge to the status quo are suppressed.

Looking at it from a different perspective, however, the commercialization of culture has created a new domain to which the public sphere approach does not give credit – the domain of popular pleasure. The popular media and their audiences provide a fruitful base from which creative and radical assessments of dominant ideologies can emerge. An example of this are horror comics which, despite often being considered as flippant and offensive (they were banned by an Act of Parliament in Britain in 1955), have acted as a vehicle for subversive ideas, as happened in the US of the McCarthy era where they satirized the prejudicial and unjust policies that were being implemented. Also, several contemporary popular television shows give a voice and a wide audience to social groups that have gener-ally been marginalized by mainstream society. For example, *Faking It USA* celebrates the taboo topics of misrepresentation and fake identity, thereby satirizing the notions of status and professional integrity, while *Queer Eye for the Straight Guy* privileges the perspective of gay men (a social and ideological minority) and allows it to direct the behaviour of straight men (the main representatives of dominant discourse).

Another example of popular texts acting as a forum of dissent to powerful discourses can be found in the role played by science fiction in the old Communist countries of Eastern Europe, as exemplified by the novels of Stanislas Lem in Poland and the films of Andrei Tarkovsky in what used to be the Soviet Union. Because these texts were considered 'fictional' and 'fantastic', they were allowed to carry symbolic messages critical of govern-ment authority in a way that the more 'serious' mainstream media were not able to, owing to strict censorship laws.

Despite their allegiance to corporate administration, the mass media are bound by certain values of quality and honour with respect to their audiences – at least in theory, even if financial and social conditions make it difficult to implement these values in practice. These are the principles or values of *diversity, independence, access, solidarity* and *objectivity* (McQuail 1992):

- *Diversity*. This suggests that the media are expected to represent the full range of public opinion and cultural practice. It also refers to the range of formats that different audi-ences may require at different times, for example entertainment, information and educa-tion.

- *Independence*. A tricky principle, this suggests that the media administration should be structured in such a way as to avoid influence from advertisers, the state and corporate stakeholders. This enables the media to take a critical stance where needed and to confront the powers that be, and also to be creative and original. However, as the main income of commercial television comes from advertising, this value is often compro-mised.

- *Access*. This requires that all members of the community have access to the media texts that are on offer. Access is often mitigated by financial factors: cable, satellite and other forms of pay-TV, for example, are only accessible to those who can afford to pay for them.

- *Solidarity*. This suggests that the media should not reinforce conflict or intolerance in society, but should attempt to promote a sense of shared values among members of the community. This too has its problematic side. In a global and multi-ethnic world, can the media promote solidarity without compromising some groups' interests? Also, should the media have a national identity or strive for an international orientation and for what reasons?

- *Objectivity*. This suggests that the media must be loyal to factual and unbiased information and must present this information impartially without evaluation. Concerns with this principle arise from the fact that the concept of objectivity itself is culture- and context-specific, and that the communication of a story (in words or images) is always based on narrative choices and can never be completely objective – a story can be told in many different ways. In many cases, allowing and encouraging different narrators, and their stories, to emerge is more faithful to 'truth' than trying to capture an absolute, but elusive, objectivity.

6.3 Audience analysis

Since it is most often of paramount importance that the information communicated be understood, awareness of the audiences' composition and their needs and desires becomes equally paramount. In fact, the close link between advertising and the media world means that media industries spend a great part of their budget and strategic planning on analysing and monitoring audiences and consumer preferences.

Generally, public audiences are analysed according to three main factors:

- *Demographics*: this includes objective aspects such as age, gender, ethnicity, education, and income level.

- *Psychographics*: this includes subjective aspects such as values, lifestyle preferences, leisure activities and consumer tastes.

- *Technical knowledge*: this becomes relevant when communicating specialist ideas, such as scientific discoveries. It refers to the level of expertise and knowledge of technical terminology that an audience is assumed to have – how technically 'savvy' they are.

An influential approach to demographic analysis, especially in business and marketing fields, is based on the generational classification proposed by William Strauss and Neil Howe, as described in their book *Generations: The History of America's Future 1584 to 2069* (1991). Examining the major historical changes in American society, the authors suggested a cyclical model of generational change based on some abstract principles that governed each generation. They distinguished four types of generations and gave them mythical names, suggesting that they were abstract representations of behavioural patterns. These names were *prophet, nomad, hero* and *artist*.

Briefly, a prophet generation shows a principled and righteous attitude, approaching social issues with idealism and missionary zeal. A nomad generation is realistic and cynical, is universalist and rootless, and attempts to deal with social issues through cunning and strategy. A hero generation is an advocate of social and civil rights, fights for technological prosperity and economic progress, and attempts to deal with social issues through rational policy-making and institution-building. Finally, an artist generation is mellow and mild-mannered, believes in fairness and equality, and tends to exhibit a rather gullible approach to life issues.

Studying major historical events and the public response to them, Strauss and Howe then divided American generations since 1584 according to this classification. Looking only at the most recent categories, we get the division shown in Figure 6.1.

Needless to say, this classification has a strong inclination to stereotype groups and to undermine social, cultural and individual differences. Also, it is largely based on the interpretation of quantifiable trends, such as economic measurement, population statistics, etc., and can therefore only provide generalizations about phenomena. Nevertheless, it has been instrumental in highlighting the importance of generational influences on consumer tastes and group values, and, if used heuristically (i.e. as a working tool rather than a mirror of reality), it can inspire, and indeed has inspired, discussion on attitudinal traits that could lead to a better understanding of audiences and markets. Researchers in the media industry often use this classification in ascribing programming to target audiences. Steve Leblang, Senior Vice President of Strategic Research and Planning at FX Networks, for example, notes that, according to his surveys, Generation Y is more spiritual than Generation X. An example that he gives to support this statement is the success among young people of television series such as *Joan of Arcadia*, which are based on a spiritual theme (Leblang 2004).

The Silent Generation Artist 1925–1942
The Silent Generation lived through World War II, saw the decline of humanitarian rationalism in the concentration camps and the rise in literary and artistic movements aiming to provide the foundations for a more enlightened life. They are sensitive and empathic but prone to pessimism and deception.

The Baby Boomers Prophet 1943–1960
The baby boomers enjoyed the rise in economic prosperity of the post-war years (their parents had more babies!) and the associated rise in optimism. Humanitarian ideals and the rise of welfare states were prominent achievements of those born in this generation.

Generation X Nomad 1961–1981
This was named after Douglas Coupland's novel *Generation X: Tales for an Accelerated Future* (1994), and is not the original name given by Strauss and Howe. Generation Xers are more cynical and cautious than their parents (they are, after all, the AIDS generation). They tend to be high achievers, especially in technological fields (they are the internet generation), but are often unappreciated as individuals. They tend to be more fearful of the future, which makes them better strategists than the preceding generation.

Generation Y Hero 1982–2003
This too is not named by Strauss and Howe, but is an alphabetical progression from X. This generation is still young and their characteristics are uncertain. They are the cellphone and text-messaging generation, technologically adept and media savvy. They are also speculated to inherit debts of various kinds, such as ageing parents and diseases (e.g. obesity, diabetes) that are due to habits formed in their upbringing.

Generation Z Artist 2004–2025(?)
This generation is literally in its infancy and not much can be said about it at this stage.

Figure 6.1 Generations

Audience analysis methods

Major ways to analyse audiences, in both media and corporate contexts, include surveys and focus groups.

Surveys

Surveys are conducted through the use of questionnaires, after a sample population has been chosen. Considerations underpinning survey research include:

- How to choose the population to be interviewed?
- How to conduct the interview?
- How to interpret the data?

The main ways to sample the population are *random*, *quota* and *purposive* sampling. Random sampling occurs when there are no fixed criteria for the sample selection, and each item, or person, has an equal chance of being selected. Quota sampling, a common method in market research, occurs when the researcher can decide which items s/he will choose from a given quota. For instance, if 50 teenage boys were selected as the quota, the researcher could choose the particular teenage boys s/he would interview (using criteria, such as type of dress, for instance). In purposive surveys, the sample is neither random nor representative. Instead it is deliberately chosen from specified groups in order to test a hypothesis or compare data. An example would be assessing the use of interactive media among high-income and low-income people by selecting samples from two neighbourhoods that represented the two income levels.

Another informed choice that has to be made when conducting surveys is the method of collecting data. For example, surveys can be conducted face-to-face, via the telephone, by mail or by e-mail. Each method has drawbacks and advantages, and its success depends on the nature of the research and the population selected.

Questions in survey questionnaires fall into these categories:

- *An open-ended question*: this allows respondents to supply their own answer with little guidance:

    Who would you like to see elected prime minister?

- *A closed-ended question with unordered answer categories*: this provides several possible answers and asks respondents to select one:

    Who would you like to see elected prime minister?

    1. A
    2. B
    3. C
    4. D
    5. E

- *A closed-ended question with ordered answer categories*: this provides several possible answers and asks respondents to rate each according to degrees of intensity:

    For each of these candidates, please indicate how much you would like that individual to be elected prime minister.

	strongly favour	somewhat favour	somewhat oppose	strongly oppose
1. A	1	2	3	4
2. B	1	2	3	4
3. C	1	2	3	4
4. D	1	2	3	4
5. E	1	2	3	4

- *A partially closed-ended question*: this provides several possible answers, but also allows respondents to select a different answer if required:

  Who would you like to see elected prime minister?
  1. A
  2. B
  3. C
  4. D
  5. E
  6. Other (specify)

- *Ladder-scale question*: this provides a scale on which respondents can rate the performance or degree of probability:

  On a scale from 0 to 10, where 0 means you rate the job the prime minister is doing as extremely poor and 10 means you rate the job the prime minister is doing as extremely good, how would you rate the job Prime Minister X is doing?

  Extremely Poor   Extremely Good

  0   1   2   3   4   5   6   7   8   9   10

- *Lickert-scale question*: this asks respondents to evaluate the likelihood of particular actions:

  How likely do you think you will be to vote for Prime Minister X in the forthcoming election?
  1. Very likely
  2. Somewhat likely
  3. Neither likely nor unlikely
  4. Somewhat unlikely
  5. Very unlikely

- *Semantic differential question*: this asks respondents to give impressionistic answers to a particular object by selecting specific positions in relation to at least nine pairs of bipolar adjectives on a scale of one to seven. The aim is to locate the meaning of the object in three dimensions: evaluation (e.g. good–bad), potency (e.g. strong–weak), and activity (e.g. active–passive). This method is useful in studying emotional reactions and attitudes and gauging the differences in outlook between cultural groups:

  How would you characterize X as Prime Minister?
  Good –Bad
  Strong –Weak
  Decisive –Indecisive
  Moral –Immoral
  Intelligent –Stupid

Focus groups

Surveys provide quantitative data that shed some light on general audience responses to questions. To understand a particular group's needs and desires, however, a qualitative approach is often more useful. Semi-structured interviews, where the interviewer has the opportunity to gain a more personal and in-depth understanding of audience opinion, are a common alternative method. As a systematic approach to data gathering, focus groups trace their origin in Robert Merton and Patricia Kendall's article *The Focused Interview* (1946). In this, the authors explained the dynamics involved and techniques used in small-group, face-to-face interviewing as a method for understanding how people interpret various issues.

Focus groups are organized by inviting a number of people to a preselected venue, such as a television network company if the research is about television viewing, and conducting semi-formal interviews under the supervision of a moderator. Although the subjects are asked specific questions, they are given the opportunity to interact and discuss matters around the question. The moderator, in this case, is an interviewer and a participant–observer, collecting both raw data (the answers to the questions) and observations (digressions, tone of voice, attitude, etc.). In some cases, focus groups are asked to perform some actions in relation to a set of instructions, in order to ascertain the clarity and accuracy of the instructions. This is what happens, increasingly, in the user documentation section of many software companies, where the designers observe how users understand instructions and how they carry them out.

Although the 'natural language' aspect of focus groups may at first sight make them a desirable method of data collection, there are some issues to watch out for. First, the environment in which the interviews take place is 'set up' and formal, making spontaneous or genuine responses unlikely. Secondly, people are not generally openly forthcoming about their views on many issues, nor do they necessarily consciously think about these views. Therefore, it is important that the focus group organizer and moderator be well prepared to direct the discussion effectively. Also, it is advisable to use the information collected from focus groups in conjunction with other material collected from other sources in order to construct a more comprehensive picture.

Stewart and Shamdasani (1990) have given a clear explanation of the theory and applications of focus-group research. These authors distinguish eight steps in the design and use of focus groups (Stewart and Shamdasani 1990: 20):

1   defining the problem and formulating the research question;
2   identifying the sample;
3   identifying the moderator;
4   generating and pretesting the interview guide;
5   recruiting the sample;
6   conducting the group;
7   analysing and interpreting the data;
8   writing the report.

Focus groups are often used in the approach to audiences loosely described as 'uses and gratifications' (explained below). In this case, groups are formed and interviewed on their reception of particular films or television shows. Producers then revise their programming plans or film content according to the feedback they receive. In the academic field, a pivotal study employing this method to discuss audience values and expectations was David Morley's *The 'Nationwide' Audience* (1980). In this, Morley set out to measure audience responses to the BBC's *Nationwide* evening news magazine programme that ran during the 1970s. Part of the research involved showing a video recording of a *Nationwide* programme to 29 groups composed of people with a range of educational and professional backgrounds, and then interviewing them. This method produced results which suggested that audiences were not passive recipients of media texts. Instead they exhibited considerable resistance to dominant discourses, both between groups and between people within groups.

Figure 6.2 shows the two sides of an invitation to attend a screening as part of a focus group. The aim is to ascertain audience reactions to a new film, in order to plan changes to the final version of the film and to map out a marketing strategy. Notice how, although this is a public invitation, it poses limitations on the composition of the focus group and shows an emphasis on secrecy.

At the end of the screening, viewers are given a questionnaire to complete. This requests personal information on demographics (age and gender), educational background and film-going habits, as well as information about the film, such as which scenes they liked, which scenes they did not like, what they thought about the ending, and how convincing each actor was for each major role.

Media researchers in the area of television use a variety of techniques to determine audience preferences – who watches what and when. Large international media research companies such as AC Nielsen and Arbitron frequently introduce new methods to measure ratings. Traditionally, the widespread method for ascertaining viewer habits was the diary. Representatives of media research companies selected households (on a random and/or demographically informed basis) and asked them to fill out diaries specifying the programmes they watched and the times they watched them. Patterns of viewing would then be traced, which would, in turn, inform the programming decisions of broadcast companies. As can be imagined, the diary method was not wholly reliable or informative.

With developments in digital technology, such measurement techniques have been updated. For example, AC Nielsen introduced a product called Panorama, which records ratings information, coupled with consumer profiles and information about product usage. This offers the purchasers what it calls detailed 'buyergraphics' and 'doergraphics' ('what the market actually buys and does') using a combination of data collected by AC Nielsen's various other media-measurement techniques. This data includes television ratings gathered via an electronic device known as a Peoplemeter installed in the homes of those participating in the survey, as well as radio ratings, readership and product-usage information gathered by means of interviews and self-completion dairies. This information from different sample groups is then statistically matched via a process described as 'data fusion' in order to provide descriptions of what different groups of people watch, read and buy. Panorama thus offers a profile of consumers, which matches demographics with patterns of media usage, opinions, tastes in food and drink, choice of car, cellphone and cable provider.

Similarly, Arbitron developed the Portable Peoplemeter, which is an electronic device attachable to equipment such as television sets and radios. This device records choices of broadcasts automatically without the need for audiences to input this information manually.

The Screening Exchange invites you to a private film screening of
"XXXXX"
(film description on the back!)
Monday 4 April 2006
Time: 7.30 p.m.
Location

Please call us with the following information:
1. Your name, including the spelling of your first and last name.
2. Whether or not you will be bringing a guest.
3. Your home telephone number.
4. Your gender and your guest's gender.
5. Your ethnicity and your guest's ethnicity.
6. Your age and your guest's age.
7. Your e-mail address.
8. Whether you and your guest have attended college for any amount of time.
9. The code in the following box: [number in box].

"XXXXX"
Description of film story, usually with an emphasis on stars or famous elements associated with
the film.

Rating status
WARNING: Under no circumstances will audience members with **CAMERA PHONES, CAMERAS**
or any **RECORDING DEVICE** be admitted into this screening.

IMPORTANT INFORMATION:
No one will be admitted if they are directly or indirectly associated with the entertainment industry,
marketing, advertising, journalism, or any media-related business including the internet. No one
will be admitted to this recruited audience test preview who appears dirty or unkempt, intoxicated,
under the influence of drugs, or who may interfere in any way with the enjoyment of the film. Since
this is a privately recruited audience, if you or your guest do not meet these criteria or any other
criteria which we feel will not fit the demographics and conditions of the screening, you and your
guest will not be admitted or given a ticket. We reserve the right to cancel the screening at any
time. We reserve the right to expel or turn away any person from a screening. We reserve the right
to refuse an invitation to any person during a recruitment. No backpacks, large bags, video recording equipment, cameras or cellphones that have cameras will be allowed in the screening. We are
not responsible for any personal items that are lost or left with theatre staff or security at the
screening. The theatre is overbooked to ensure capacity.

Figure 6.2 Screening invitation

6.4 Approaches to mass communication

Media effects

The group of approaches classified under 'media effects theory' is primarily concerned with
the ways in which media content influences the behaviour of consumers (Bryant and
Zillman 2002). Not surprisingly, media effects research looks at taboo topics, such as
violence and sexuality, and asks if individuals' violent or aberrant behaviour in society is a
result of exposure to such behaviour on television and film. This conceptualization of the

Spotlight on the history of radio

The foundational scientific principles for the development of a system that sends electronic signals through the air were formulated by British physicist James Clerk Maxwell (1831–79). However, these principles were first systematically applied by Italian engineer Guglielmo Marconi (1874–1937). It was not until about twenty years after Marconi's first experimental device that the radio was commercialized as the first electronic mass medium. The first regularly scheduled public radio broadcast was made in 1920 from station KDKA in Pittsburgh, Pennsylvania, in the US. Shortly afterwards, other companies emerged and established radio networks for broadcast programming – including the Radio Corporation of America (RCA) and Westinghouse. Because of its oral and immediate transmission, radio became a popular medium of communication very quickly, and is the first mass medium whose content was designed with mass appeal. With the development of other media, such as television, film and the internet, radio has been backgrounded in appeal in many countries and cultural contexts. As with the other media, radio technology has been greatly influenced by the digital revolution. Radio stations now use digital technology to broadcast their programmes through such technologies as digital-audio broadcasting (DAB).

media as persuasive, or even prescriptive, tools of social control (in other words, that we 'learn through the media') traces its origins to the post-World-War-II era in the US, when scholars such as Paul Lazarsfeld et al. (1968 [1944]) attempted to ascertain the influence that the media had on political campaigning and on public opinion regarding presidential candidates. This interest was then extended to other areas of media (especially television and film) content.

'Priming', a key concept in media effects research, describes a form of conditioning that the media is purported to carry out on audiences. It supports the idea that people react to a stimulus as a result of having been conditioned by a preceding stimulus. When applied to media theory, priming refers to the effects of the content of media on people's later behaviour or opinions. Experiments carried out to test this idea include cases where subjects are tested to see if they are markedly violent after viewing violent content (Anderson 1997). Many results seem to suggest that some subjects are affected by media content, but that this influence dissipates over time, while others suggest that only those subjects who have specific behavioural dispositions are influenced to any significant extent (for instance, those who exhibit violent behaviour prior to testing may become more aggressive after viewing violent content). On the whole, the results of priming research are conflicting and nonconclusive, and are very much dependent on such factors as the context of the experiment and the composition of the subject groups.

The 'third person effect' is another phenomenon highlighted by media effects research. This refers to the widely attested claim of media consumers (researchers, regulators and non-specialists) that media content influences others but not themselves. This is a significant finding in relation to policy makers and censorship legislators, because it shows how the concern to protect society from media influence that often motivates broadcast regulation stems from the ungrounded belief that 'others' or 'people' are susceptible to corruption and need to be protected. It also shows that if we are to believe that the media are harmful to some, we need to justify why others (including ourselves) may be exempt from this rule, or else we need to reconsider the rule itself.

Because of its emphasis on behavioural responses to external stimuli, media effects research has been popular in the US, where there is a stronger psychological orientation to the study of sociocultural phenomena than in Europe. This does not mean to say, however, that European scholars have not flirted with the idea. Notably, in 1994 Elizabeth Newson, Professor in Developmental Psychology at the University of Nottingham in the UK, published an essay entitled 'Video Violence and the Protection of Children', which came to be known as the Newson Report. In this, Newson denounced the irresponsible portrayal of violence in the media for entertainment purposes by putting forth an argument about the harmful effects such texts can have on children. The report was prompted by the torture and death of two-year-old James Bulger in 1993 by two ten-year-old children. Blame for this act had been put on violent films that the children had allegedly been watching, and had added fuel to the debate on the effects of media violence, especially on children.

Newson claimed that media violence not only desensitized children but also exposed them to behaviour that they were induced to assimilate without having experienced it, thereby distorting the real impact and consequences of this behaviour. Despite its merits in contributing a lucid argument to this controversial issue, the report did not answer some pertinent questions, including the following:

- Is there really an increase in violence among children with the advent of mass media depictions of violence, or did cases like the James Bulger incident occur in pre-mass-media times too? Could it be that we are becoming more aware of such incidents because of mass-media coverage?

- Accepting the claim that children are more suggestible and vulnerable to impressionable images than adults, should not the argument be that a consistent effort should be made to enforce ratings regulations rather than to censor or ban violent media content (as Newson's article suggests)?

- What would the consequences of strict censorship laws be on art and freedom? Would not such laws produce autocratic restrictions on civil rights that would trigger a whole new set of social problems? Is there a justified need to create draconian laws in light of evidence that remains, in the final analysis, inconclusive?

In general, the media-effects approaches show some weaknesses that need to be addressed. First, by focusing on an abstract value in the content (such as violence), they fail to assess the overall narrative and semiotic structure from which this value emerges (that is, the whole film, programme or game), and therefore cannot adequately evaluate the way the medium was used to construct the particular message. For example, what is the difference in the use of violence in a film as opposed to a computer game? Or, what is the difference in the use of violence in, say, Stanley Kubrick's *Clockwork Orange* (1971), Frank Miller and Robert Rodriguez's *Sin City* (2005) and a porn movie that depicts rape and violence?

Secondly, by attempting to establish a causal link between media content and behaviour, they neglect other elements that could be equally responsible for the behaviour. For example, consider the case of a youth committing a murder after watching 18 hours of television, seven days a week for a prolonged period. Would not the fact that this is how he was spending his time seem as significant as (if not more significant than) the content of the broadcasting that he was viewing? Social factors that lead to young people's isolation, frustration and boredom would then emerge as more significant than media content.

Thirdly, the time element between the use of the medium and the behaviour is often unacknowledged. Much experimental media-effects research, where a group is shown particular content and then observed after the viewing, describes the effects of the content directly after exposure. The claimed influence, therefore, can only be contained within the time limits of the experiment, in which case other psychological factors could also be at play. As philosopher Albert Camus once noted, it is easy to detect those who have just seen an action movie because of the way they walk in the street!

In all, although media-effects research can be thought-provoking, it assumes a one-way direction of influence from the media to the audience, and this makes it limited in perspective. A broader view would recognize that media content is influenced as much by social currents, expectations and trends as the other way round. Alan McKee puts this aptly (2003: 46):

> The media texts, like the sense-making practices of individuals, have to work within the practices that already exist, although they can also try to alter those. The process is like a feedback loop – texts in the media have to draw on existing ways of making sense of the world: these are then interpreted by people, and feed back into the texts that they themselves produce (speech, writing, dress codes), and then these feed back into mediated texts.

Uses and gratifications

The 'uses and gratifications approach' (U&G) to mass media is a broad term that is applied to methods that focus on the ways in which audiences use the media for information and/or entertainment purposes. It tends to be contrasted with the media-effects approach, whose focus is on the influences of media content on audience behaviour. To put this distinction simply, U&G looks at what audiences do with media objects, whereas the media-effects approach is more interested in what media objects do to audiences.

U&G developed during the 1960s and 1970s, and reflects the emancipation of media consumers, who were increasingly being seen as independent selectors of media content, rather than as passive recipients. The key source representing the concerns of this approach was Blumler and Katz's *The Uses of Mass Communication* (1974). A model derived from this research and elaborated on by McQuail (1994: 134) poses the following sequence: U&G researchers study (1) the social and psychological origins of needs, which generate (2) expectations of the media, and which lead to (3) different patterns of media exposure, resulting in (4) other consequences. This sequence is represented graphically in Figure 6.3.

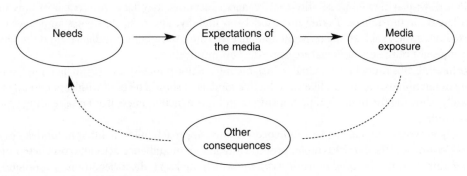

Figure 6.3 Uses and gratifications model

This approach acknowledges that, when it comes to media selectivity and response, audience behaviour is influenced by needs and motivation, and, indeed, by the pursuit of pleasure. The basic notion underlying U&G research is that the media are seen by audiences as offering rewards which are valued (or, of course, the opposite, that they contain messages that are negatively evaluated and therefore avoided).

Stuart Hall (1973 and 1980), the director of the celebrated Centre for Contemporary Cultural Studies (CCCS) at the University of Birmingham, formulated a model of audience positions in relation to mass-media texts that has been influential in understanding what audiences do with texts. In line with the inclination in structuralist and some post-structuralist thought of tracing analogies between language and text (both visual and verbal), Hall described these audience reactions in terms of 'reading' a text, and distinguished three main types:

- *Dominant or hegemonic reading.* Here the audience accepts the reading that is inscribed in the coding and sign structure of the text. This happens when the audience shares the values propounded by the text and understands the code used to present these values as being natural or transparent. In this type of reading there is no resistance to the meanings created in the interface between text and reader–spectator, and the audience can be seen as friendly.

- *Negotiated reading.* Here the audience accepts parts of the message of the text, while resisting other parts. The audience tends to agree with some values of the texts, but still finds some contradiction between these values and the audience's own experiences and beliefs. So, it modifies certain aspects of the text to make it more in tune with its positions and interests.

- *Oppositional or counter-hegemonic reading.* Here the audience rejects the message because its own values clash with those inscribed in the coding and sign structure of the text. Although the readers–spectators understand the meanings created in the text, they resist them and bring into focus their own frame of reference, based on their ideologies and experience. In this case, the audience can be seen as hostile.

A criticism that has often been raised in relation to this model is that it assumes meaning to be inherent in the text, somewhat like the older, sender-based communication models (as described in Chapter 2). To be sure, the audience is seen as active in that it can accept, negotiate or reject this meaning, but it is still passive in relation to constructing or interpreting the signs with which it is presented. This model also reifies or essentializes the reading position, downplaying the possibility that readers-spectators may take different positions in different circumstances. Taking this model too literally, one risks classifying audiences in fixed categories, such as 'the resistant audience' or 'the contradictory audience', and thereby losing sight of the dynamic nature of media communication.

In all, Hall's model gives valuable insights into major possibilities of audience positioning in relation to a text, but, like all reductive models, it should be used with care and eclectically, allowing for more flexible transitions and more inclusiveness from one reading type to another.

Other writers interested in an audience-response approach follow a different model. Levy and Windahl (1985), for example, propose a typology of audience activity constructed on two dimensions, the *qualitative dimension,* which looks at the orientation of audience members towards the communication process, and the *temporal dimension,* which asks whether audience activity occurs before during or after engagement with the media. The qualitative dimension is given three values: *selectivity, involvement* and *utility*. Selectivity is the non-random selection of one or more behavioural, perceptual or cognitive, media-related alternatives. Involvement is the degree to which an audience member can identify a connection between himself/herself and media content, and the degree to which the audience member interacts psychologically with a medium or its messages. Utility is how audience members use the media for different purposes (Levy and Windahl 1985:112). These values are then combined with the two dimensions:

- *Selectivity before exposure* describes the individual's decision to receive a media message, usually because, through experience with that particular type of media content, s/he has come to expect a certain level of gratification.

- *Selectivity during exposure* means that the individual pays attention only to certain messages or parts of messages, disregarding the rest. Studies of magazine and newspaper readers, for example, have shown that different individuals reading the same text have in fact chosen to receive different sets of messages. This selectivity during exposure can be conscious and active or unconscious and less active.

- *Selectivity after exposure* designates the amount and type of information that an individual remembers after exposure to the media message. Research has shown that only a fraction of the information received by an individual is actually retained for a substantial amount of time.

- *Involvement before exposure* suggests that the individual anticipates a set of media messages. This is what happens, for example, when an individual says s/he is looking forward to seeing a particular television show, movie or whatever. Another example of this involvement may be fantasizing about or trying to guess what will happen in, say, the next episode of a television series. Researchers believe that this type of involvement may well have important consequences for exposure patterns, particularly repeat viewing.

- *Involvement during exposure* describes the different levels of consciousness on which media messages are received. On the subconscious level, message stimuli elicit a small number of neurological responses, and the individual is unaware of the message. This is what might happen, for example, when there is television background noise but the individual pays no attention to the broadcast. On the preconscious level, the individual is aware of the presence of the stimulus and responds to it. However, the individual is unable to report verbally on what just happened in the message or what it did to him/her. This could be exemplified by an individual not being able to remember the details of a television show. The conscious level is where the individual is able to verbalize the experience of his/her interaction with the media message. The preconscious level is usually associated with affective responses, while the conscious level is associated more with cognitive responses.

- *Post-exposure involvement* is when the individual's behaviour is influenced by a message after s/he has received it. Examples include children who take on the identity of a fictional superhero when playing, and those whose daydreams or fantasies are based in part on the content of media messages.

- *Utility before exposure* occurs when an individual uses his/her interpersonal and social contacts to anticipate upcoming media presentations. This happens, for example, when future media presentations become the topic of conversation, or when opinion leaders alert others to expected media messages that offer the opportunity for specific types of gratifying experiences.

- *Utility during exposure* is using the media presentation to obtain affective and/or cognitive gratification. This happens, for example, when an individual uses a television programme to assure himself/herself that s/he is right in some opinion, attitude or stereotype. Actually, the media are often used to make sense of reality, by explaining or affirming aspects of the world. A related use occurs when an individual can identify with what s/he learns by making connections with his/her own life.

- *Post-exposure utility* occurs when an individual talks about things s/he has seen or read, and reflects on or assimilates received information into his/her behaviour.

Much of the audience analysis conducted by U&G researchers focuses on the ways in which audiences use the media, but also on psychosocial aspects ruling individual and group behaviour, and the motivations that incite people to carry out certain actions or to seek certain media objects. One influential approach to human needs and motivations, relevant to U&G research, is that developed by Abraham Maslow in 1954 (Maslow 1987). Maslow found that unsatisfied needs motivated behaviour, and organized a description of needs in a hierarchy going from physiological at the bottom to self-actualization at the top. Maslow's method was original in that he studied the behaviour of successful and well-adjusted people to understand motivation, as opposed to the more common approaches that focused on the socially maladjusted or deviant.

Maslow' hierarchy of needs is represented graphically in Figure 6.4.

Physiological needs encompass the basic requirements of life, such as food and water, and anything affecting survival. *Safety* needs are those whose attainment allows protection from danger and deprivation. *Social* needs become important when the needs on the two lower levels are satisfied. They include companionship, belonging and friendship. *Esteem* needs comprise the desire to achieve self-esteem and to gain the approval of others. The highest level is that of *self-actualization* needs, where individuals strive to achieve the full degree of their potential and become fully integrated individuals.

Figure 6.4 Maslow's hierarchy of needs

This is a useful model for heuristic and analytical purposes, but it is rather basic and simplistic to be taken at face value. For example, its hierarchical nature suggests that each level of needs must be satisfied before moving on to the next and that an individual cannot have both basic and high-level needs, or even conflicting needs, simultaneously. The model, therefore, fails to acknowledge the complexity of human nature. To take a few examples that contradict the implications of the model, some individuals value the satisfaction of ideological needs more than the satisfaction of physiological needs, political hunger strikers and suicide bombers being two examples. Also, many professionally ambitious individuals will place esteem and self-actualization needs above social or even safety needs.

A different approach to human needs was developed by William Schutz (1966). Schutz concentrated on social needs, leaving out basic biology, and identified three main needs that ground communication: *inclusion, control* and *affection*. Schutz's main argument was that people's needs were closely tied in with their individuality: that is, the desire to be seen to be distinct from others. Inclusion is the need to gain attention, rather than simply to be accepted by others. Control is the need to exercise some form of power over oneself and/or one's environment. Affection is the need to give and receive friendship and love.

These needs are placed along a continuum reflecting the idea that individuals' needs have different degrees of intensity. For example, a high degree of inclusion would produce an individual who wanted attention from others at all costs, and for whom punishment would be preferable to neglect. Similarly, a high degree of need for control but low need for inclusion would produce an individual who was content to 'work behind the scenes'.

Schutz's concept is shown in diagrammatic form in Figure 6.5.

Like the previous model discussed, this classification tends to rely on stereotypical categories based on a high degree of abstraction. This produces a 'black and white' approach with little space for those who do not quite belong to any category or whose disposition changes according to time and context. Nevertheless, as was noted also in previous chapters, modelling of social behaviour is a very common approach in the academic study of communication trends, and can be useful in helping to image and articulate ideas about identity and interaction. It should be emphasized, though, that such models do not refer to or describe

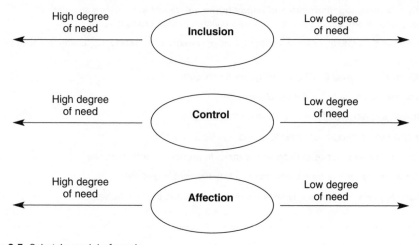

Figure 6.5 Schutz's model of needs

reality; rather, they construct ways in which to talk about reality. One way to avoid the potential rigidity and reductiveness of abstract modelling would be to adopt an inclusive, eclectic approach that blends different methods and does not attempt to reach a high degree of certainty about the world.

In U&G and in marketing research, models of human inclinations are used to shed light on what people want and how they use particular products to satisfy their needs and desires. The most common human needs which advertising executives recognize, for example, and which underlie the branding and marketing of products are listed in Figure 6.6.

Assumptions about personality, however, do not always underlie U&G research. Some writers choose a less introspective approach in studying audience expectations and desires. Conducting interviews with focus groups or getting personal testimonies from audience members are other ways to compare data and trace patterns in the ways in which media are used. Major studies following this approach include Ien Ang's work on the popularity of the television series *Dallas* (*Watching Dallas* 1985), and Barker and Brooks's work on the film *Judge Dredd* (*Knowing Audiences* 1998) .

Ang set out to examine why *Dallas* was popular in the social context of Holland. To this end, she published a letter in a women's magazine asking readers to send her descriptions of their experiences watching Dallas, their expectations of the series, and the gratification it gave them. She found that there was not one universal reason for the series' popularity, but common justifications included escapism from the mundane, identification with the characters' situations and the narrative continuity of the text.

Acquisitiveness: desire for money, power, prestige, material possessions

Comfort: desire for physical comfort, rest, leisure, peace of mind

Convenience: desire to eliminate work, to do tasks more easily

Curiosity: desire for any kind of new experience.

Egotism: desire to be attractive, popular, praised.

Family affection, togetherness and happy home life: desire to do things as a family unit, to please members of the family, to help children in their growing years

Fear: fear of pain, death, poverty, criticism, loss of possessions, beauty, popularity and loved ones.

Health: desire for good health, longevity, youthful vigour

Hero worship: desire to be like people we admire.

Kindness and generosity: desire to help others

Love and sex: desire for romantic love and a fulfilling sex life

Mental stimulation: desire to improve the mind, to broaden mental horizons.

Pleasure: desire for fun, travel, entertainment, enjoyment in general

Sensory appeals: desire for any stimulus received through the five senses

---

Figure 6.6 Basic human needs for advertising and marketing

Ang argued that watching television soap operas often involves a psychological or emotional realism for viewers, which exists at the connotative (as opposed to the denotative) level. Viewers find some representations emotionally true and realistic, even though at the denotative level the treatment may actually seem unrealistic or improbable.

Ang's findings supported the hypothesis that audience preferences are diverse (i.e. not reducible to a common denominator) and that audiences interpret texts according to their personal experiences (i.e. they are not passive recipients of inherent messages). They also highlighted the distinction that Ang discusses in the book between mass-culture ideology and populist ideology. The former supports the idea that the impersonal relations created by global institutions control trends in consumer tastes, whereas the latter 'supplies a subject position from which any attempt to pass judgment on people's aesthetic preferences is a priori and by definition rejected, because it is regarded as an unjustified attack on freedom' (Ang 1985: 113).

In *Knowing Audiences*, Barker and Brooks examined how audiences responded to *Judge Dredd,* what they expected from it, and how this compared with the strategies the producers used in making the film. This research, which was funded by an Economic and Social Research Council project grant in 1995, involved interviewing 136 people from various English youth clubs. A significant contribution of the study lay in the writers' detailed reflective documentation of their concerns in formulating questions and in interacting with the focus groups. In their approach, Barker and Brooks deliberately avoided searching for results that would substantiate the belief that audiences were passive recipients of media and that their reactions either reflected the ideology of the media (i.e. violent people watched violent media), or were influenced by it (i.e. violent media encouraged copy-cat behaviour in society).

Instead, they formulated a list of guiding research questions to enable them to focus on the complex interrelationships between audience, media object, producers, genre and socio-cultural context. This list is as follows (Barker and Brooks 1998: 8–9):

1   What qualities in a cinema are seen by audiences to best 'suit' films such as *Judge Dredd*? How likely are these to affect actual decisions to attend a screening?

2   What is the relationship between the film and comic book (in terms of storylines, characters, cultural status, etc.)? What is the evidence of the effects of film adaptations on comic book sales?

3   How does *Judge Dredd* relate to people's images of law and order? What role do fantasies about crime and its control play in the lives of delinquents, and non-delinquents?

4   What part in Sylvester Stallone's career is *Judge Dredd* perceived to have played? For how many was it perceived as continuous, a new development or a disruption?

5   What role do images of the future play among different age-groups, and how do science fiction images (such as *Judge Dredd*) contribute?

6   Who made the key decisions in planning and producing the film? On the basis of what information were these decisions made?

7   How do people process information to gain understanding from films, compared with other media?

8   How does 'hype' affect film-going? What kinds of talk get generated by films, and how do these work to turn some films into box office hits?

9 What combinations of stars generate particular expectations and hopes in audiences, and how far do these translate into improved cinema attendances?

10 What legal devices (copyright and trademarks, for instance) surrounded the film version of *Judge Dredd*? What effects did these have on the nature of the film and in spin-offs?

11 How did the British and US publicity regimes for the film differ? What measures are there of the effectiveness of each?

From this general research framework, they extrapolated a list of questions for the focus groups. Here is an abridged version of this (Barker and Brooks 1998: 38):

1 Do you go to the cinema? Describe for us a typical evening out to the cinema that you would have. Do you visit the cinema alone and/or with others? What difference does it make? Do you watch videos? What are the main differences between seeing things on video and at the cinema?

2 What prompts you to see a film? What would put you off going?

3 What had you heard about *Judge Dredd*? What had you expected it to be like? Had you had any contact with the comics, with Stallone films, with action movies before?

4 Who did you go with? What did you do that was connected, before and after?

5 Imagine you were telling a friend about the film – how would you describe it to them?

6 Did you enjoy it? What was good or bad about it?

7 What were your reactions to the start of the film? How did you feel about the ending of the film?

8 Did the film seem to you to have any point or argument? Did it leave you thinking about anything?

9 Would you watch it again? At the cinema? On video?

10 Dredd's story is set in our future. What kind of future was it? What did you feel about it?

11 Who do you feel the film was aimed at?

12 Have you come across much of the merchandising? What did you think of it?

13 Did you come across magazine or TV reviews of the film? What did you think of them?

14 What would you do with a *Judge Dredd II*? What should it be like?

Interestingly, the project was received with derision by some conservative popular press, the 'tabloids', who saw both it and the culturalist, media-studies approach it represented as frivolous, unscientific and a waste of money. This is significant in itself for anyone interested in the media in society because it is a good example of a section of the populist media attacking a section of academic culture that actually follows a populist and media-friendly approach. In other words, Barker and Brooks were criticized for not being high-brow enough by a populist journalism which claims to present the angle of 'the people'.

A second reaction to their research was from those who unquestioningly assumed that the research would involve a media-effects approach, unveiling the negative effects that

Spotlight on the history of television

The scientific principles underlying the development of television were formulated by British engineer John Logie Baird (1888-1946). The first television sets for mass use were produced in Britain and the US in the later 1930s, but the boom in television's influence took place after World War II. By 1948, the United States had 34 all-day stations operating in 21 major cities. Most industrialized countries had well-established television networks broadcasting regular programming by the late 1950s.

The development of television has evolved over several stages: the 1960s saw the development of cable television, and the 1990s the development of direct-broadcast satellite (DBS) television, which united the world by means of the transmission of the same programmes at the same time internationally. In 1998, television became digital, which allowed networks to increase their channels significantly. Digital broadcasting produced high-definition television

(HDTV), which allowed more precise picture and sound than was possible with analogue formats. Combining visual representations with sound, television quickly became and has remained one of the most popular mass media globally. In fact, an interesting point is that there is no place in the world where television has been introduced only to be rejected or not valued. Other than its functions of entertaining and informing, the universal popularity of television could be due to the idea pointed out by David Marshall (1997: 129) that it 'is intensively involved in making the world familiar'.

Because of its ubiquity and universal popularity, television is, in many ways, a privileged source of information about popular culture. As John Hartley (1999: 13) notes, what 'makes television an especially complex and satisfying object of study is that it is possible to think through large-scale issues while taking due account of the detailed technical processes and social organization of the popular media'.

violent media have on audiences. This produced such headlines as 'Stallone study on violence' and 'Stallone violence probe' (Barker and Brooks 1998: 2). As the authors noted, 'if it wasn't that, then it had to be a waste of money' (1998: 2).

Diffusion of innovations

Research on ways that innovations, such as new ideas, styles and inventions become known and are accepted in society was pioneered by Everett Rogers (1995), who defined diffusion as 'the process by which an innovation is communicated through certain channels over time among the members of a social system' (Rogers 1995: 35). His diffusion approach asked questions about what communication channels were involved in making an innovation known, how people were persuaded to adopt an innovation, and what groups of people were early or late adopters.

From his research using case studies of communities adopting or rejecting technological innovations, Rogers found that diffusion took place in five stages: the *knowledge* stage, the *persuasion* stage, the *decision* stage, the *implementation* stage, and the *confirmation* stage.

- *The knowledge stage.* This occurs when an individual is exposed to an innovation's existence and gains some understanding of how it functions. Knowledge about an innovation can be of three types; *awareness knowledge* (what the innovation is), *how-to knowledge* (how it works), and *principles knowledge* (why it works). How-to knowledge is important in showing the adopter the use, facility and relevance of an innovation. If not enough information is available on how to use an innovation, it is likely that the innovation will be rejected or discontinued. Principles knowledge is not generally necessary for adoption, but lack of it may cause the innovation to be misused, which would lead to negative

The British mathematician Charles Babbage (1792–1871) designed the first computing machine, called the Analytical Engine, in the 1830s. Ada Byron, the Countess of Lovelace, known as Ada Lovelace, is held by many to be the first programmer because of her work with Babbage. In 1843 she translated Luigi Menabrea's paper 'Sketch of the Analytical Machine' from the French and greatly expanded on it with her own thoughts. These notes – about three times longer than the original manuscript – are the reason for her reputation as the first programmer. Some 120 years before the age of computers, Lovelace predicted that the analytical machine would one day be able to create images and music. She also quickly grasped the fact that computers and programming languages needed to be kept separate, something that Babbage and subsequent scientists failed to understand until the 1950s. As credit to Lovelace's contribution to the development of computers, the world's first programming language, written in 1979, was named Ada.

It was not until about a century later that Babbage's theories were given physical form and applied to produce relatively complex machines using electrical punched-card operating systems. Engineers working at International Business Machines (IBM) in the US produced this machine for business purposes in the 1930s. British mathematician Alan Turing made great developments in computing science while working for the Secret Service during World War II, mostly in an effort to break German military codes. The Universal Turing Machine was a simple device that could carry out any conceivable computational or mathematical operation, and is the predecessor of the computer.

The first computers were huge; one computer would occupy a whole room. With advances in technology, computers became smaller and smaller. The memory and processing power of thousands of circuits were compressed into tiny chips, called semiconductors. By the 1970s it was possible to manufacture a computer small enough for personal,

home use. These were the first PCs, which were used basically as an improvement to typewriters. However, for a long time, military considerations were the greatest impetus for progress in computer science. In addition to making computers smaller and faster, the other major consideration was to connect them in networks

Engineers in the Advanced Research Projects Agency (ARPA) of the US Department of Defense collaborated with researchers in various universities to produce a network of computers in the 1960s – the ARPANET network. This used telephone lines and satellite links to share data. In the 1970s, the National Science Foundation connected universities and non-military sites to ARPANET and turned it into the first network using digital technology to connect various centres for more purposes than just defence, renaming it the internet. The internet uses telephone lines, computer cables and microwave and laser beams to carry digital information to all connected computers. Developments in digital technology have allowed all mass media to overlap and interact in the phenomenon called 'convergence'. For example, audiences can access mail, view videos and listen to music on their computer monitors. Also, communications using the internet have facilitated the advent of the 'global village' predicted by communication expert Marshall McLuhan, making it possible for people around the world to interact with each other, irrespective of the distance between them.

The increased awareness of global phenomena created by the internet can lead to a more critical attitude towards national or local conditions. Media activities, such as surfing the internet and watching cable television offer the potential for this attitude to develop in an unprecedented way. For example, the Chinese government imposed restrictions on internet use in 2001 and again in 2002, which demonstrates the power of this mass medium in increasing critical awareness among populations.

results occurring and the innovation being discontinued. Principles knowledge gives information on the laws governing the functioning of the innovation. For example, germ theories explain the importance of sanitation, hygiene and disease prevention in cooking, building construction, vaccinations, etc.

The mass media are key elements in the knowledge stage of the diffusion process: that is, they are instrumental in informing the public that an innovation exists. For example, in a study conducted in New Mexico after the 11 September terrorist attacks in New York, Everett Rogers (2003) found that television was the main medium through which people found out about the event. This was followed by interpersonal channels (people telling others and trying to find out more information from others). When people became informed of the event, they sought more information from television. Newer media, such as cell phones and the internet were found to be less prominent.

- *The persuasion stage.* This occurs when an individual forms a favourable or unfavourable attitude towards the innovation. Whereas the mental activity at the knowledge stage was mainly cognitive (or knowing), the main type of thinking at the persuasion stage is affective (or feeling). In other words, Rogers found that logical arguments were rarely enough to persuade people to adopt an innovation; what was needed was a link of emotive affinity between the adopter and the innovation, so that the innovation became meaningfully relevant to the adopter's needs and motivations.

  Diffusion research has repeatedly found that the mass media are not as important in the persuasion stage as it may seem at first sight. Although the public learns about innovations largely through the media, individuals and groups are persuaded of the benefits of an innovation through interpersonal channels. So, although the mass media can create and spread knowledge, and change weakly held attitudes, interpersonal communication is more effective in forming and changing strongly held attitudes.

- *The decision stage.* This occurs when an individual or group performs activities that lead to a decision to adopt or reject the innovation. This is the stage at which individuals or groups try out the innovation to see if it suits their needs and expectations, before adopting it more fully.

- *The implementation stage.* This occurs when an individual or group puts an innovation into use. For example, when a new information management system is introduced into an organization, it is first tested by some sections or individuals or is partially used over a specified period of time (the decision stage). If the new system seems promising and effective, it is implemented for full use.

- *The confirmation stage.* This occurs when an individual or group seeks reinforcement of a decision already made, or changes a previous decision to adopt or reject the innovation, especially if s/he is exposed to conflicting messages about the innovation. This is the stage at which the individual or group seeks to avoid a state of disagreement or conflict. The confirmation stage, therefore, is also a conformity stage: adopters of an innovation seek approval or support for their decision. Opinion leaders and those who have a high degree of credibility in the areas related to the innovation are especially important during this stage.

As regards the time aspects of adoption, such as who becomes aware of an innovation early in the innovation's life and who comes into the scene later, up until now diffusion research has found that early knowers generally have:

- more formal education than later knowers;
- higher socio-economic status than late knowers;
- more exposure to mass media channels of communication than late knowers;
- more exposure to interpersonal channels than late knowers;

- more social participation than late knowers;
- a more internationalist orientation than late knowers.

Key notions used in diffusion theory are *change agents*, *opinion leaders* and *critical mass*:

- *Change agents* are individuals or groups who are strategically positioned to facilitate change from the knowledge stage through to the decision stage. For example, mass media are change agents in awareness knowledge because they spread information. Interpersonal change agents become distinctive in the persuasion–decision stages, especially if they concentrate on how-to knowledge, which demonstrates the value of the innovation.
- *Opinion leaders* are those sought by others for information or advice about a topic. They are usually experts whose knowledge and experience give them high credibility and status. Their reputation allows them easy access to information sources. Opinion leaders have the highest powers of persuasion, and the most influential change agents are recruited from their ranks. Opinion leaders can conform to the norms of a particular group or organization, in which case they motivate others to maintain the status quo and act in the accepted tradition. At other times, opinion leaders can break away from the norm and revolutionize the accepted order of things.
- The concept of *critical mass* originates in physics, where it is defined as the amount of radioactive material needed to produce a nuclear reaction. In diffusion theory (as in social psychology) it is used to describe the point at which enough individuals or groups have adopted an innovation that the innovation's rate of increase becomes self-sustaining. When a critical mass is achieved, the rate of adoption accelerates, demonstrating the importance of social acceptance and/or imitation for the continued existence of a type of activity.

■ Summary

◆ The 'audience' is a central concept in the study of mass communication. Audiences have been classified in different ways according to such criteria as size, composition and location.

◆ Mass communication is generally considered to be unilinear, going from a media organization to an anonymous mass of people. Some researchers, however, have opted for a more 'personalized' approach to mass communication, one that sees the 'mass' as groups of individuals with distinctive needs and tastes.

◆ The 'public sphere' originally designated the social arena where information was exchanged with no direct control by government or corporate interests. In the increasingly corporatized environment of media communication, however, the notion of public sphere needs to be revised to take into account oppositional or subversive uses of media texts.

◆ Audiences are generally segmented according to demographics, psychographics and degree of education. Methods to analyse audience needs and responses include surveys and focus groups.

◆ The relationships between media organizations and audiences have been studied using different approaches, depending on whether the focus is on the influence of media texts on audiences or on the uses to which media texts are put by audiences.

◆ The 'media effects' theory examines the ways in which media texts influence the behaviour of audiences.

◆ The 'uses and gratifications' theory explores the ways in which audiences satisfy their needs and desires through media texts.

◆ The 'diffusion of innovations' theory studies the ways in which the media are used to communicate, and often to 'sell', new technologies and innovations to audiences.

▮ Topics for discussion

▶ Select a popular film that has been advertised widely and has created expectations. Then select a sample of ten individuals from your peer group and ask them to participate in a focus group that will study how a recent, popular film has been received. Arrange a screening or make sure that all focus group participants see the film. Then arrange a focus group meeting and gather information on the topics listed below. Make sure you prepare well-constructed questions, but do not ask the participants to write answers. The questions are for your guidance. The focus group should be conducted as informally as possible, in the form of a friendly conversation. Find out:

- How much the participants knew about the film before seeing it. How they knew.
- What their expectations of the film were. Why they saw the film.
- How their expectations were met and whether they were pleased or disappointed. Get specific information on this.
- If they were to make some changes to the film what they would be and why.
- What they specifically liked about the film. Whether they thought it worked well and why.
- How they would compare this film with others in its genre.

If possible, record the conversation. If not, write down some characteristic phrases that the participants used.

Write a report that describes and discusses the results of your focus group. Reflect upon your results. Were your initial hypotheses supported? Were you surprised by what you discovered? What proved to be particularly difficult in conducting this experiment?

▶ Brainstorm some ways in which you find out about the existence of new entertainment and news items. These could include new music albums or songs, films and computer games, as well as 'hard' news events. Write down specific examples. Then interview five members of your generation and five members of a different generation to find out how they learn about similar new items. Discuss your results. Are generational differences significant? How different are entertainment items from news events in the way people learn about them? What are some possible reasons for the choices people make in how they get information? Can you see any relationships between the ways in which the media are organized (i.e. how they present news events and how they advertise new products) and the ways in which people get information?

▶ Interview five people from the same demographic to find out how they use different media, such as the internet, television, radio and the telephone (both land and cell). What do they use for entertainment/recreation, what do they use for business, and what do they use for both? Divide your analysis into the categories of time, duration and purpose.

■ References and further reading

Abercrombie, N. (1996) *Television and Society.* Cambridge: Polity Press.

Abercrombie, N. and Longhurst, B. (1998) *Audiences.* London: Sage.

Adams, Michael H. (1995) *Introduction to Radio: Production and Programming.* Madison, WI: Brown and Benchmark.

Albaran, Alan B. (2002) *Management of Electronic Media,* 2nd edn. Belmont, CA: Wadsworth.

Anderson, C. A. (1997) 'Effects of Violent Movies and Trait Hostility on Hostile Feelings and Aggressive Thoughts', *Aggressive Behavior,* 23, pp. 161–78.

Ang, Ien (1985) *Watching Dallas: Soap Opera and the Melodramatic Imagination.* London: Methuen.

Ang, Ien (1991) *Desperately Seeking the Audience.* London: Routledge.

Barker, Martin and Brooks, Kate (1998) *Knowing Audiences: Judge Dredd, its Friends, Fans and Foes.* Luton: University of Luton Press.

Bennett, T. and Woollacott, J. (1987) *Bond and Beyond: The Political Career of a Popular Hero.* New York: Methuen.

Berger, A. A. (1996) *Manufacturing Desire: Media, Popular Culture, and Everyday Life.* New Brunswick, NJ: Transaction Publishers.

Blumer; H. (1951) 'Collective Behaviour', in A. M. Lee (ed.) *New Outline of the Principles of Sociology.* New York: Barnes and Noble.

Blumler, J. G. and Katz, E. (1974) (eds) *The Uses of Mass Communication.* Beverly Hills, CA: Sage.

Bolter, J. D. and Grusin, R. (1999) *Remediation: Understanding New Media.* Cambridge, MA: MIT Press.

Briggs, A. and Cobley, P. (eds) (1998) *The Media: An Introduction.* Harlow: Longman.

Bryant, J. and Zillmann, D. (eds) (2002) *Media Effects.* Hillsdale, NJ: Lawrence Erlbaum.

Burton, G. (2000) *Talking Television: An Introduction to the Study of Television.* London: Arnold.

Compaine, Benjamin, M. and Gomery, Douglas (2000) *Who Owns the Media? Competition and Concentration in the Mass Media Industry.* 3rd edn. Mahwah, NJ: Erlbaum.

Coupland, D. (1994) *Generation X: Tales for an Accelerated Future.* New York: St Martins.

Croteau, D. and Hoynes, W. (2000) *Media Society: Industries, Images and Audiences,* 2nd edn. Thousand Oaks, CA: Pine Forge Press.

Cunningham, Stuart and Turner, Graeme (eds) (2002) *The Media and Communications in Australia.* Sydney: Allen and Unwin.

Danesi, M. (ed.) (2000) *Encyclopedic Dictionary of Semiotics, Media and Communications.* Toronto: University of Toronto Press.

Devereux, E. (2003) *Understanding the Media.* Thousand Oaks, CA and London: Sage.

Dichter, E. (1985) *The Strategy of Desire.* London: Garland.

Febvre, L. and Martin, H. (1984) *The Coming of the Book: The Impact of Printing 1450–1800.* Verso: London.

Fiske, J. (1987) *Television Culture.* London: Methuen.

Frank, T. (1997) *The Conquest of Cool: Business Culture, Counter Culture and the Rise of Hip Consumerism.* Chicago: University of Chicago Press.

Goldstein, J. H. (1998) *Why We Watch: The Attractions of Violent Entertainment.* New York: Oxford University Press.

Gray, A. (1992) *Video Playtime: The Gendering of a Leisure Technology.* London: Routledge.

Habermas, J. (1979) *Communication and the Evolution of Society*, trans. by T. McCarthy. Boston: Beacon Press.

Hall, Stuart (1977) 'Culture, the Media and the "Ideological Effect"', in James Curran, Michael Gurevitch and Janet Woollacott (eds), *Mass Communication and Society.* London: Edward Arnold.

Hall, Stuart (1980) [1973] 'Encoding/Decoding', in Centre for Contemporary Cultural Studies (ed.), *Culture, Media, Language: Working Papers in Cultural Studies, 1972–79.* London: Hutchinson, pp. 128–38.

Hartley, John (1999) *Uses of Television.* London and New York: Routledge.

Katz, E. and Lazarfeld, P. F. (1955) *Personal Influence: The Part Played by People in the Flow of Mass Communication.* Glencoe, IL: Free Press.

Kaufer, D. S. and Carley, K. M. (1993) *Communication at a Distance: The Influence of Print on Sociocultural Organization and Change.* Hillsdale, NJ: Lawrence Erlbaum.

Lazarsfeld, P. F., Berelson, B. and Gaudet, H. (1968) [1944] *The People's Choice: How the Voter Makes up his Mind in a Presidential Election.* New York: Columbia University Press.

Lazarsfeld, P. F. and Menzel, H. (1963) 'Mass Media and Personal Influence', in W. Scramm (ed.) *The Science of Human Communication.* New York: Basic Books.

Leblang, S. (2004) Personal interview. Los Angeles, CA.

Levy, Mark and Windahl, Sven (1985) 'The Concept of Audience Activity', in K. E. Rosengren, L. A. Wenner and P. Palmgreen (eds) (1985) *Media Gratifications Research: Current Perspectives.* London and Beverly Hills: Sage, pp. 109–22.

Livingstone, Sonia and Lunt, Peter (1994) *Talk on Television: Audience Participation and Public Debate.* London: Routledge.

Manovich, L. (2001) *The Language of New Media.* Cambridge, MA: MIT Press.

Marshall, P. D. (1997) *Celebrity and Power: Fame in Contemporary Culture.* Minneapolis: University of Minnesota Press.

Maslow, A. (1987) [1954] *Motivation and Personality.* 3rd edn. New York: Harper Collins.

McKee, A. (2003) *Textual Analysis.* London: Sage.

McKee, A. (2005) *The Public Sphere: An Introduction.* Cambridge: Cambridge University Press.

McLuhan, M. (1964) *Understanding Media.* London: Routledge and Kegan Paul.

McLuhan, M. and McLuhan E. (1988) *Laws of Media: The New Science*. Toronto: University of Toronto Press.

McQuail, D. (1992) *Media Performance*. Newbury Park, CA and London: Sage.

McQuail, D. (1994) *Mass Communication Theory: An Introduction,* 3rd edn. London: Sage.

McQuail, D. (1997) *Audience Analysis*. Thousand Oaks, CA and London: Sage.

McQueen, D. (1998) *Television: A Media Student's Guide*. London: Arnold.

Merton, R. (1949) *Social Theory and Social Structure*. New York: Free Press.

Merton, R. K. and Kendall, P. L. (1946) 'The Focused Interview', *The American Journal of Sociology*, 51, 6, pp. 541–57.

Meyrowitz, J. (1985) *No Sense of Place: The Impact of Electronic Media on Social Behavior*. Oxford: Oxford University Press.

Morley, D. (1980) *The 'Nationwide' Audience: Structure and Decoding*. London: British Film Institute.

Newson, E. (1994) 'Video Violence and the Protection of Children', *Journal of Mental Health*, 2.

Rogers, E. M. (1995) *Diffusion of Innovations,* 4th edn. New York and London: Free Press, pp. 17–30.

Rogers, E. M. (2003) 'Diffusion of News of the September 11 Terrorist Attacks', in A. M. Noll (ed.), *Crisis Communications: Lessons from September 11*. London and New York: Rowman and Littlefield.

Rosengren, K. E., Wenner, L. A. Palmgreen, P. (eds) (1985) *Media Gratifications Research: Current Perspectives*. London and Beverly Hills, CA: Sage.

Schutz, W. (1966) *The Interpersonal Underworld*. London: Science and Behaviour Books.

Stewart, D. W. and Shamdasani, P. N. (1990) *Focus Groups: Theory and Practice*. Newbury Park, CA: Sage.

Strauss, W. and Howe. N. (1991) *Generations: The History of America's Future 1584 to 2069*. New York: William Morrow.

Williams, R. (1974) *Television: Technology and Cultural Form*. London: Fontana.

Film

CHAPTER 7

> Photography is truth. And cinema is truth 24 times a second.
>
> Jean-Luc Godard

The links between communication and film are controversial. Generally, film is considered an artistic medium with mostly an entertainment function and aesthetic criteria of evaluation. Communication, on the other hand, assumes a message-centred basis of social interaction. Certain characteristics, however, link film to the objectives associated with communication projects, especially the shared concern with the creative and the technical, and the increasing appreciation of the effectiveness of visual signs for audience appeal (Lester 1995). In fact, visual communication design now drives much corporate image-building and advertising.

Within the framework of visual communication, film holds an important position. The capacity to combine image with motion and sound in creative ways, as well as story-telling power, have made cinematic techniques the basis for the design of a variety of new media objects, including multimedia applications, web interfaces and computer games. As Lev Manovich (2001: 79) points out, film and its terminology have become a 'visual Esperanto' for the developing digital media.

This chapter overviews main issues concerning the role of film as a communication medium. It describes the codes through which film is expressed and the processes through which it reaches an audience, and discusses some ways in which artists have used film to communicate ideas about identity and the world.

7.1 Background to film theory

Structuralist analyses (which were some of the first attempts to apply systematic theoretical analysis to film) traced analogical connections between the structure of language and those of film. Their aim was to examine the ways in which the deep structures of language, hard-wired in the human cognitive faculties, translated into cinematic texts (Metz 1974; Monaco 1981; Mitry 2000). For example, analysing a film syntagmatically (i.e. according to its constituent units as these are combined in sequential order), we can distinguish three basic meaning-producing units: the *shot*, the *scene* and the *sequence*. The shot is a continuous, uninterrupted segment of film producing a meaningful image; it is analogous to a sentence in language. The scene consists of images of a particular setting and time, so that an effect of continuous action is produced; this is analogous to a paragraph in (written) language. Finally, the sequence is a group of scenes that may cover more than one place and time but are still contained within one logical or thematic section, so a chapter in a written text would be the closest analogy. Having divided a film into its syntagmatic components, a structuralist analysis would then proceed to examine the relationships between parts.

Approaches to film in terms of linguistic terminology still persist, as common expressions such as 'film language' and 'reading a film' testify. However, in post-structuralist times (since the 1980s) there has been a steady shift in emphasis in textual analysis from uniformity to difference. Whereas structuralist approaches attempted to trace a common basis in media texts, using language as the blueprint, many contemporary approaches look for distinctive traits and unique characteristics in each medium (Vernet 1992; Bordwell and Carroll 1996; Casetti 1999). This attitudinal shift makes more sense when we keep in mind that symbolic systems, such as film, language and other representational media, are means of expressing relationships between abstract thought and physical reality. The question then becomes whether to look for common codes among all systems and trace these codes to underlying, universal cognitive structures or whether to explore how each system uses codes specific to the nature of the medium and describe individual manifestations.

The immense popularity of film is constantly attested world-wide. In fact, many contemporary viewers encounter classic works of literature through their film adaptations, and many modern writers model their writing on screen-based action. Of course, some of the popularity of film could well be due to the business practices of producers and to advertising principles that have been successful in selling film to the public. However, audience responses indicate that film activates emotional and cognitive processes and taps into the collective imagination, making it more meaningful to audiences than most other media products. It is worthwhile, therefore, to have a closer look at the distinctive characteristics of the filmic sign.

So, what is the difference between the filmic and the linguistic sign? And is *imaging* a piece of reality equivalent to *articulating* this piece of reality? Consider this example. The word /money/ has no physical relationship to the metal and paper objects of value that it signifies. It is an arbitrary linguistic signifier (following Saussure's definitions, described in Chapter 4), which knowledge of the English language enables us to understand as denoting valuable metal and paper objects. In film, on the other hand, the situation is different. To show a chair in a film, for example, the director uses an actual chair. On a certain level, therefore, the chair is both signifier and signified; it signifies itself as chair, so to speak. For similar reasons, film is also different from other visual media such as painting. A chair in a painting is a constructed representation of a physical chair, so it is a signifier of 'something else'. The painter has mentally processed an image and reproduced it using the code of paint; the painted chair bears an iconic resemblance to the object it signifies but is not identical to it.

Of course this does not mean that film is a direct reflection of reality and not a representational medium. Even though the signs in a film narrative may be identical to the objects they denote, the 'reality' presented is still mediated by technical means and the artistic choices made by the director. The film does not record or reproduce reality, but creates one of an infinite number of possible versions. Thus, the chair that has been chosen is one type from a number of possible chairs, and in this sense it interprets or evaluates reality as much as it represents it; a different type of chair would evoke a different set of meanings. A more poignant example is offered by film adaptations of books. In this case, the film interprets the verbal information presented in the written text by providing images of signifieds for the book's signifiers: the verbal description of 'a tall, blond man dressed in a black suit' becomes embodied in the actor chosen to represent the character. It is the director, and not the individual reader's imagination, that provides the signified and seals the sign.

In fact, some theorists have gone as far as to suggest that film is unique among representational media in that its system of signification, relying as it does on showing concrete objects with motion and sound, cannot be reduced to a set of invariable abstract properties present in all 'texts'. Torben Grodal (1997), for example, claims that film does not *signify* objects, as linguistic texts do, but allows viewers to *experience* reality in a certain way. It works on a level that connects the emotive with the cognitive, and enables viewers to interpret the meaning of the images through strong empathic identification. In this way, film acts as a kind of filter, rather than a description or a representation of reality. He notes:

> The images are not of something else, but a kind of 'software' which establishes and grounds our knowledge in the world. For this very reason, film does not possess a semblance of reality; it is not an illusion, as has been claimed by numerous film scholars and critics; on the contrary, film is part of reality; its experienced power connected to the way in which it uses experiences of central processes in the mind–body–world interaction. From this point of view, narrative structures or schemata are not in principle imposed from without, for instance on images, emotions or memories, but are related to the synthetic–functional processes by which our different mental faculties and different aspects of the world are connected (Grodal 1997: 10-11).

So, how does film communicate? The next section describes the processes through which films are produced, and the medium-related techniques that film-makers have at their disposal.

7.2 **Film-making in context**

Traditionally, the process of film-making is divided into three stages:

- *Production*: when the film is actually made – this stage is further subdivided into preproduction, production proper and post-production.
- *Distribution*: when the film is made public by gaining access and being promoted to an international forum.
- *Exhibition*: when the film is shown to audiences in actual physical settings, such as theatres.

In the US from the 1920s to around 1960, film production was dominated by the major studios, such as Universal, Paramount and Warner Bros. The 'studio era', as it has come to be known, meant that actors and film crews, including directors and writers, were contracted to work exclusively with a studio, thus minimizing independent initiative.

Studios controlled the whole process of film-making, from pre-production to exhibition, which led to financially less-risky business procedures, but also to more standardization of film narrative and presentation – to the creation of 'classical Hollywood cinema' and the genesis of the star system.

Since the 1960s, film production has become more and more decentralized, and now each film is produced as a unique project. This has increased the potential for experimentation, on both narrative and presentational levels, and has allowed the emergence of independent producers who have a more ideological, and less commercial, interest in film. The major studios have now become mainly distribution companies, working for the promotion and marketing of film internationally, although most still also partially or wholly fund films and provide the material resources (studio space and equipment) for films to be shot and edited.

Studios still play an important role in film production in the US, a role that in other countries is taken up by state-owned or independent organizations set up to support film art. In France, for example, the Institute for Financing of Cinema and Cultural Industries (IFCIC) provides funding for film projects and so do television networks, such as Canal+. Since French regulation decrees that at least 40 per cent of visual media must be in the French language and include at least 50 per cent French input, the media have a vested interest in co-operating. In fact, national television networks are required by law to invest a minimum of 3 per cent of their total sales in the film industry and to broadcast a minimum of 60 per cent European films. Similarly, television is a significant source of funding for film in many European countries, including the UK, where Channel 4 is a well-known patron of film.

The division of film production into *commercial* (studio-backed) and *independent* colours much of US regulation as well as attitude towards film, in stark contrast to television, which has more co-operative and less competitive practices. Barry Collin, founder of the Association of Independent Feature Film Producers, pointed out that networking in the film industry, as opposed to the television industry, is considered dangerous because of competitiveness. He made an analogy with gold mining, explaining that those who discover gold were not likely to tell others where to look. Collin suggested that a reason for this competitiveness in the film industry is that the number of films made is limited in comparison to television, which is always expanding. Because of this, and because television is more process-based (i.e. it develops series of shows), it provides a more co-operative environment, as opposed to the film industry, which is more product-based (Collin 2004). This observation is supported by the fact that representatives of film studios were reluctant to be interviewed during the researching of this book, whereas representatives of television networks showed no hesitation.

Collin also noted, however, that despite the apparent friendliness of the television industry, most non-commercially-oriented artists avoid it because of its strong advertising basis, which suggests that film remains the preferred medium of expression for the idealistically inclined. This does not mean to say that independents do not enjoy commercial success or that they do not change sides. For example, Quentin Tarantino's *Pulp Fiction* (1994) is the quintessential independent production that was successful commercially, and Steven Soderbergh is an example of a film-maker who started off as an independent and turned commercial (Collin 2004).

7.3 Pre-production

Film-making is characterized by a collective effort involving a large number of people in specialized tasks – one only has to look at the list of credits in a film to realize the extent of collaboration involved. Skill and imagination, therefore, are pivotal factors when making a film. In addition to these, film uses advanced technical equipment to create its content, making technology another major player in the process. Finally, skilled people and technology require money, so funding also comes into the picture.

> Some productions, such as James Cameron's *Titanic* (1997), for example, list about 1500 names in their final credits.

Gathering all these factors is the main objective of the pre-production phase. Novices and unknown aspiring film-makers with no appropriate connections in the film industry would have the most difficulty in persuading investors to support their project. This is why the role of the 'elements' (famous people associated with the film) is important. Film-makers have more of a chance of making a financially successful film if the actors, writers or director are famous. The success of first-timer Sofia Coppola's *Lost in Translation* (2003), for example, owes much to the presence of Bill Murray in the cast, and to the indirect support of established director Francis Ford Coppola. Similarly, one reason that sequels of successful films have become widespread is that they rely on the reputation and established clientele of the original.

Funding is a major issue in the decision to produce a film. With even a very low-budget film costing, at a modest estimate, around one million US dollars, raising money assumes centre stage. Basic costs consist of below-the-line expenses, referring to materials and the technical aspects of the film, as well as extras, such as personnel, set construction, wires, lights, cameras and transportation, and above-the-line expenses, referring to the more creative aspects of the film, such as the property itself, writers, producer, director, stars and principals. All this costs millions of dollars, making film production a very high-risk business.

The main reason that investing in the film industry is high-risk lies in the inherent unpredictability of the market. Many other industries have accurate indications of their market when they set out each year, and can therefore plan and budget accordingly. As Barry Collin points out, in the film industry 'everything that makes sense is most certainly incorrect' (Collin 2004). Many examples support this. Certain films that were thought to be 'flops' while in their pre-production stage actually went on to become great successes. For instance, George Lucas's *Star Wars* (1977) was abandoned by Universal, and Chris Columbus's *Home Alone* (1990) was abandoned by Warner.

Commercial films, backed by major studios, have lower-risk practices, mainly because they rely on the reputation of stars and famous directors and writers. Investing in such projects is therefore more straightforward than in independent productions. However, as Barry Collin emphasized, independent film production, contrary to popular perception, is not

> The only business that comes close to film with regard to unpredictability would probably be fashion, where trying to judge what styles will sell next year – how to tailor an inventory, how much cloth to buy, how much to cut, etc. is uncertain and relies to a large extent on educated guesses and speculation.

necessarily low-budget. For example, George Lucas is technically an independent because he is not tied to a studio, does not make studio deals and does not use studio resources (Collin 2004). Rather than studio backing and the associated advertising that goes with it, the commercial success of the *Star Wars* films is actually due to Lucas's skill and talent in tuning into the social imagination and creating popular characters and stories.

However, the fact remains that many independent productions may never leave the pre-production stage because of a lack of funding interest. Collin pointed out that as many as 98 per cent of independent film projects are not marketable. Also, for those that do make a 'one-hit wonder,' it is often difficult to sustain success if the film-maker's orientation is essentially anti-commercial. This is why it is common advice to aspiring film-makers to begin their careers within a more commercially oriented framework and then move to alternative ideologies. An example of this at work is Mel Gibson's *The Passion of the Christ* (2004), which would not have been likely to have received studio backing had it not been for the director's reputation (Collin 2004).

When the development process is completed, the producers must decide whether the project will go forward to the production stage. This usually happens when there is a workable script, budget, director, producer and major casting. If the project is studio-backed, it is up to the studio managers to greenlight the film. If the answer is no, a process known as 'turnaround' usually begins. Turnaround is the effort, after abandonment, to carry the project elsewhere, repay prior investments and begin production. If an 'element' changes during this process, it is expected that the producers will return to the abandoning studio for reconsideration. For example, if a project was developed at Columbia without a star, then moved to Paramount with, say, Sean Penn attached, Columbia should have another chance to commit to the project.

7.4 Production

The production stage involves shooting the film. Films tell stories using codes that arise from the technical nature of the medium. These codes include *shot, angle, lens, camera movement, editing, scene composition, narrative techniques, light, colour, sound,* and *digital effects.* This section looks at some of these codes in relation to the effects they produce.

The shot

A shot is an uninterrupted segment of film, which may or not include camera movement. A shot ends with a transition, such as a cut, to another shot. The duration of a shot varies: films with rapid editing have quick shots (music videos, for example), whereas films whose meaning and effect do not rely on the rapid juxtaposition of images tend to have longer takes of a shot. Shots are classified according to the distance, angle position and perspective taken by the camera in relation to the image. The main types of shot and their purposes, going from the ones with the longest distance to the ones with the shortest, are:

- *Extreme long shot*. This has the longest distance from the subject. It tends to be used to show a whole setting with all or most of its objects, but not in detail. An extreme long shot captures a wide perspective and suggests distance between the seer and the seen. A *long shot* has a similar function but uses a shorter distance from the subject. Also, the perspective narrows and more details are discernible. Long shots tend to be used for natural settings to capture the expanse of a landscape, especially if there is also camera movement, such as panning from one side to another. If human subjects are used in a long shot, they appear small and distanced.

- *Medium shot*. In this, less of the subject is captured but it appears closer to the camera and so more detail is seen. If the subject is a standing human, a medium shot usually captures him/her from the thighs or waist up. Medium shots produce a neutral effect, since action is seen in enough detail to attract attention and provide information on the story, but not so much detail that the image becomes overbearing. Therefore, medium shots are favoured by directors who want to produce a realistic effect, such as the French New Wave directors (described later in the chapter).

- *Medium close-up shot*. Here the subject fills most of the height of the frame and appears to be a step closer to the camera. If the subject is human, the medium close-up usually captures the head and shoulders. This type of shot reveals more detail of fewer objects and therefore elicits a stronger involvement of the viewer. Medium close-ups have a more compelling and 'urgent' look than medium shots.

- *Close-up*. This focuses on a limited number of objects (usually one), excluding most of the background or surroundings. If the subject is human (the term *insert* is often used for close-ups of non-human subjects), the close-up tends to capture one part of the body. In an *extreme close-up*, the part shown is emphasized very strongly, to the point of exaggeration. A close-up reveals considerable detail of its subject, and, if it is of a face, it has a very strong emotional effect. As it is part of our instinctual framework to attribute emotional meaning to faces, a face in a film becomes particularly compelling because it encourages empathic identification with the character (Grodal 1997). Charlie Chaplin alluded to this power when he recommended long shot for comedy and close-up for tragedy (Phillips 1999: 96). In long shot, a subject is more likely to be formalized (i.e. presented in abstract, with distinguishable contours but without the emotive expressiveness that would make the subject 'real' for the viewer), and therefore easier to ridicule or caricature. A subject in close-up, on the other hand, is more likely to assume a sense of urgency that invites a more intense emotional response.

Close-ups tell the viewer what to see and so exhibit the strongest directorial control of all shots. Thus, it is no surprise that they are the favoured shot in films where such control is valued, such as in Hollywood mainstream, or 'classical', cinema. In recent times, a practical reason for the extensive use of close-ups is media convergence: close-ups are effective in the transference of film to the television screen.

Illustration 7.1 Three shots of the same object – a bush with flowers. The medium shot shows more of the object, and from a longer distance than the others. The medium close-up moves closer, and the close-up captures an aspect of one of the flowers in close proximity to the viewer.

Illustration 7.2 A medium close-up shot from the last scene of Truffaut's *The 400 Blows*. The shot focuses on the human figure with some background. *Les Films du Carosse*

Camera angle

In addition to the distance chosen from which to represent the subject, the *angle* of the camera is instrumental in revealing the contents of a shot. The four main angles are bird's eye (or 'top-down'), high, low and eye-level.

In the bird's eye angle, the shot is taken directly from above the subject, with the camera usually mounted on a crane. This angle can cover a wide breadth and show the extent of an image. For example, documentary shots of disaster scenes are top-down shots taken from a helicopter or light plane. Also, this angle can be used to show depth, to conceal the identities of subjects and to increase suspense and mystery.

In a high angle shot, the camera looks down on the subject, but not from as high a position as in a bird's eye shot. A common use of this angle is when the camera takes the point of view of someone taller or in a more elevated position than the subject. High angle shots make the subject appear smaller and often, by extension, vulnerable or insignificant.

Low angle shots, in contrast, have the opposite effect. Taken from a lower level than the subject, they give the impression of looking up, so they could indicate that the subject is seen from the point of view of someone shorter. They can also attribute more power to the subject, which is seen as 'larger than life', so to speak. As shots from this angle maximize the sky or ceiling in a setting, they can also signify freedom and openness.

The eye-level angle is the most inconspicuous because it imitates the angle at which we normally interact with others. Therefore, it tends to be associated with representations of reality or normality, where the image shows natural objects in the world, rather than representations of the distorted imaginings of a character's mind.

Lens and camera

Cameras have lenses on the front, and the choice of lens can affect the optical nature of the shot. The *perspective* of the shot affects the apparent size and depth of the objects shown.

Perspective changes when the camera distance and the lens are modified at the same time. This alters the relationship between the subject and other elements in the image, including the background, and can make objects appear as more or less distant and more or less distinct. For instance, a dramatic effect is created when the lens zooms out on a subject (that is, goes from normal to wide angle) while the camera dollies forward. The result is an increase in the size of the subject because of the approaching camera, while the background recedes from the zooming effect.

A well-known example of this comes from Steven Spielberg's *Jaws* (1975): when Chief Brody sees a shark attacking a swimmer at the beach, his concern and confusion are signified by the camera moving forward and the lens zooming out, making it seem as if the world is disappearing from him and leaving him helpless and disoriented. Spielberg dubbed this technique a 'trombone' shot because it resembles the moving slide of that instrument.

A *wide-angle lens* can focus equally on objects in both the foreground and background, and can produce an effect of depth. Also, the apparent distance between objects in the foreground and background will increase. If objects are held close to the lens they will distort and be magnified (as happens when an image is reflected on a spoon). *Deep-focus* shots play on the balance of objects depicted and allow the viewer to focus on different aspects of the scene. Unless done expertly and with a narrative purpose, a deep-focus shot can appear cluttered and confusing.

Lighting

Lighting is in many ways the central code in film. If we take the camera to be the narrator of a film narrative, then light becomes the words in which the story is told. In addition, lighting is a basic and very productive way to produce different effects. Lighting adds mood and tone to the events shown, so all one needs to do is change the lighting in a scene and the whole story changes, even though the actions and characters may remain the same.

Hard lighting is strong light that falls directly on the subject. This produces an intense but harsh effect that maximizes details and produces shadows with sharp edges. *Soft lighting*, in contrast, softens the borders between shadow and light and produces a mellow tone. Soft light does not fall directly on the subject, spotlight fashion, but reflects off at least one other object, taking the edge off the intensity.

In *backlighting*, the light falls on the subject from behind. The use of strong backlighting can create sinister and mysterious figures, since it hides individual features. *Sidelighting* falls on the subject from the side and can give an ethereal tone to a scene, adding artistic overtones.

Top lighting uses a single light from above the subject. As with hard lighting this does not produce a flattering effect. It tends to emphasize shadows and details and makes objects look lighter on top: for example, if top lighting falls on a human subject the hair looks lighter but shadows tend to appear under the eyes. The opposite is *bottom lighting*, where the subject is from below. This produces the most frightening effect, if used on a human face, because it creates a sharp contrast between dark and light tones and makes the subject look menacing.

Camera movement

Camera movements can alter shot composition, revealing or concealing significant details. Some common camera movements are *dollying*, *panning*, *swish-panning* and *tilting*. When the camera dollies, it moves backwards away from or forwards towards the subject on a

George Romero's *Night of the Living Dead* (1968) did not use any special effects other than black and white cinematography, and light-ing and camera angle effects. These were enough to produce an eerie mood and make the film a classic of the horror genre.

wheeled platform; when it pans, it moves from one side to another within one shot; when it swish-pans, it moves fast from one setting to another within one shot and thereby produces a blurred image; finally, when it tilts, it moves up and down on its base. Also, hand-held cameras are often used when a documentary-style spontaneity is desired. To avoid the trembling of a hand-held camera, a commonly used alternative is a Steadicam, a device that includes a body frame and torsion arm, allowing the operator to stabilize the camera around the waist and so produce a smoother effect.

Scene composition

Also known by the French term *mise en scène*, this refers to the theatrical arrangements of objects to be captured in a shot: the positioning of actors, objects, costumes, make-up, light-

Illustration 7.3 A deep-focus shot. Notice how all the elements in the shot are shown clearly, and the background is not blurred. The deep focus gives the illusion of another dimension to the scene, making it seem as if the scene was shot from different angles simultaneously. Deep focus gives equal weight to elements in the scene composition, and allows the viewer to choose where to look. It becomes significant when a shot shows different things happening at the same time.

Illustration 7.4 A long shot in the last scene of Truffaut's *The 400 Blows*. The shot captures the boy and the background. This way, the human figure is shown as part of the environment. *Les Films du Carosse*

ing, props, colours. Scene composition becomes especially important when less editing and longer shots are used, because in such cases the positioning of objects is more significant than movement or changes in setting in the way the story is told. Films with extended scene composition techniques have a photographic effect, and cinematography (the cinematic version of photography) assumes prominence in these cases.

7.5 Post-production

In post-production, the film is edited and reworked digitally to produce the final version that is shown in cinemas. Given that most shots have different takes (differently constructed versions) after shooting, unedited film runs to many hours – *Crimson Tide* (1995), for example, was 148 hours long after shooting; the final version after editing was 113 minutes (Phillips 1999: 122). During the editing stage, the film is cut and put together in its final shape; in fact, it is often said that the film is made in the editing room (which is somewhat of an exaggeration, of course, since the editor needs something to edit).

The ways in which shots are joined together can create different effects. In addition to the *straight cut* (connecting the ending of one shot to the beginning of another), other commonly used techniques are the *match cut*, which matches two shots from different scenes that contain similar shapes, and the *jump cut*, which joins shots from two scenes, producing an impression of abrupt change or discontinuity. A famous match cut occurs at the beginning of Stanley Kubrick's *2001, A Space Odyssey* (1968) where a bone flying in the air after being thrown by an ape is transformed through a match cut into an orbiting space-craft. The match cut here suggests the flow of time and the development of technology from prehistoric times, when the first scene is set, to 2001, when the second scene is set. A frequently cited jump cut occurs in Jean-Luc Godard's *Breathless* (1959) when the lead character, driving a car, pulls off the road to avoid two pursuing motorcycle policemen. One policeman pulls off too and then the man shoots him and runs away. This scene is presented through a series of jump cuts, giving the scene a jerky look, as if something is missing between the shots.

Cuts to *reaction shots*, which show a character's reaction to something s/he has just witnessed, are an effective way to encourage an emotional response. Reaction shots provide a comment on a previous shot that shows the witnessed action, but they have even more impact when they are shown before the witnessed action.

Another function of editing is to set the tempo of a scene. Rapid editing makes events seem to move faster and can produce an exciting effect, especially in action scenes. As Bordwell (2002: 24) points out, 'rapid editing obliges the viewer to assemble discrete pieces of information, and it sets a commanding pace: look away and you might miss a key point'.

In contrast, avoiding cuts produces long takes, creating an effect of continuity in the action that can sometimes appear more realistic. Alfred Hitchcock experimented with long takes in *Rope* (1950), which consists of takes of around ten minutes each (when a cut had to be made to change the reel of film). To compensate for the lack of editing, Hitchcock used camera movement strategically to imitate the viewer's eye panning a stage, thereby producing a theatrical effect and a feeling of witnessing (rather than just seeing) the events. A more recent example of a long take can be found in a scene in Mike Leigh's *Secrets and Lies* (1996) where two women talk in a restaurant for several minutes. The scene consists of two medium shots, the second one about eight minutes long, taken with a static camera. Of course, as happens in theatrical productions, such techniques require strong acting, suggestive scene composition and compelling content to sustain audience attention.

Editing of film is no longer done on film itself, as was the case before the 1970s. The AVID system of editing, which is based on digital video, is being increasingly used by both mainstream and independent film-makers. In fact, many films are now being shot entirely on digital video and then blown up to 35 mm for distribution, making the future of 35mm film doubtful and challenged by new developments in digital technology.

The advent of digital technology has revolutionized not only editing but also the whole process of film-making, with the division into pre-production, production and post-production becoming increasingly problematic as the boundaries between stages are blurring. For instance, here is what George Lucas has to say about his experience with computer-based filming (cited in Kelly and Parisi 1997: 2):

> Instead of making film into a sequential assembly-line process where one person does one thing, takes it and turns it over to the next person, I'm turning it more into the process of a painter or sculptor. You work on it for a bit, then you stand back and look at it and add some more onto it, then stand back and look at it and add some more. You basically end up layering the whole thing. Filmmaking by layering means you write and direct, and edit all at once. It's much more like what you do when you write a story.

Assuming that we want to keep the traditional division into stages, the post-production stage attains a marked emphasis in the digital era. For example, the production stage in George Lucas's *Star Wars Episode One: The Phantom Menace* took 65 days. The post-production stage, where the film was manipulated digitally, took two years. In the end, 95 per cent of the film was computer-made (about 2000 out of a total of 2200 shots) (Manovich 2001: 302).

7.6 Distribution and exhibition

Distribution remains the deciding factor in the success or failure of a film because, regardless of its artistic merit, it is distribution that allows audiences to access the film and give it public recognition. For independent film production in particular, distribution is pivotal. As Barry Collin explained, independents work outside the established studios, so they do not have the same access to studio-owned theatres as mainstream producers do. An effective way to gain distributors' attention for independents is a film festival. Sundance, for example, has been the main venue where independent producers and distributors meet (Collin 2004).

With the development of video and digital technology, video production is becoming cheaper and more widespread, which facilitates both production and exhibition. Also, the portability and flexibility of low-cost video production supports those working as independents. However, the increased costs of distribution make it more difficult for the work of independent producers, who have no studio backing, to reach an international audience. Also, recent corporate mergers, like that of Time Warner/AOL in 2000, suggest that the boundary between conventional television and web-interactive television is blurring. As home-based delivery systems are changing, so are conventional cinema screening methods and therefore exhibition procedures. If the 35mm prints are replaced with digital formats, films can be downloaded directly from satellite and stored in computer memory at the cinema to be screened as needed, without the problems usually associated with 35mm prints.

A milestone in digital film exhibition was marked when George Lucas opened his film *Star Wars Episode One: The Phantom Menace* in four cinemas on 18 June 1999 in an entirely digital format. In the same year, Lucas, a fervent advocate of digital film-making, demonstrated the commercial and aesthetic advantages of the digital medium at the ShoWest Convention in Las Vegas, where he showed 35mm and digital projection of the same images to display the value of each medium. Spectators were impressed, despite some problems with colour, which were forecast to improve with the rapid developments in technology.

7.7 Artistic movements in film

Since its inception, film has had strong ideological overtones. Its immediate appeal to mass audiences and its emotional power ensured that it attracted the attention of those interested in propagating an ideology or world-view, or that it drew public attention to sociopolitical situations. This section describes some major artistic movements in film, especially *surrealism, expressionism, montage theory, New Wave, realism* and *classical Hollywood*.

Surrealism

Some directors have dedicated their careers to expressing their dissatisfaction with cultural trends and attitudes, using the medium of film. Spanish director Luis Buñuel, for example, said that he wanted his films to show the damage that people had inflicted on the world and on each other in the name of God, and he remained loyal to his mission throughout his 50-year career. Buñuel made over thirty films between the late 1920s and the late 1970s, all of which were sharply critical of religious and bourgeois hypocrisy and narrow-mindedness. He was especially keen on showing how Christian dogma, as disseminated through the Church, suppressed human emotions turning them into cruel perversions that manifested themselves in irrational and obsessively destructive behaviour.

In *Un chien andalou* ('An Andalusian Dog') (1928), his first film, co-directed with his artist friend Salvador Dali, Buñuel shocked audiences not only through the absence of narrative continuity or storyline, but also through such disturbing shots (for their time!) of a man slicing a woman's eyeball and of decomposing donkeys being carried in two pianos. This film is now an icon of the movement known as *surrealism*, where images are more evocative than meaningful, and have no logical connection between them. Buñuel (1968: 30) described the film as 'a passionate call to murder', and commented that it 'has no intention of attracting or pleasing the spectator; indeed, on the contrary, it attacks him, to the degree that he belongs to a society with which surrealism is at war'.

In *Simon of the Desert* (1965), Buñuel attacked the hypocrisy of religion through the depiction of Simon, a self-centred and socially indifferent monk, who isolates himself from the rest of humanity more out of contempt than out of love, while at the same time not ceasing to glorify his own supposedly superior deeds (such as the fact that he only eats lettuce). The film is bitter towards the clergy as well as towards its followers, who use religious faith to advance their own ignorant and selfish interests. For instance, when Simon restores to a peasant the use of his hands, the first thing the peasant does is to hit his child. The film's extreme attack on the Church did not go unpunished by the powers that be: funding was withdrawn before the filming was over, resulting in a hasty and incomplete ending.

Also, in his last film *This Obscure Object of Desire* (1977), Buñuel plays on ideas of sexuality that has become compulsive and sinister because of suppression, by interweaving the story of a man who is sexually obsessed with a woman with episodes depicting the acts of terrorists. Interestingly, the woman is played by two actresses who have no physical similarity, suggesting the blindness and absurdity of urges that have become grotesquely exaggerated because they were not given the social legitimacy that would have allowed them to develop without guilt.

The closest parallel to surrealist story-telling is dreaming. Surrealist film parallels the process of dreams where images are linked with subconscious impulses that do not have to be conventionally meaningful on the level of consciousness. By extension, surrealism questions the definition of the individual as a rational being with deliberate intent. Instead it focuses on random and symbolic behaviour and depicts the imagery that is associated with this behaviour. In surrealist films, things function according to a logic that is unconventional and not immediately recognizable.

Stylistically, surrealist film is eclectic. Favoured devices include superimpositions and dissolves (typical dream-like forms of expression), as well as montage editing, which juxtaposes shots depicting different, and even contradictory, scenes. The heyday of surrealist film was in the 1920s and 1930s, but many thematic and stylistic techniques have trickled down to contemporary times. David Lynch (*Eraserhead* 1977, *Lost Highway* 1997, *Mulholland Drive* 2001) and Steven Soderbergh (*Schizopolis* 1996) are examples of directors whose work shows undisputable traces of surrealist tendencies. This work, however, remains largely on a personal level of expression, functioning as a sign of artistic idiosyncrasy, and lacks the moralist and socially critical inclinations of Luis Buñuel.

Surrealist writer André Breton pointed out that surrealism was 'based on the belief in the superior reality of certain forms of association, heretofore neglected, in the omnipotence of dreams, in the undirected play of thought' (Breton 1969: 25).

Expressionism

If we take surrealism to glorify the state of the dream, *expressionism* would glorify the state of hypnosis. Expressionism is an artistic movement developed mostly in Nordic countries, such as Germany and Norway, in the early part of the twentieth century. Expressionist film, like its counterpart in painting, presents images that have been created in a mind, not in the real world. In fact, in expressionism there are no objects that exist in objective reality. Everything is specially designed to reflect the extreme states of mind of the narrator. Natural settings are not used, preferring instead elaborate and explicitly fake (i.e. unrealistic) set designs – which explains why the role of the art director was very important in early expressionist productions. Sharp and angular shapes predominate in the constructed designs, and are set off more intensely by hard lighting that brings into focus corners and edges.

Also, acting is not spontaneous or 'natural' but highly stylized, with actors wearing heavy make-up and moving in formally choreographed rhythm. In fact, the characters themselves are not presented as 'real' in these films, but as objects that blend in with the rest of the décor. For example, a famous scene from *The Cabinet of Dr Caligari* (Wiene 1919) shows the actor's arms and posture as a direct reflection of the painted trees through which he moves. This way the film draws attention to itself as a constructed piece, a work of art that captures the imagination of its creator.

Both surrealism and expressionism deal with their themes ambiguously and indirectly, on a symbolic level, but whereas surrealism brings to the fore issues of moral double standards and sexual repression, expressionism brings into play issues of power, control and domination. In fact, depictions of excessive or extreme personalities (such as the 'madman', the 'crazy inventor' or the 'eccentric outsider') are favourites in expressionist films, as are depictions of intergroup and interclass conflicts.

A significant difference between dreaming (surrealist-style) and being under hypnosis (expressionist-style) is that the former is a purely individual activity, whereas the latter is induced by someone who has control over the hypnotized. Accordingly, expressionist narratives revolve around characters trapped in intense situations that are controlled by at best eccentric, at worst evil outside forces. For example, in Robert Wiene's *The Cabinet of Dr Caligari* (1919), which even takes hypnosis as its theme, Dr Caligari is a circus performer but could also be a psychiatrist, depending on who we believe the narrator of the story to be. Since, as a circus hypnotist, he sends his assistant Cesare to murder people while under his spell, there are serious doubts also about his secret activities in his more authoritative role as clinical hypnotist. Dr Caligari's identity depends on how much credibility we attribute to the character whose point of view orients the narrative: this character could be a circus spectator or an inmate of an insane asylum. In either case, the story, told in characteristic style, with sharp angles, radiating patterns and stylized scene composition, is strongly coloured by this narrator's vision.

In a similar vein, Fritz Lang's *Metropolis* (1926) is set in a future society where workers work like automata to sustain a conceptually advanced but socially indifferent ruling class. A key figure is Rotwang, the society's inventor, who attempts to replace the workers with robots. To succeed in this, he creates a robot in the image of the workers' inspirational leader, Maria, which is directed to destroy the workers' society. The story plays on the expressionist themes of forced or constructed identity that lead to betrayal and revolt. The setting is extravagantly designed, with the typical absence of natural objects, and actually involved the most expensive set design of any film up to that time, almost bankrupting the producing studio.

The expressionist movement in film is generally associated with the films made at the UFA studios in Germany from 1919 to the late 1920s. However, this does not mean that expressionism was a trend, now defunct and existing only in the archives of film history. Ideas and the imagery associated with them are part of our collective, mythic consciousness, so they continue to inspire artists, who recycle them into different manifestations. In addition, such ideas and forms can be accessed through the artistic objects that embody them and can find their way in new creations by means of intertextual allusions.

For example, the work of Alex Proyas (*The Crow* 1994, *Dark City* 1998, *I, Robot* 2004) shows clear traces of expressionist influence. In *The Crow*, black-clad Eric Draven's identity is forcefully transformed (by his murder) and he dedicates his new existence to revenge. In *Dark City* the world is ruled by an alien species, the Strangers, who experiment on humans by switching memories and identities. Both humans and the world they inhabit are controlled by an external and evil power, and nothing is actually as it seems to be. Buildings are reconstructed by the Strangers' willpower every time identities are switched, reflecting the ideology espoused by expressionism that mind controls matter (Marsen 2004). Proyas's style is characterized by montage editing and jump cuts, which emphasize discontinuity and different points of view in the narrative. Instead of the seamless transitions between one scene and another, associated with 'classical' film narrative and produced by longer shots and continuity editing, Proyas opts to tell the story through abrupt changes in scene and setting. This parallels changes in mental state and makes feelings and attitudes towards events more important than the events themselves.

Tim Burton (*Edward Scissorhands* 1990, *Ed Wood* 1994) provides what we might call a light-hearted take on expressionism, with gothic and fantastic themes presented in playfully humorous tones. Edward, in *Edward Scissorhands*, is an artificially created 'person' who was literally put together from different materials by an eccentric inventor, reworking the theme, typical of expressionism, of a deliberately designed reality. Also, David Cronenberg (*Existenz* 1999, *Spider* 2002) has contributed to expressionist imagery with depictions of characters that live more in their minds than in reality, and with narratives constructed in images emanating from a troubled consciousness. In *Spider*, for example, the lead character, Spider, walks through streets that are empty, suggesting that these are the streets of his mind, where he exists, rather than the streets of London, where he lives.

Montage theory

Other approaches shifted the emphasis from set design and lighting to the combination of images. Where fantastic sets and extraordinary make-up prevailed with expressionist directors, other directors focused on perfecting editing techniques. Probably the most famous and influential proponents of this approach were the Soviet montage directors who flour-

Editing a film so that the sequence of shots is
not linear according to a narrative temporal
unity was thought by montage theorists to
combine dynamically different details of the
idea expressed and to create a powerful
impression.

ished in the 1920 and 1930s and included Vsevolod Pudovkin (*Mother* 1924), Lev Kuleshov (*Death Ray* 1925, *By the Law* 1926) and, the most famous of all, Sergei Eisenstein (*Strike* 1924, *Battleship Potemkin* 1925, *October* 1927, *Ivan The Terrible* 1945).

For these directors, film was a means to raise people's consciousness about their situation in society and about political issues. Reality, for them, as it was experienced in everyday life, was obscure and not easily interpretable. It was the role of film, more than of any other medium, to reconstruct reality in such a way that it could generate meanings with the greatest possible emotional effect. The way that film could best achieve this was through the creative combination of shots, which was believed to produce meanings that would not be possible if each shot were seen in isolation. In the words of Eisenstein (1959: 16), 'editing is for me the means of giving movement to two static images'.

Eisenstein's approach to film was emphatically political and Marxist; in fact, he even made a connection between editing techniques and dialectical materialism, seeing a direct link between the thesis–antithesis–synthesis paradigm of dialectical materialism and the shot-by-shot structure of a film. When translated into montage terminology, the thesis becomes the shot. As the thesis exists in relation to an antithesis, which leads to a synthesis of the two, so the shot attains meaning through its juxtaposition with another shot, although the two shots may have nothing in common. The viewer is induced to synthesize the two by providing an interpretation that unites the two different meanings, most often by finding an analogical or metaphorical connection between the signs composing the two juxtaposed shots.

An often-cited example of this technique from Eisenstein's own work is the juxtaposition in *Strike* of a shot of striking workers being beaten by police with a shot of animals being slaughtered in an abattoir. In this example, the shots are semiotically linked through a different use of the signs of 'executioner' and 'victim'. Also, *Battleship Potemkin* contains a famous shot combination of the battleship approaching harbour followed by three consecutive shots of a marble lion aroused from sleep (achieved by using three shots of the lion in a different position, evoking movement). This equates the approach of the battleship with the people's dormant power and strength being awoken.

In a famous laboratory experiment conducted in Moscow in the early 1920s, Lev Kuleshov set out to demonstrate the power of image combination by eliciting interpretations of two shots from a number of respondents. The first shot was variable and included a plate of food, a woman in a coffin, and a child playing; the second shot was that of an actor's face (the actor was told to remain expressionless) and remained invariable. Subjects interpreted the man's expression in the first combination (plate of food + man) as hunger, in the second combination (woman in coffin + man) as grief, and in the third combination (child playing + man) as affection. Subjects were convinced that the man's expression changed each time in response to the situation that he was observing, whereas, in actual fact, the shot of the face was the same.

Of course the interpretations of the facial expression could vary (and certainly would in an experiment conducted in contemporary times or in different cultures). Kuleshov's point, however, was that the same image could attain totally different meanings depending on how it collocated with another image. What was of special interest to him was that the subjects not only had no problem attaching a meaning to the face but also that they did so with certainty, and even marvelled at the actor's talent in modifying his expression to suit the circumstances. These results lent support to the montage theorists' hypothesis that cognition relied on the perception of contrastive stimuli, and that meaning was created by transposing signification from one context to another.

The significance attributed to editing techniques in producing emotional reactions has not diminished since the time of the montage theorists, despite the fact that the systematically formulated ideology attached to montage editing as an awareness-raising tool has faded. Also, the idea that metaphorical and metonymical meanings attract attention and have more impact than literal meaning has been repeatedly attested, and explains the extensive use of metaphors and metonymy in persuasive texts, such as those created in advertising. Rapid or montage-style editing is now mostly associated with advertising and music videos, and, in fact, many directors known for this stylistic preference (such as Alex Proyas and David Fincher) began their careers as MTV video producers. Moreover, rapid editing goes well with digital special effects and therefore gives new film-makers grounds for experimentation.

New Wave

Other film-makers adopted a different stance with regard to the relationship between film and reality. The French New Wave directors, including François Truffaut (*The 400 Blows* 1959, *The Bride Wore Black* 1968), Jean-Luc Godard (*Breathless* 1960, *Alphaville* 1965) and Claude Chabrol (*The Butcher* 1970, *A Piece of Pleasure* 1975), see film as a means through which the director can express his/her vision. For them, film parallels the function of literature, which illustrates the artistic perspective of the writer. In fact, in a famous article in 1948, New Wave theorist and film-maker Alexandre Astruc (Astruc 1968) made an explicit connection between film and writing by describing the camera as a pen and encouraging film-makers to use film as they would literary writing.

In contrast to the juxtaposition of images, which is the domain of the montage followers, New Wave directors exploited the qualities and functions of dramatic space, camera movement and real time. Scene composition (or *mise-en scène*, literally 'setting the scene') became their privileged tool of expression. For these directors, the reality that the film depicted should be a blend between objects and phenomena as they existed in the world, and the director's imagination through which these objects and phenomena were filtered.

New Wave directors were against the fragmentation of the world through close-ups and montage editing. Instead, they favoured techniques of storytelling such as camera movement (panning), and deep-focus shots, where the content of the scene and the movement within it became meaningful. The viewer's eye was allowed to roam around the screen and select the objects that stood out for the particular viewer, without direct control or manipulation by the director. Therefore, what occurred in one sequence of events should be shown in one uninterrupted shot in order to reflect the unity of meaning and the integrity of the events described. For example, a scene in Truffaut's *The 400 Blows* shows two boys going out of a cinema and into another in a different part of town. Instead of cutting from one shot to

The journal *Cahiers du cinéma*, which was founded in 1951 by André Bazin, continues to this day to publish quality film criticism and analysis. In fact, it has recently received the support of the National Centre of Cinematography (CNC) and the Institute for the Financing of Cinema and Cultural Industries (IFCIC) to design an online version (www.cahiersducinema.com) and to digitize a valuable stock of original articles dating back to the 1950s. These are now available to the public free of charge, continuing the mission of New Wave artists and theorists to promote an appreciation of the power of the cinema.

another, Truffaut respects the temporal flow between the two events and uses a swish pan (fast camera movement showing a blurred image) to follow the two boys running from one location to another. The camera thus becomes a running companion to the boys, participating in the action that it shows.

Like true aesthetes, French New Wave film-makers valued the balance between artistic interpretation and perceptual reality, espousing the idea that film should show reality in such a way that it could be perceived through the senses and not through the mind or the emotions. They believed that graphic and exaggerated presentations of extreme conditions, such as poverty, deformity and violence, were pretentious and, although they might produce temporary shock reactions, did not amount to an insightful or even objective depiction of the world.

For example, consider the famous concluding scenes of Truffaut's *The 400 Blows*, which tells the story of a teenager, Antoine, who rebels against the injustice and indifference of the adult world. In the final scene, Antoine runs from a soccer ground towards the sea in an attempt to escape the cruel constraints of his society. In one moving shot, the camera follows him at enough distance to be able to grasp his figure within the natural environment of which he is part: he runs along a country road, ducking under a road sign, and then towards the sea, with no specific destination in mind. When he is at the beach, the camera stands still and pans from right to left, taking in the desolate beach and the waves of the sea. Then it moves behind Antoine as he faces the sea, suggesting the contrasting sadness and beauty in his life. At this point, Antoine turns towards the camera, which zooms in and freezes his face, bringing a tension between the previous running of the boy, the movement of the sea, and the frozen shot of the face, and evoking the moral ambiguity that exists between impulse, action and consequence.

In line with phenomenology and existentialism, which provided the philosophical backbone for New Wave film-makers, ambiguity is a privileged concept. For the New Wave ideology, reality was considered to be inherently ambiguous and open to interpretation, and film should respect this ambiguity and not attempt to attach pre-fixed interpretations to phenomena; this would signal a lack of artistic vision and an invitation to distortion. For example, leading New Wave theorist André Bazin criticized the experiments conducted by Kuleshov to support the hypothesis that meaning arose in the combination of images and not in the content of the images themselves. For Bazin, the fact that Kuleshov's subjects found exact meanings in the images proved the inadequacy of the montage ideology. When shots are taken out of their context, the ambiguity of reality is destroyed, and the viewer can only fill the gap by looking not for subjective interpretation and personal meaning, but for certainty and definite meaning.

Illustration 7.5 The last frame of Truffaut's *The 400 Blows*, a close-up of Antoine's face, is a freeze. The camera follows Antoine at the seaside with a long shot before slowly moving to a medium shot. Finally, a zoom freezes on this close-up. *Les Films du Carosse*

The French New Wave was distinctive in being a school of film with a strong theoretical inclination. The directors wrote systematic methodologies of film and militant critical essays of world developments in film, which they published in the journal *Cahiers du cinéma* ('Cinema Notebooks'). Although the New Wave reached its heyday in the 1950s and 1960s, it continues to have many admirers and followers internationally. Actually, most contemporary French film claims direct descent from François Truffaut and Jean-Luc Godard. It is interesting to note, for example, that 'metteur en scène' ('scene setter') and 'mise en scène' ('setting the scene') are the French words for film director and for direction respectively, underlining the close relationship in French culture between scene composition and film directing, and the value attributed to the director's personal touch and vision in filmic representations of reality.

Realism

For New Wave directors, reality should be shown adorned with the director's craftsmanship. In contrast, for another group of film-makers, the neo-realists, reality should be shown unadorned and basic. Roberto Rossellini (*White Ship* 1941, *Rome Open City* 1945), Luchino Visconti (*La Terra Trema* 1947) and Vittorio de Sica (*Shoeshine* 1946, *Bicycle Thieves* 1948) attempted to present reality without symbolic representation, in a quasi-documentary style that chronicled, rather than explained, the described events. Neo-realists generally had radical (left-wing) political views and wanted to use film in order to show that the world was actually an unfair and often brutal place, and it was only simple people's genuine feelings that could bring some warmth and joy to it. Interestingly, Bazin (1968: 33) described neo-realism as a form of humanism rather than a form of direction, adding that it was a style that supported self-effacement before reality.

Neo-realist films described 'a slice of life', often seen through the eyes of simple and poor people; they left many stories open-ended and with unanswered questions, to suggest the ongoing and unpredictable flow of life. The favoured techniques of neo-realist directors included using amateur actors whom they chose literally from the street (the protagonist of *Bicycle Thieves* was a factory worker), avoiding studio filming and shooting, instead filming on location in natural settings, using natural lighting and writing simple, everyday dialogue, often allowing actors to improvise their own lines. The direction was aimed to be as unobtrusive as possible, telling mostly chronological stories with few, if any, close-ups which suggested directorial comment. Such films gave attention to the details of everyday life and settings, and emphasized the here-and-now aspects of reality as it was experienced by ordinary people.

In *Bicycle Thieves*, for example, a long-term unemployed man finally finds a job pasting film posters (an indirect way to pay homage to the art of film). However, he has his bicycle stolen, which makes his job very difficult. The remainder of the film consists of a series of mini-episodes, with the man and his son searching for the bicycle in different parts of Rome. In the end the two characters are still wandering the streets, the bicycle is still missing, and their future is unknown.

Neo-realism was popular in Italy just after World War II, but did not have a long history. One reason for its demise was that the Cinecitta studios, which were destroyed during the war, were rebuilt, and many directors found it more practical and productive to shoot in studio settings. Another reason was that Italian audiences showed a preference for foreign films (American and French) with more elaborate plots and sets. In all, many neo-realist directors found that creating 'realistic' films actually involved more deliberate effort than acknowledging the representational nature of film and working accordingly.

The tendency to see film as an opportunity to depict reality in an unmediated fashion and as a vehicle of truth is not restricted to one group of film-makers. It can be traced in the work of various directors throughout the history of film, a likely reason being the identification of the signified with the signifier in film, which gives the illusion that what happens on the screen is real. In many respects, films can *show* more unequivocally and less ambiguously than written fiction, and this fact appeals to those interested in showing the unadulterated 'truth' to an audience.

In contemporary times, a group of film-makers who have taken up this idea and attempt to implement it systematically in their work are the Danish Dogma 95 directors, led by Lars Von Trier (*Breaking the Waves* 1996, *Dogville* 2003). Whereas neo-realists produced films 'documentary-style', with the camera aiming to capture scenes of life as it happens, Dogma 95 directors tend to go for a more 'group-therapy' style, where the unobtrusiveness of the camera and the absence of stylized techniques aim to bring out the hidden emotional depth of the actors. Their ideology of capturing 'pure' reality on film reaches levels of almost religious fanaticism and is summed up in their statute of rules, aptly named The Vow of Chastity, as shown in Figure 7.1.

Nevertheless, the attempt to capture reality 'as it is' in its pure form is doomed to failure

Although neo-realism as a movement developed during and immediately after World War II, neo-realist tendencies and patterns survived in much Italian cinema till the 1970s. Such patterns are present, for example, in the films of directors such as Pier Paolo Pasolini and Michelangelo Antonioni.

I swear to submit to the following set of rules drawn up and confirmed by DOGME 95:

1. Shooting must be done on location. Props and sets must not be brought in (if a particular prop is necessary for the story, a location must be chosen where this prop is to be found).
2. The sound must never be produced apart from the images or vice versa. (Music must not be used unless it occurs where the scene is being shot.)
3. The camera must be hand-held. Any movement or immobility attainable in the hand is permitted. (The film must not take place where the camera is standing; shooting must take place where the film takes place.)
4. The film must be in colour. Special lighting is not acceptable. (If there is too little light for exposure the scene must be cut or a single lamp be attached to the camera.)
5. Optical work and filters are forbidden.
6. The film must not contain superficial action. (Murders, weapons, etc. must not occur.)
7. Temporal and geographical alienation are forbidden. (That is to say that the film takes place here and now.)
8. Genre movies are not acceptable.
9. The film format must be Academy 35 mm.
10. The director must not be credited.

Furthermore I swear as a director to refrain from personal taste! I am no longer an artist. I swear to refrain from creating a 'work', as I regard the instant as more important than the whole. My supreme goal is to force the truth out of my characters and settings. I swear to do so by all the means available and at the cost of any good taste and any aesthetic considerations.
Thus I make my VOW OF CHASTITY.

Copenhagen, Monday 13 March 1995

On behalf of DOGME 95, Lars Von Trier, Thomas Vinterberg

Figure 7.1 The Vow of Chastity
Source: http://www.dogme95.dk/the_vow/vow.html

for two main reasons. First, reality is very much a philosophical concept, so it is not certain that it refers to something concrete and undisputable in the world. As the existentialist philosopher Søren Kierkegaard (1987: 56) creatively pointed out, 'reality' is like a sign in a shop window saying 'Ironing Done Here'. If you brought your clothes to be ironed, you would be duped because the sign would actually be for sale. Also, film semiotician Jean Mitry (2000: 83) has made a similar observation: 'I will not go so far as to cast doubt on the reality of the real world, but . . . this reality is only ever a datum of our senses picking up fragments of phenomena which our consciousness turns into a reality which is "effectively real" for us.'

Secondly, even if we were to accept that the term 'reality' refers to an objective fact, it is still not possible to present it 'as it is'. Even simple factors such as how and when to begin and end a story have an arbitrary aspect that points to the choices made by an artist. Other elements, such as the duration of each scene, and the casting of actors (regardless of whether they are professional or amateur) to embody particular roles are even more complicated choices which mould the reality that is presented. Realism is actually an idealist approach to film, attempting to overlook the material aspects of production that contribute to the final presentation of 'reality'. For example, Lars Von Trier filmed *Breaking the Waves* on 35mm film, then transferred the footage to video and reworked it digitally to extract most of the colour. He then transferred the result back to film, producing images that were desaturated and shimmered. An effect of 'lived' or 'experienced' (worn out!) reality was thus produced, but only through calculated technical manipulation.

That reality cannot be presented as an unmediated whole, however, should not over-shadow the fact that different approaches to reality and to the function of art in relation to reality do produce contrastive effects. An expressionist film does affect viewers totally differently from a Dogme 95 production, and both make a statement about humans' relationships with each other and with the world. It is not a case, therefore, of identifying which is the most 'real' or the most 'artistic', but of attributing equal merit to them as possible ways to use film in order to represent aspects of life – ways that are meaningful to different audiences depending on their own ideological standpoints.

In certain cases, ideologies about the function of film in society develop as a reaction to existing situations that are perceived as constraining. The Dogme 95 ideology and various other contemporary European approaches to film, for instance, are implicit criticisms of the virtual colonization of film by the US-based studios, referred to using the umbrella term 'Hollywood'. Although Hollywood film-making is often defined in opposition to the notion of ideology, any institution that has successfully sustained a system of procedures and techniques over a period of time can be seen to have an ideological foundation that nurtures it. I believe, therefore, that it would be appropriate to end this section with an overview of the Hollywood ideology.

Classical Hollywood

As a physical location, Hollywood is now a run-down suburb of Los Angeles. As a term used in film criticism as well as in everyday language, 'Hollywood' refers to the films made by the main studios, when they were actually in Hollywood from the 1920s through to the late 1950s, and now to the films made by the large media corporations that replaced the studios, starting in the 1960s (Nelmes 1996; Wasko 2003; Decherney 2005). Having as its main aim to entertain rather than to challenge, Hollywood is characterized by high innovation in technological advancement but strikingly low innovation in narrative formulation. In fact, such films tend to remain loyal to the basic narrative structure, consisting of an initial situation, a complication or twist, a series of actions resulting from the complication, and finally a resolution. As Kristin Thompson (1999: 8) notes: 'Hollywood continues to succeed through its skill in telling strong stories based on fast-paced action and characters with clear psychological traits. The ideal American film still centers around a well-structured, carefully motivated series of events that the spectator can comprehend relatively easily.'

On the level of the story, prevalent techniques of Hollywood films include:

- A unified narrative with a clear causal link between events: events are explained or justified either explicitly through dialogue or implicitly through elements in the film.

Although Hollywood is arguably the most widely recognized model of film-making world-wide, Hollywood itself does not produce the most films. India comes first in film production with an estimated 800 releases each year, way ahead of Hollywood's estimated 250 (Plate 2002). The Indian film industry's status as a major competitor of Hollywood is reflected in the title 'Bollywood', referring to the booming film industry of Mumbai (formerly Bombay).

- An emphasis on the personality and individual traits of the characters: not much is left to the viewers' imagination as to who the main characters are, where they came from, and what they want to achieve.

- The basic actantial structure is clearly evident and remains constant with few changes: heroes, opponents and helpers have distinct roles that rarely overlap (the actantial model is described in detail in Chapter 4).

- A clear motivational structure: characters' actions, goals and problems are explained in terms of causes that originate in the characters' biography and are personal rather than social.

- A clear temporal structure producing a recognizable chronology of events, even though the events may be presented in analepses (flashbacks) and prolepses (flashforwards) (as explained in Chapter 4).

- A strong tendency to provide closure: events are resolved and questions answered, and it is usually relatively easy to understand 'what happened in the end'.

On the level of the presentation, things are somewhat more complicated because, as was noted above, Hollywood pioneers and experiments with new technologies, or visually stunning styles. For example, in the 2000 remake of Mike Hodges' 1971 film *Get Carter,* director Stephen Kay retains the original story, but revamps the presentational style by including jump cuts and overexposure to symbolize the pressure and pace of the protagonist's life. This is in line with contemporary audience's expectation that they will see an exciting story shown in an exciting style.

On the whole, some prevalent Hollywood techniques that can be distinguished on the presentational level include:

- A preference for continuity editing so that the camera narration is as unobtrusive as possible, and the transitions from one shot/sequence to another flow seamlessly.

- A strong use of face close-ups and reaction shots. This reinforces the Hollywood emphasis on individual characters, presented as 'persons', as central motivators for the development of the narrative. As noted above, this also suggests strong directorial control, where the director attempts to manipulate viewers' emotions by showing them how they should feel through the strategic use of a face.

- A reliance on the reputation of stars, consistent with Hollywood's emphasis on personality over story. In many instances, the presence of a famous star in a film can guarantee this film's success. In fact, it is common for contemporary audiences, when eliciting information on new film releases, to ask 'Who is in it?' rather than 'What is it about?'

7.8 Analysing film

Ideology does not force values and attitudes on to passive recipients in an obvious and open manner. If it is to be effective, ideology is presented subtly, as a natural, transparent or even inevitable consequence of particular events. A fruitful way to analyse film in terms of its ideology is to examine the values that are assumed, those that are affirmed and those that are negated. Four main areas to focus on when analysing ideology in film are:

1 *Identity*. Arguably, all stories are based on issues of identity, which is further subdivided into:

- *Individual identity*: are characters determined by biography and personality or do they change in response to circumstances and intention? How much responsibility for the outcomes of events is placed on individuals and how much on social factors? What is the role of agency in the development of events, i.e. how free is a character to choose particular actions?

- *Gendered identity*: which roles and behaviours are allocated to women and which to men? What physical characteristics do characters of each gender display and are these characteristics pivotal to the development of the story? What differences would need to be made to the story if the gender of key characters were changed?

- *Ethnic identity*: to which ethnic/racial groups do the main characters belong? How is their ethnicity linked to actions and events in the story? What differences would need to be made to the story if the ethnicity or race of key characters were changed?

2 *Motivation*. This describes the reason why something happens or why something appears in a film, and is subdivided into:

- *Compositional*: is a specific, non-negotiable reason given for a character's behaviour and actions? If yes, is this reason given as conscious or unconscious? Is this reason pivotal in advancing the plot or is it coincidental? How many of the behavioural patterns present in the film are attributable to specific motivations and how many remain ambiguous or mysterious? Films that have a strong causal structure where actions are reduced to one event in the past of a character usually have conservative ideologies, for which the world works in simplistic ways. The same occurs in films that attempt to provide 'logical' answers to every question raised in the narrative unfolding.

- *Realistic*: are some elements or props designed to reflect objects as we know them in the real world, or are they imaginary? For example, the sets representing outdoor locations in Proyas's *I, Robot* do not denote an actual city but a futuristic one, so the designs are artistic. Some indoor locations, however, such as the protagonist's home, denote indoor settings in contemporary Western societies, so the designs used are realistic and remind us of the objects we use in our own homes (tables, chairs, dishes, etc.).

- *Artistic*: the opposite of realistic, this describes the presence of elements whose raison d'être is to draw attention to themselves as creative or imaginary devices. As noted above, for example, expressionist films used artistic sets to symbolize the interiority and subjectivity of reality. Also, props or events that have no obvious function in the narrative but are playfully distractive would fall into this category. Finally, self-reflexive devices, those that refer to the film's identity as film, also belong here. For example, in Burton's *Ed Wood*, Ed wears strongly visible eyeliner and the film is shot in black and white, both self-reflexive devices signifying the medium of cinema through their association with silent films.

- *Intertextual*: does the film include certain elements in order to make allusions to another film, or to the conventions of its genre? Such allusions could take the form of a piece of dialogue, costume, action, etc. that is recognized as having occurred in another film, or in more than one film.

3 *Closure.* This describes the conclusions or consequences of events making up the story. The representation of how things end shows the implicit values of the film. How do things turn out for the main characters at the end? Who gets punished and who gets rewarded, and for what actions? Does everything 'fall into place' or are there loose ends left when the film finishes? Films that have a clear and final closure tend to present simplistic world-views, especially if this closure restores order as it is envisioned by the status quo.

4 *Knowledge.* Besides identity, knowledge is another fundamental aspect of narrative: identity encompasses 'what is', while knowledge encompasses 'how we know what is'. In film we know what we hear in the dialogue and sometimes in voice-over narration, and also what we see and how we see it. Therefore, the identity of who imparts knowledge is significant, as are camera movements, points of view, and the influence of the soundtrack. Is the story presented from a fixed point of view or is the point of view mutable and diverse? Is the knowledge presented attributed to specific sources, or does it come from an all-knowing, unspecified origin? Are actions judged or criticized in a cliché d fashion?

■ Summary

◆ Concepts developed in film have permeated other areas of communication, especially the digital media.

◆ Early approaches to the theoretical study of film focused on how film was a kind of language, and used linguistic concepts and terms to analyse films. More recently, film researchers have shifted the focus on to how film and other visual media possess distinctive features that set them apart from their verbal counterparts.

◆ The process of film-making is divided into four stages: pre-production, production, post-production and exhibition/distribution. In the digital era, post-production is especially important as much special-effects editing and image-manipulation is carried out at this stage.

◆ The elements through which films tell stories are *shot, camera angle, lens* and *movement, lighting* and *scene composition.*

◆ Many film-makers have used film to make statements about the nature of reality and about social issues. Prominent movements in the history of film include surrealism, expressionism, montage theory, New Wave, realist movements and the Hollywood model.

■ Topics for discussion

▶ Write a screening report of a scene from a film of your choice. A screening report is a detailed analysis of a scene (a scene being a self-contained sequence of the story, which may or may not include more than one shot). Describe the scene composition and the use of colour, movement, and camera angle, as well as how many shots make up the scene and how the shots were edited. A screening report does not include any evaluation or comment on the scene; it just describes how it was created.

▶ Analyse a film of your choice using the criteria outlined above. Pay attention to assumptions that the film makes in choosing characters and their actions, what motivations for actions are given, and how predictable or not the development of events is. Compare the story structure with the way the story is told in terms of special effects and visual elements.

▶ Compare two films, one of a mainstream, Hollywood-style orientation and one with more artistic overtones. Select two films that deal with a similar topic, for example childhood, interracial marriages or alienated personalities. Discuss the differences and similarities between the two. Include both story structure and presentation in your discussion.

■ References and further reading

Armes, R. (1985) *French Cinema*. New York: Oxford University Press.

Astruc, A. (1968) [1948] 'The Birth of a New Avant-Garde: La Camera-Stylo', in P. Graham (ed.), *The New Wave*. London: Martin Secker and Warburg.

Barlow, J. D. (1982) *German Expressionist Film*. Boston, MA: Twayne.

Bazin, A. (1967) [1958] *What is Cinema?*, trans. by H. Gray. Berkeley, CA: University of California Press.

Bazin, A. (1968) [1957] 'The Evolution of Film Language', in P. Graham (ed.), *The New Wave*. London: Martin Secker and Warburg.

Bordwell, D. (2002) 'Intensified Continuity: Visual Style in Contemporary American Film', *Film Quarterly*, Vol. 55, 3, pp. 16–28.

Bordwell, D. and Carroll, N. (1996) *Post-Theory: Reconstructing Film Studies*. Madison, WI: University of Wisconsin Press.

Bordwell, D. and Thompson, K. (2001) *Film Art: An Introduction*, 6th edn. New York: McGraw Hill.

Breton, A. (1969) [1962] *Manifestoes of Surrealism*, trans. by R. Seaver and H. R. Lane. Ann Arbor, University of Michigan Press.

Buñuel, L. (1968) [1947] 'Notes on the Making of "Un Chien andalou"', in F. Stauffacher (ed.), *Art in Cinema*, 2nd edn. New York: Arno.

Cardullo, B. (1997) (ed.) *Bazin at Work: Major Essays and Reviews from the Forties and Fifties*. New York: Routledge.

Casetti, F. (1999) *Theories of Cinema: 1945–1995*, trans. by F. Chiostri, E. Gard Bartolini-Salimbeni.

Austin, TX: University of Texas Press.

Collin, B. C. (2004) Personal interview. Los Angeles, CA.

Decherney, P. (2005) *Hollywood and the Culture Elite*. New York: Columbia University Press.

Eisenstein, S. (1959) *Notes of a Film Director*. London: Lawrence and Wishart.

Elsaesser, T. (2000) *Weimar Cinema and After: Germany's Historical Imaginary*. New York: Routledge.

Evans, P. W. (1995) *The Films of Luis Buñuel: Subjectivity and Desire*. Oxford: Clarendon Press.

Grodal, T. (1997) *Moving Pictures: A New Theory of Film Genres, Feelings and Cognition*. Oxford: Clarendon Press.

Karriker, H. (2005) *Film Studies: Women in Contemporary World Cinema*. New York: Peter Lang.

Kelly, K. and Parisi, P. (1997) 'Beyond "Star Wars"', *Wired*, Vol. 5, no. 2.

Kierkegaard, S. (1987) [1845] *Either/Or*, ed. and trans. by H. V. Hong and E. H. Hong. Princeton, NJ: Princeton University Press.

Kinder, M. (2002) 'Hot Spots, Avatars, and Narrative Fields Forever: Buñuel's Legacy for New Digital Media and Interactive Database Narrative', *Film Quarterly*, Vol. 55, 4, pp. 2–15.

King, G. (2000) *Spectacular Narratives: Hollywood in the Age of the Blockbuster*. London and New York: Tauris.

Lester, P. M. (1995) *Visual Communication: Images with Messages*. Belmont, CA: Wadsworth.

Leyda, J. (1963) (ed.) *Film Form: Essays in Film Theory*. London: Dennis Dobson.

Manovich, L. (2001) *The Language of New Media*. Cambridge, MA: MIT Press.

Marsen, S. (2004) 'Against Heritage: Invented Identities in Science Fiction Film', *Semiotica*, 150–1/4, pp. 141–57.

Metz, C. (1974) *Film Language: A Semiotics of the Cinema*, trans. by M. Taylor. New York: Oxford University Press.

Mitry, J. (2000) [1987] *Semiotics and the Analysis of Film*. London: Athlone.

Monaco, J. (1981) *How to Read a Film*. New York: Oxford University Press.

Nelmes, J. (1996) *An Introduction to Film Studies*. London: Routledge.

Phillips, W. H. (1999) *Film: An Introduction*. New York: Bedford St Martins.

Plate, T. (2002) 'Hollywood Faces New Competition: World Film Industry is Globalization at its Best', UCLA International Institute. Retrieved 2 September 2005 from http://www.international.ucla.edu/article.asp?parentid=2059

Salt, B. (1992) *Film Style and Technology: History and Analysis*, 2nd edn. London: Starword.

Stam, R. (2000) *Film Theory: An Introduction*. Oxford: Blackwell.

Stam, R. and Miller, T. (2000) (eds) *Film and Theory: An Anthology*. Oxford: Blackwell.

Thompson, K. (1999) *Storytelling in the New Hollywood*. Cambridge, MA: Harvard University Press.

Wasko, J. (2003) *How Hollywood Works*. Thousand Oaks, CA: Sage.

Wilson, G. M. (1986) *Narration in Light: Studies in Cinematic Point of View*. Baltimore, MD: Johns Hopkins University Press.

Wollen, P. (1998) [1968] *Signs and Meaning in the Cinema*. London: British Film Institute.

Vernet, M. (1992) *Aesthetics of Film*, trans. by R. Neupert. Austin, TX: University of Texas Press.

The Mass Media

> The media. It sounds like a convention of spiritualists.
>
> Tom Stoppard

Communication guru Marshall McLuhan (1964) suggested that the dominant media in a society are powerful forces that shape social structure by imposing mental frameworks. McLuhan implied that the media we use regulate the way we think – the random-access aspect of digital texts, for example, produces a non-linear orientation that challenges the previously dominant structure of texts, which was mostly sequential. In addition to their more abstract function of cognitive remodelling, however, the media have a concrete manifestation in corporate administration, societal and legal regulation, and technological organization. This chapter discusses pertinent social and professional aspects of mass-media communication. It begins with a discussion of the digital media and issues of globalization, and then takes a closer look at the business organization of media corporations. The chapter ends with a list of commonly used terms in broadcasting.

8.1 The digital media

Developments in computer technology have enabled all electronic media to utilize at least some digital elements in their operation. A question that has occupied many researchers of what is known as 'the digital revolution', however, concerns the originality of the communicative interaction between users and digital text. Do people use the digital media differently from how they use other electronic media? Are the 'new' media replacing the 'old' media, or do they complement them by enhancing their capabilities? And is the digital text unique among media in the presentation of its content?

In an influential study on the characteristic features of digital media, Bolter and Grusin (1999) made two interesting observations. First, they pointed out that the digital media attempt to make transparent the interface through which the user accesses media content. This aims to establish a sense of immediacy and presence for the user, who feels as if s/he 'is there'. Secondly, they described how digital media combine content from other sources and reassemble it in the new, digital environment. They referred to this representation of one medium in another as *remediation*. Furthermore, they distinguished some ways in which remediation occurs, including the following:

- Digital media reproduce other media forms, such as photographs and text, and provide new ways to access them. This is what happens, for example, when photographs are scanned, or analogue video is digitized, and stored as files in a computer.

- Digital media enhance other media by adding multimedia elements. This is what happens, for example, when online encyclopedias combine content with sound and video.

- Digital media absorb other media content and reproduce it in the digital or networked environment. This is what happens, for example, when interactive computer games use film techniques and conventions.

8.2 The internet

The internet is the fastest-growing medium that has ever been recorded. Some estimates include that from 1995 (30.6 million users) to 2002 (605.6 million users) the number of internet users had grown by almost 2000 per cent (NUA Internet Surveys 2004).

The internet blends different communication objectives, making it a hybrid medium: it is partly an information system where people can search for information by means of search engines; it is also a medium where people can create their own content and distribute it widely using the platform of the World Wide Web. The term internet refers to the architecture of the system, and the World Wide Web is the software that facilitates the sending of individual e-mails, the creation of group electronic directories and the formation of online chat groups and forums. It is also a tool for the commercial exchange of goods and services, known as electronic commerce or *e-commerce*.

The internet traces its ancestry to a US Department of Defense project begun in the late 1960s. Developments initiated there were taken a step further by the innovative work carried out by researchers at the Centre for European Nuclear Research in the late 1980s. The internet and web-based applications then started to be adopted widely in the 1990s, especially through the highly popular medium of electronic mail or *e-mail*.

Access, community formation and *convergence* are key notions when studying the distinctiveness and power of the internet as a communication medium. To start with access, an inherent strength of the internet is the structural anarchy on which it is based, in comparison with the institutional models of ownership and control of older media. In contrast to print and broadcast media, the internet has few 'gatekeepers' of either content or form – nobody actually owns the internet. The ability to connect to the internet and some technical skill are all that is needed for one to become an author and express an identity (real or made-up!) to fellow users dispersed throughout the world. This capacity has not only enabled users to access previously unavailable information, it has also enabled minority groups to state their presence, inform the world of their existence, and voice their opinions. In the words of economists John Browning and Spencer Reiss (1998: 105):

Old media divides the world into producers and consumers; we're either the authors or the readers, broadcasters or viewers, entertainers or audiences, one-to-many communications in the jargon. New media, by contrast, gives everybody a chance to speak as well as to listen. Many speak to many – and the many speak back.

The downsides of potentially unlimited access? For one, the lack of control means that the quality and credibility of information found on the internet is of varying standards, ranging from state-of-the-art presentations of valid and practical information to very low-quality and unreliable material. Secondly, although access to the internet is available to all in theory, it is not always so in practice. Access to internet-connected computers and, in the case of uploading data, access to server space are prerequisites, and these are not readily available in some parts of the world. Also, authorities are not always lenient in allowing citizens free access to the world. For example, the restrictions imposed by the Chinese government in 2001 and in 2002 on internet use demonstrate both the power of the internet and its vulnerability to external control. Thirdly, free access often also means lack of privacy. In fact, although exchanging information and carrying out business deals on internet-connected computers is increasingly becoming a routine procedure, serious fears of 'cyberterrorism', such as privacy abuses, security breaches and fraud, persist.

The second key notion associated with the internet is the formation of common interest groups, which has become easier now than at any other time in the history of communication. People with similar interests, consumer tastes and lifestyle habits have the chance to exchange ideas with the similar-minded internationally. This way the notion of community, originally associated with locality, is now being redefined in terms of global connectivity. This change goes hand in hand with the fragmentation of audiences observed by market analysts. As discussed in Chapter 6, the digital era has shifted the emphasis from demographic segmentations of audiences and markets to a psychographic distribution. The traditional division of populations into age and gender is being replaced with classifications according to lifestyle values and consumer tastes. For example, such communities as sailing clubs, science fiction groups and Beatles fans include members of all nationalities, most ages and both genders – and all find a hospitable venue in cyberspace.

Also, the internet has enlarged the public domain by enabling counter-cultural, alternative and even anti-social groups to express their views and communicate with each other in a public forum. For example, in addition to numerous special-interest sites, ranging from stamp collecting to treasure hunting, terrorists also routinely post their ideologies and activity calendars on the internet. Also, the 2004 trial of Armin Miewes in Germany, who ate another human, Bernd Brandes, at the latter's request, revealed an online community of cannibals.

Shenton and McNeely (1997) suggest that some reasons for individuals participating in online discussion groups and forums include:

- the opportunity to form relationships that are perceived as being more difficult to develop in the physical environment;
- the ability to experiment with different identities;
- the ability to exchange ideas with like-minded peers;
- the opportunity to find others who share the same interests or value system, however, non-mainstream these may be;

- the search for romantic and sexual experiences;
- the ability for the marginalized and socially excluded to disseminate ideologies and opinions that could not be communicated through mainstream media outlets.

The internet is also a major contributor to the phenomenon of *convergence*. Convergence is the integration of different media capabilities, forming new combinations. It is now possible, with the help of digital technology, to mix and convert content from video, radio, computer and other media into new forms. Although this is not per se an internet phenomenon but a more widely digital one, such new forms of multimedia technologies ground many web-based applications, such as computer games. Computer games have changed from autonomous products to networked applications that can often be transformed and developed by their players. In addition to the individual games produced by major companies such as Nintendo and Microsoft, there are many multi-user games played on the internet, bringing together thousands of players from around the world.

Finally, the internet has been a forum for collaborative online publishing, as evidenced by the construction of blogs and wikis. Blogs evolved from listings of websites that people liked to collaborative notebooks and multimedia educational tools, where participants could contribute ideas and information on a topic, on a peer-to-peer basis.

Writing in 1999, Mark Stefik (1999: 20–1) assigned ten identities to the internet based on functions that it had started to develop in the twentieth century, many of which it had fully developed by 2005. These identities, which are based on the values of ubiquity, portability and wearability, are:

- *The Big Screen*: accessing news and entertainment in comfort.
- *The Personal Document Reader*: accessing news and entertainment through a lightweight, portable display with interactive wireless communication.
- *The Web Watch*: accessing e-mail, calendars and photos through a screen on the wrist.
- *The Web Tricorder*: accessing and recording pictures and videos from a palm-sized computer and posting pictures and videos on the internet through a wireless connection.
- *The Insighter*: researching through a hand-held device that can scan documents, search for data and summarize information.
- *The Hiker's Companion*: remaining informed about travel events and opportunities, accessing a global positioning system, and summoning help from remote locations if stranded – all on a pocket-sized device.
- *The Net Phone*: communicating with others telephonically through internet-based applications.
- *The NetMan*: listening to music, or accessing e-mail and other internet sources by voice command.
- *The StreetSmart*: getting directions and finding out about local attractions by means of a videophone-internet device built into street lampposts.
- *The Web Suit*: interactively accessing information about one's environment and the world through wearable appliances. These provide information through eyeglasses and earphones with which the user may interact by means of forearm keyboards and voice commands.

Although the internet is one of the most rapidly evolving technologies, its destination remains controversial. Many have pinned hopes on the internet becoming the main medium of message exchange and engulfing or replacing telephone, fax and mail services. However, the nature of digital technology is such that it defies causal progression and therefore prediction. In fact, prophecies of the future are futile in the information age. For example, when the internet started developing in the 1990s it was forecast that we would soon be living in a paperless world, since most of our communicative interactions would be using digital bytes. This has not happened and we now use much more paper than in the pre-internet days.

Various studies have confirmed this. For instance, in a famous environmental experiment in the early 1990s, eight 'bionauts' lived for two years in a sealed glass dome in the Arizona desert, from where they were allowed to communicate with the outside world only through electronic media. Despite their reliance on e-mail and fax messages, the volunteers found that they could not avoid using paper. In particular, they found that they needed hard copies of documents, printed on paper, to read (Dizard 2000: 152–3). One reason for the ubiquity of paper in communication is that it is physically difficult to read off a screen. In fact, reading off a screen takes about three times longer than reading print, possibly because the flatness of the screen and the light that it projects do not suit the human optical system. Editors, for example, routinely print text to edit and proofread, and there is no indication that this is about to change, at least in the near future.

8.3 Globalization

The last thirty years or so have seen the rise of world-wide phenomena such as international conglomerates and the accumulation of capital in a small number of multinational corporations. Brands such as McDonald's and Starbucks, mostly of US origin, have spawned franchises around the world, fostering a standardization of tastes and consumer habits. These phenomena are classified under the umbrella term 'globalization'.

Globalization describes mainly trade practices, extending also to the communication patterns and cultural systems that underlie these practices. The most significant features of globalization include:

- *An increasing ease of information exchange between individuals, groups and nations.* This is mainly due to the developments of technology that underpin many global practices. The rise of the internet and other media, referred to as Information Communication Technologies (ICTs) play a major role in this. In turn, this ease of information exchange leads to a greater awareness of intercultural approaches to various issues, and thereby to a more critical approach towards social conditions, than was possible in earlier times.

- *An accumulation of wealth in the hands of a few.* World resources are increasingly owned and exploited by powerful multinational corporations. This aspect of globalization has come under attack by protesters who claim that this kind of economic distribution prevents poorer countries from developing and imposes blueprints of business management that stem from the culture of the large multinationals.

The development of satellite technology was a major factor in the growth of globalization, since this enabled the transmission of Western-produced media texts world-wide. The first international satellite transmission was marked by the broadcast, in 1967, of the Beatles' song *All You Need is Love*, which was seen live by 400 million viewers in 24 different countries. Given the subsequent criticisms of globalization and the internationalization of the mass media, the title and lyrics of the song assume an ironic form.

- *A gradual corporatization of the world.* In addition to the economic consequences of a few corporations engulfing smaller trade and business organizations, globalization also affects culture. Certain cultural world-views, emanating mainly from the US and Western Europe, tend to dominate social trends internationally, and, many believe, contribute to the undermining of non-Western cultures. One symptom of this is the emergence of English as the international language.

The mass media are directly involved in globalization processes for two main reasons: first, they connect the world through content that is broadcast or accessible in most parts of the globe; audiences world-wide watch the same television programmes, and communicate with others internationally in real time through the internet. Secondly, the media, in their business capacity, are often owned by multinational corporations, and are regulated according to international standards generally set by agencies that support global uniformity and equivalence in media communication. For these reasons, studying the media helps to shed light on social conditions in the global era.

In his analysis of the uses of television, John Hartley (1999: 13), for example, lists some areas that contain the main changes currently taking place in most modern nations. These areas are:

- capitalization of entertainment and leisure, and extensive division of labour in text-making of all types;
- internationalization of trade in information, communication and entertainment;
- privatization (domestication and feminization) of the public sphere, and suburbanization of both family and civic life;
- virtualization of power – the conversion of governmental power from direct to 'virtual', from armies to information, from control of land to control of airwaves.

These four areas neatly encapsulate the points of interface between media texts (and the power structures that underlie them), and public audiences, within the global context. They indicate the new social spaces created through free international trade and enabled by developments in technology, where information and meanings are constructed and exchanged. They also underline the role of the mass media in grounding these changes.

8.4 Mass communication

Ownership and regulation are key factors in how media are organized and how much influence they exert in society. *Publicly owned media* may be funded from direct or indirect taxation, a licence fee, revenue generated from advertising, sponsorship or commercial ventures. *Privately owned media* are largely funded by advertising and other commercial activities, such as the production and selling of content to other media organizations. *Community-based media* are usually organized on a non-profit basis by specific interest groups, and are funded by subscriptions and small amounts of advertising and sponsorship.

As regards television, which is undoubtedly the most influential and popular of the mass media, in most countries publicly and privately owned networks coexist. These are now being challenged by the proliferation of cable channels, which started emerging in the 1980s. Cable and satellite television, high-definition television (HDTV) and such technologies as compressed digital television and digital audio are creating their own successful programming, while many public networks are finding it increasingly difficult to invest in high-cost programming because of the audience's shift to satellite-distributed cable networks and digital home playback.

In most countries in the early twenty-first century, public, commercial and cable television co-existed, with varying degrees of power attributed to each. At the same time, technological advancements have made it possible for formerly separate sectors of the communication industries (such as broadcasting, print media, computing, publishing and film) to merge or form alliances in order to exploit more effectively the creative potential offered by technology. This is *synergy* – a business strategy with collaborative focus that brings together, under one management, different sectors of industry. According to Turow (1992: 683), synergy is 'the co-ordination of parts of a company so that the whole actually turns out to be worth more than the sum of its parts acting alone, without helping one another'.

Synergy is facilitated by two factors evident in the modern business world: first, companies share a common technological infrastructure, which means that formerly autonomous sectors are now connected through computer networks, enabling collaboration and exchange of expertise. Secondly, as was noted in Chapter 6, audiences are becoming fragmented and characterized by a plurality of tastes and motivations, as well as by a global orientation. Within this context, different companies, or branches, of the same conglomerate can produce a range of products to appeal to the diverse audiences that make up the contemporary market. Disney, for example, is a company that pioneered synergy among its products even before the onslaught of the digital breakthroughs that ground synergistic practices today. Disney trademark products such as Mickey Mouse and Donald Duck have evolved for over half a century in different avatars projected through various media, such as comic books, films, theme parks and toys. Also, the staggering profit of over a billion dollars of the more recent *Lion King* was only partly due to the film itself; substantial amounts were made from such 'tie-ins' as videocassette sales, clothes, toys and other products – the film made $730 million, while the rest poured in from the synergistic ventures (Dizard 2000: 136).

Another example of successful synergy is Vivendi Universal. Vivendi is a transnational corporation whose interests lie in both media and non-media sectors. Its parent company is Compagnie Générale des Eaux, which was established in France in 1853 to supply water to Lyons. Now, Vivendi's international companies are involved in music, publishing, television and film, telecommunications, the internet and the environment. As well as owning a diverse range of companies such as the French cable network Canal+, Houghton Mifflin publishers and a part of Universal Studios, Vivendi is involved in transport, energy, waste and water supply industries (www.vivendiuniversal.com).

Digital Video Broadcasting (DVB)

International Standardisations Organization (ISO)

International Electrotechnical Commission ((EC)

European Telecommunications Standards Institute (ETSI)

International Telecommunications Union (ITU)

Moving Pictures Experts Group (MPEG)

Figure 8.1 International organizations regulating broadcasting

Companies can be integrated vertically or horizontally. According to Croteau and Hoynes (2000: 41), 'vertical integration refers to the process by which one owner acquires all aspects of production and distribution of a single type of media product'. Vertically integrated media corporations usually own and control a number of companies that are involved in various stages of the production and distribution of a specific kind of media product. For example, a vertically integrated television network may own and control the production company, the television station and the cable channel that broadcasts a particular programme.

Conversely, horizontal integration 'refers to the process by which one company buys different kinds of media, concentrating ownership across differing types of media rather than 'up and down' through one industry' (Croteau and Hoynes 2000: 41). Media corporations engage in horizontal integration when they own and control a diverse range of media companies involved in print, broadcast and digital media sectors. For example, global media corporations such as AOL-Warner own and control a wide variety of media companies. Their horizontal nature often extends to owning companies that produce and sell merchandise associated with their media products.

Although some international organizations (see Figure 8.1) attempt to impose worldwide standards of regulation in order to maximize equity and accountability in the practices of the media industries, regulation and classification of the media remain the responsibility of individual countries. Taking television as a focal point, most countries have a broad division between public and private, but widely different subdivisions and regulation. As James Watson (2003: 212) points out, 'the issue is less about the *categorization* of ownership and control, public or private, and more about the *degree* and *extent* of that control'. The following sections describe the situation of television in the UK, the US, Australia and France.

Television in the United Kingdom

Britain has public, commercial and cable television. The British Broadcasting Corporation (BBC), formed in the 1920s, is a public corporation run as a quasi-independent body. The BBC has been founded, in both theory and practice, on a public service philosophy that colours its public image as well as the programmes it is associated with. The BBC is a producer, a broadcaster and a distribution network. It is funded by a licence fee, paid by all who own a television set.

In 1954, the Television Act introduced commercial television, known as Independent Television (ITV). Although it is founded on a commercial ideology, ITV is supervised and guided by a public body (the Independent Broadcasting Authority), with ideological foundations of public service, and norms of quality and balance. It is therefore more protected from the harsh realities of market competition than other commercial television networks around the world. ITV developed Channel 4 in the early 1980s, primarily as a broadcaster. Channel 4's statute allows it to include in its repertoire a range and diversity of programmes with experimental, innovative and often controversial content not catered for by the other commercial stations. Channel 4 has now also become a significant contributor to film production.

Cable television is widespread and catching up with public and commercial television, although, at least at this stage, the reputation, innovativeness and quality of the BBC, ITV and Channel 4 ensure the stability of their position with British audiences.

Television in the US

The US does not have a publicly owned television system equivalent to the BBC. Instead, television networks are divided into three categories: one category includes what is known as 'the big three' national networks, ABC, NBC and CBS, another category includes the three national networks that are sponsored by Hollywood studios, Fox, UPN and USA, and the last category includes numerous cable networks, which are rapidly multiplying. The big three national networks are owned by corporations: Disney Corporation owns ABC, General Electric owns NBC, and CBS Corp (previously known as Westinghouse) owns CBS. The national networks are facing serious problems with the development of cable, mainly because advertisers support cable networks owing to their large numbers of channels, which attract larger audiences. As the revenue for all networks comes from market sources, it is advertisers that call most of the shots in American television.

Synergy and corporate mergers are major phenomena in the world of American television. Owners of television networks usually also own other media and entertainment facilities. Disney Corporation, for example, among other ventures, owns ABC, the Disney Channel (which is broadcast by cable), produces a variety of films through Disney Productions, and owns amusement parks in California (Disneyland). The most important merger to date occurred when Time Warner and AOL joined forces in 2000, making them the number one media company in the world in terms of revenue, and a leading proponent of convergence. Major mergers in media corporations are shown in Figure 8.2.

Television in Australia

Australia has a system of television made up of three parts: public, commercial and subscription ('pay-TV'). The Australian Broadcasting Corporation (ABC), modelled largely on the British Broadcasting Corporation (BBC), provides a national service and is non-commercial, i.e. a public service broadcaster. The statutory body of the ABC legally requires it to be both a broadcaster and a major producer of programmes. The ABC is financed by a direct government grant rather than by a licence fee, which makes its interests closely aligned with its political administrators, resulting in frequent criticisms of political bias.

Public television includes the Special Broadcasting Service (SBS), an innovative venture that helps to promote the multicultural policies and social orientation of the country. SBS broadcasts subtitled programmes in more than sixty languages, and more than 50 per cent

To face the challenge posed by cable stations in the US, many commercial networks have been venturing into original scripting programmeming, with the aim of providing programming that equals that of cable stations, such as Home Box Office (HBO). FX Network's *The Shield* is an example of a successful series with this aim.

of its transmission is in languages other than English. Broadcasts include news, sports, films and documentaries. In addition, SBS is the producer of a limited number of programmes, especially documentaries, short films and animation, with content that celebrates multiculturalism and diversity.

Commercial television, on the other hand, is made up of a series of private stations, many of which are organized into networks, particularly in the major cities, the principle ones being Channel 7, Channel 9 and Channel 10. These commercial stations and networks act mainly as broadcasters rather than producers. Programme schedules are made up of a combination of imports, station-produced programmes and programmes brought in from external agents, known as 'packagers', who make and sell programmes. The Australian Broadcasting Authority (ABA) regulates all broadcasting and online content, while the Broadcasting Services Act of 1992 regulates the ownership and control of commercial and subscription broadcasting services.

Although Australia has access to cable networks similar to those in other countries, cable television does not pose as serious a threat to the public and commercial networks as it does elsewhere, such as in the US. One reason for this could be cultural: Australians tend to expect a free entertainment and information service from authorities in return for their tax

2000	Vivendi acquires Seagram/Universal for US$35 billion AOL and Time-Warner merge for US$350 billion
1999	Viacom and CBS merge for US$35 billion
1998	AOL buys Netscape for US$4.2 billion AT&T buys TCI for US$45 billion
1997	WorldCom buys MCI for US$37 billion
1996	Bell Atlantic buys NYNEX for US$22.1 billion Westinghouse buys CBS television network for US$5.4 billion Microsoft and NBC establish MSNBC online site and cable channel
1995	Disney buys Capital Cities/ABC for US$19 billion Time Warner merge with Turner Broadcasting
1994	Viacom buys Paramount Communication for US$9.6 billion and Blockbuster Entertainment for US$8.4 billion.
1989	Time Inc. merge with Warner Communications for US$14.1 billion

Figure 8.2 Major mergers in media corporations 1989–2000

contributions, and are inclined to think of television as a public, rather than a private, enterprise.

Television in France

The television system in France is divided into three categories: public/commercial, commercial and cable. France 2, France 3, La Cinquième and the Franco-German Arte channels are subsidized by state sources as well as by advertising. France 2 and France 3 are generalist channels with the aim of informing and entertaining. Arte is an upscale cultural channel with a European focus, and broadcasts films, debates and news programmes on European topics. La Cinquième is educational, with documentaries targeting mostly students.

Purely commercial stations, funded by advertising, are TF1 and M6. The oldest and most established channel, TF1, has a generalist orientation with a strong entertainment focus, while M6 attracts mostly the under-35s and specializes in films and music. Canal+, owned by Vivendi Universal, is the largest French cable network, also famous for sponsoring sports events and funding film productions. In addition to these, there are several networks, both French and foreign, that are accessible through cable and satellite and include the BBC, CNN and MTV.

French television has a strong tradition of supporting the film industry, with both commercial television, such as TF1, and Canal+ being regular contributors to film funding.

Although many developments are taking place in the digital field, which will make television more interactive, researchers in the media industry have found that change in the ways people use television may not be as far-reaching or fast as some people predict in the next five to ten years. Steve Leblang, Senior Vice President of Strategic Research and Planning at FX Networks in the US, for example, pointed out that television is basically a passive medium and that this gives it its entertainment value. Turning it into an interactive medium will require time and discipline (Leblang 2004).

8.5 The structure of media companies

This section gives an overview of the business structure of the media industry. Although individual companies may differ in some respects, this outline provides an accurate description of commonly attested trends. In broadcast companies, as indeed in most companies of all types, there are three levels of managers:

- *Top* managers coordinate the company's activities and provide the overall direction for the accomplishment of its goals. In broadcasting, a top-level manager would be the general manager.

- *Middle* managers are responsible for carrying out particular activities to further the overall goals of the company. In broadcasting, middle managers are the heads of sales, programme, news engineering and business departments.

- *Low* managers supervise the routine work of employees. Examples of low managers in broadcasting would be the radio station local sales manager, who reports to the general sales manager, and the television production manager, who answers to the programme manager.

Commercial broadcast stations, typically, are organized into a number of departments.

Sales department

The sale of time to advertisers is the principal source of revenue for commercial radio and television stations. This is the responsibility of a sales department, headed by a sales manager. Many stations subdivide the department into national sales and local sales. Sales to national advertisers are entrusted to the station's sales representative company or 'sales rep'. Local sales are the responsibility of the station's salespersons, typically called *account executives*.

Programme department

Under the direction of a programme manager, or director, the programme department plans, schedules, and, with the assistance of the production staff, produces programmes. The programme manager engages in four basic tasks: planning, acquisition, execution and control of programmes.

Here is a list of the main activities carried out by this department, applicable to both television and radio stations:

- the production or acquisition of content that will appeal to targeted audiences;
- the scheduling of programmes to attract the desired audience;
- the production of public service and promotional announcements and of local commercials;
- the production or acquisition of other programmes to satisfy the public interest;
- the determination and execution of policies for news, sports and public affairs programmes;
- decisions on what to cover and how to cover it;
- reporting and newscasting;
- the selection of topics and guests for public affairs programmes;
- the hosting of interview programmes.

In addition, for television, the programme department carries out these activities:

- researching and shipping films and videotapes and maintaining appropriate records;
- screening films and videotapes for quality and adherence to the station's programme and advertising standards;
- marking films for commercial and other breaks;
- designing sets;
- producing graphics for programmes, commercials and public service and station identification announcements
- producing graphics for advertising and promotional materials for use in other visual media.

Recently, there has been a backlash against reality TV. This now appears to many as less real and more contrived than scripted shows. For example, Steve Leblang's research at FX Networks showed that scripted shows are viewed as more realistic and compelling. This suggests that many people consider television to be an entertainment medium, and not a venue where they can view reality voyeuristically. Because of such results, many programmes that imitate reality shows like *Survivor* have been rejected by television stations.

For radio, the programme department carries out these activities:

- additions to and deletions from the station's playlist of music;
- preparation of the playlist and supervision of its execution;
- auditioning of new recordings;
- liaison with representatives of recording companies to obtain new releases;
- contact with music stores on sales of CDs and cassettes;
- cataloguing and filing of CDs.

As the saying goes 'being in the right place at the right time' is what determines success. Similarly, with broadcast companies, scheduling is paramount in ensuring that the right kind of audiences are attracted at the right time. Scheduling is one of the functions assigned to the programme department. This involves a set of strategies:

- *head-to-head*: scheduling a programme at the same time and of the same nature as the competitors do. For example, early and late-night newscasts are usually scheduled against each other on different stations.

- *counter*: scheduling at the same time as the competition a programme that appeals to a different audience from that targeted by the competition. An example would be a programme with principal appeal to adults at the same time as a children's programme on another station.

- *Strip*: scheduling a programme series at the same time each day, usually Monday to Friday. This practice, also known as *horizontal programming*, encourages habit formation.

- *Checkerboard*: scheduling a different programme series in the same time slot daily.

- *Block*: scheduling several programmes with similar audience appeal back to back, usually for two hours or more. This strategy is also called *vertical programming* and seeks to attract special-interest audiences.

News department

As noted in Chapter 6, the ideal functions of the media in society are to inform, educate and entertain. In many stations, the information function is kept separate from the entertainment function and is supervised by a news director. The department is responsible for regularly scheduled newscasts, news and sports specials, and documentary and public affairs programmes.

Engineering department

This department is headed by a chief engineer or technical manager. It selects, operates and maintains studio, control room and transmitting equipment, and often oversees the computers. In some stations, studio production personnel report to the head of this department.

Business department

The business department carries out a variety of tasks necessary to the functioning of the station as a business. They include secretarial, billing, bookkeeping, payroll and, in many stations, human resources responsibilities.

Broadcast stations engage in several other activities, which may be assigned to separate departments or subdepartments, or may be included in the duties of the departments described above. The following are among the most common.

Promotion and marketing

This department, often called the sales department, is concerned with programme and sales promotion. The promotion section seeks to attract and maintain audiences, while the marketing section aims to attract advertisers. Some stations assign programme promotion to the programme department and sales promotion to the sales department.

Some of the main activities in which the sales department engages include:

- selling time to advertisers;
- providing vehicles whereby advertisers can reach targeted audiences with their messages at a competitive cost;
- developing promotions for advertisers;
- generating sufficient revenues to permit the station to operate competitively;
- producing a profit for the station's owners;
- contributing to the worth of the station by developing and maintaining a strong base of advertiser support.

The executives working in the sales department include:

- the *promotion and marketing director*, whose tasks include creating and planning audience and sales promotion campaigns, coordinating the station's overall graphic look, and maintaining media relations;
- the *general sales manager*, whose duties include developing overall sales objectives and strategies and controlling the department's budget;
- the *national sales manager*, who coordinates the sale of time to national and regional advertisers through the station representative companies, and maintains contacts with local offices of national and regional accounts;
- the *local sales manager*, who plans and administers local sales, and carries a list of clients.
- a number of *account executives*, whose job it is to seek out and develop new accounts, and prepare and make sales presentations.

Traffic

Traffic is often carried out by a subsection of the sales department, and is headed by a traffic manager. Its activities include the daily scheduling on a *programme log* of content to be aired by the station, and the compilation of an *availabilities sheet* showing times available for purchase by advertisers. It is also responsible for the monitoring of advertising content to ensure compliance with commercial contracts.

Continuity

Continuity is concerned chiefly with the writing of commercial copy and, in many stations, constitutes a subsection of the sales department. The continuity director supervises the section's activities and reports to the sales manager.

8.6 Influences on the management of media companies

The management of broadcast companies is mainly influenced by these sources:

- *The licensee.* The main responsibility for the operation of a radio or television station rests with the licensee, the person or persons who have made a financial investment in the station and are therefore considered owners. The general manager must seek to satisfy their expectations and weigh up the financial impact of all actions.

- *The competition.* Radio and television stations compete against each other and against other media in the market for advertising, and, similarly, for audiences. Stations are aware that their initiatives and projects will produce a reaction from competitors, and need to take this into account in their enterprises.

- *The government.* This exerts influence on broadcasting in many ways, depending on the individual governments of different countries. The main areas of influence on broadcasting come from public sectors, as well as through independent regulatory agencies.

- *The labour force.* As with all industries, the success of broadcasting is influenced by the number of people available for work and their skills. The station's ability to hire and retain qualified and productive employees is a major contributor to the station's performance.

- *Labour unions.* The unions to which employees belong exert a significant influence on the general manager's decisions on policy. The company is required to abide by the terms of a union contract covering, among other things, wages and fringe benefits, job jurisdiction and working conditions.

- *The public.* The public is a major force in decision-making concerning programming. Since advertising is, in most cases, the main contributor to the company's revenue, the opinions and needs of consumers are always taken into account in programming policy. In fact, the media constitute a major source for audience and consumer research and devote large amounts of funding towards this end.

- *Advertisers.* The financial fate of commercial broadcast stations lies in its support from advertisers. Therefore, proof that they attract audiences is very important for stations to ensure the continued financial flow from advertisers.

- *Economic activity.* The state of the economy, locally and nationally, determines the amount of money consumers have to spend on advertised products and their spending priorities. When the economy is slow, businesses often reduce their advertising expenditures, which is problematic for broadcast stations and other advertising-intensive media.

- *Social factors.* Since broadcast stations must take into account and respond to the interests of the communities in which they function, social factors play an important role in programme decisions. Stations must analyze and interpret trends in the size, demographics and psychographics of the local population (as described in Chapter 6), employment practices, income and spending habits, and changing morals.

- *Technology.* Technology is instrumental in the competitive and up-to-date functioning of the broadcast media. Advances in technology resulted in the emergence of radio and television broadcasting and continue to play a major part in station practices. To be successful, broadcast companies must respond to the influence of new technologies, as well as those technologies that are being introduced into the home and that provide alternative leisure-time pursuits for the public.

8.7 Organization of cable stations

Like commercial stations, a cable television system is organized according to the major functions that must be carried out to ensure its successful operation. While differences exist in organizational structure, the functions are similar and are allocated to departments. The following departments are found in many systems:

- *Government affairs and community relations.* These activities are often performed by a director. The focus of community relations is on the planning and execution of public relations campaigns designed to create and maintain a favourable image.

- *Human resources.* This section's responsibilities include recruiting and interviewing job applicants, orienting new employees, developing and implementing employee training and evaluating programmes, and processing benefits.

- *Business operations.* This section processes revenues and expenditures, and handles computer operations and the collections of funds.

- *Advertising sales.* The sale of local availabilities in advertiser-supported networks is a major responsibility of this department. Many systems also sell classified advertising and spots on local channels.

- *Technical operations.* Tasks of this section include the maintenance and operation of the 'headend' (the facility that receives, processes and converts video signals for transmission on the cable) and trunk and feeder cables; maintenance of the standby power supply; testing and adjustment of signal strength; installation and repair of drop cables and 'hookups' (connections) to cable boxes and videocassette recorders; the planning and construction of extensions to the cable system in new subdivisions and apartment complexes; and the dispatch of technicians.

- *Marketing*. This section is in charge of the sale of the system's programme services to subscribers, and the planning and execution of advertising and promotion campaigns in furtherance of the goal. The department engages in market analyses to assess customer preferences and potential, determines the packaging of services and their price structure, and conducts door-to-door and telemarketing sales campaigns.

- *Customer service*. This section deals with all customer service and repair calls, enquiries and complaints.

There are major differences between cable and commercial television. In commercial television, advertisers are the primary market. In cable, the audience is the market and the system's financial success is tied closely to the number of subscribers it can attract and the number of services they purchase. These realities impose on cable managers an obligation to ensure that the technical quality of the signal is of the highest quality. Viewers tend to subscribe as long as they feel that they are receiving value for their money. If they do not feel that this is the case, the system will experience subscriber disconnects, or 'churn'. Accordingly, the marketing and technical staff must co-operate closely, since the retention and addition of subscribers depend heavily on a signal that is technically acceptable when delivered to the home.

Cable is a capital-intensive business. Everything, from the 'headend', or origination source, to the miles of cable is very costly. It is significantly more difficult to construct a new cable system than a new broadcast station. Coupled with the front-end capital costs is the likelihood that it will be years before the revenue exceeds the cost and debt service. Usually, it is estimated to take around six years to break even on a cable start-up. For this reason, cable construction often falls to large companies that are already in the business and have adequate capital to realize the tax benefits accruing from interest and depreciation.

Although audience-subscriber support is vital to the prosperity of a cable station, it is also very difficult to predict or plan. For example, in an often-cited marketing failure, Time Warner attempted to 'sell' an advanced, interactive cable television venture in Orlando, Florida in the mid-1990s. This system gave access to a wide range of video and print services delivered directly to television sets. Although the project was technically successful and actually seemed like 'a good idea', it attracted only around 4000 subscribers, indicating that this service was not valued by the market at which it was directed.

8.8 Advertising

Advertising is generally agreed to be the backbone of all commercial media. More than just providing the main source of income for most of the media industry, advertising gives both print and broadcast media their characteristic look and sound. In addition, advertising concerns influence media decisions on the types of entertainment and information that they produce to keep in tune with the audiences that advertisers want to reach. Advertising is part of the marketing process, and connects the product with the potential buyer. According to the Federal Trade Commission of the United States, for example, the aim of advertising is to 'provide consumers with the information they need to make rational decisions in the marketplace'.

Although advertising often comes under attack by many who see it as a form of manipulation and exploitation of the public in the service of corporate interests, its power and sociological significance in contemporary culture is acknowledged by others. Marshall McLuhan (1964), for instance, identified the creative aspects of advertising, noting that 'the historians and archeologists will one day discover that the ads of our time are the richest and most faithful daily reflections that any society ever made of its entire range of activities' (cited in Nadin and Zakia 1994:78). Its significance in the functioning of the media industry justifies its inclusion in this chapter.

Advertising is a major component of the mass media. Programming takes place according to consumer preferences, and is used to attract advertisers. Market researchers in the media industry conduct both quantitative and qualitative research in order to track people for advertising purposes.

Advertising agencies (and many marketing departments of major corporations) are divided into the following major roles:

- The *creative director* generally has the final say about major advertising decisions.
- The *art director/designer* provides the technical support and artistic layout for the packaging and publicizing of products.
- The *marketing director* oversees existing promotional methods, and analyses trends and consumer habits. S/he is actively involved in the creative output of the organization in terms of ensuring that it is relevant, 'hard-hitting' (targeted to specific consumer tastes) and customer-focused.
- The *account director (or client services director/new business director)* is principally found in advertising agencies (although equivalents exist in other business contexts). Job responsibilities revolve around maintaining existing client accounts and seeking new ones. These people tend to command respect from clients because it is their duty to service the account, keep tabs on the market and develop a mutually productive working relationship.
- The *financial director* is often also the one who decides whether the organization can afford proposed projects, and the one who goes hunting for external and internal funding.
- The *copywriters* and *editors* are generally responsible for writing text that accompanies products as part of the packaging, as well as the text, or 'copy', that complements catchy headlines and impressionable images in print advertising (as found in magazines, for example), and web content.

8.9 Public relations

'Public relations' (PR) is the conventional term for a wide range of activities which are initiated by organizations and which use the media with the aim of influencing public opinion. There are three main functions ascribed to public relations (Grunig 1992; Grunig and Hunt 1984; Fearn-Banks 1996). The first is influencing what the public thinks or does in order to serve the interests of an organization. This might involve publicly beneficial activities, such as coordinating the promotion of a concert tour for a famous musician or orchestrating a series of events in support of a charity. The second is responding to public concerns, developments or initiatives on behalf of an organization or individual. A common example of this is handling a crisis in relations between an organization and the public. The third is the pursuit of mutually beneficial relationships among different sections of the public, such as negotiating settlements between mining contractors and landowners.

These functions are pursued through a number of different models of practice, going from the least desirable (in that it is the most ethically controversial) to the most desirable (in that it allows for negotiation and feedback):

- *Press agent/publicity model.* In this model, the organization attempts to publicize its clients or products in as many ways as possible, but typically by turning publicity press releases into news stories. This is a one-way model, where the organization uses mostly entertainment to influence the public in favour of its products. It is akin to propaganda, where the information presented is biased, one-sided and exaggerates the qualities of the object or company being publicized. PR ventures based on this model subscribe to the belief that all publicity is good, and tend to pursue it at all costs. Usually, there is no audience research done, and there is certainly no feedback.

- *Public information model.* This is similar to the previous model in that it is one-way, requests no feedback and attempts to influence the public in favour of the product or organization that it represents. However, it differs from the previous model in that it has a more ethical basis, requiring its practitioners to communicate true information, however disappointing, without recourse to entertainment factors. This is the model of practice most often required by government agencies when informing the public of policies and legislation. In non-government contexts, this model is used when the company uses the media only to distribute news releases without excessive commentary or advertising tactics.

- *Two-way asymmetric model.* This model is sometimes also called the scientific persuasion model because the PR practitioner uses quantifiable data reflecting social science research, such as surveys. This model to some extent takes into account feedback, but the organization is not likely to change its policies or procedures because of it. Examples would include the justifications of practice presented to the public by organizations that are perceived to damage the environment, such as those dealing with mining or oil refinery. The notion of 'public opinion' is important for this model, and extensive research is often carried out for the purpose of changing the public's attitude about the product or organization.

- *Two-way symmetric model.* Practitioners of this model attempt to negotiate and compromise with public demands. The model is based on a dialogic relationship with the public, where information collected from representative groups is used as feedback, which means

1. AOL-Time Warner (Turner, HBO, Warner Brothers)
2. Walt Disney Company (CapCities ABC, ESPN)
3. Vivendi-Universal (USA Networks, Universal, Canal+)
4. Viacom-CBS (Paramount, UPN, Infinity, MTV)
5. Sony (Columbia TriStar)
6. News Corp Ltd (Fox)
7. AT&T Broadband (TCI, MediaOne, Liberty Media)
8. Comcast
9. Tribune (Times Mirror)
10. Cox

Figure 8.3 Top media companies in 2006

that it can affect the organization's policies and procedures. Typically, the desired outcome is the establishment of harmonious relationships between conflicting or competing interests so that the two parties (whether they be company and public or different sectors of an organization) can reach a mutually beneficial agreement.

As with other models, these constitute abstract representations of the actual programmes of PR practitioners, and are rarely found in pure form. In most cases, PR campaigns follow a mix of the four designed for particular purposes and targeting different audiences. A general observation on PR practice using these models is that in countries or social–corporate contexts where PR approaches to public communication are prevalent, there is usually a mix of the four models. For example, Grunig and Hunt (1984) estimated that, in the US, 15 per cent of PR was based on the publicity model, 50 per cent was based on the public information model, 20 per cent was based on the two-way asymmetric model, and 15 per cent was based on the two-way symmetric model.

In other countries or contexts where PR procedures to communicate with the public are not prevalent, the public information model tends to predominate.

Figure 8.3 shows the top ten media companies in terms of annual revenue.

Figure 8.4 defines some frequently used terms in broadcasting.

Definitions of frequently used terms in broadcasting
AC   adult contemporary, a soft rock music format targeting the 25–54 age category.
Access   public availability of broadcast time; in pay-TV, one or more channels reserved for non-commercial use by the community, educators or local government.
Access time   the hour preceding *prime time* (usually 7–8 p.m.).
Actuality   an on-the-spot news report or voice of a newsmaker (often taped over the phone) used to create a sense of reality.
Adaptation   a film or video treatment of a story that appeared in print (such as a novel or play).
Affiliate   a commercial radio or television station receiving more than ten hours per week of network programming, but not owned by the network.
Anthology   a weekly series consisting of independent, unrelated programmes classified under an umbrella term. Examples include playhouse series with dramas by different authors. Sometimes, this technique is used by networks to package unused programme pilots.
AOR   album-oriented rock, a rock music format appealing to a strongly male audience, aged 18 to 34, generally consisting of songs by avant-garde rock artists. ⇨

Appeals   elements in broadcast content (for example, sentimentality, comedy, romance and suspense) that attract audiences.

Arbitron Information on Demand (AID)   a computer system that identifies the best times for airing specific programmes based on input on content and target audience.

Audience flow   the movement of audiences from one programme or time period to another.

Audimeter   Nielsen's in-home television rating meter, used up to the late 1980s (also called the *peoplemeter*).

Avatar   a computer-generated self in humanlike form that carries out its 'real' self's wishes.

Backsell   telling the audience what songs have just been played on the radio.

Barker channel   a cable television channel that lists programmes.

Beautiful music (BM)   a radio format emphasizing low-key, popular music, generally with extensive orchestration.

Big Seven Studios   the major Hollywood studios: Columbia Tri-Star, Walt Disney Studios, MGM-US, Paramount, 20th Century Fox, Universal and Warner Brothers.

Block booking   licensing several programmes or films as a package deal.

Blocking   placing several similar programmes together to create audience flow.

Blunting   broadcasting a programme of the same type carried by another source so as to share the audience.

Branding   creating an image for a channel that persists even after programme changes. This technique serves to identify the channel with a particular set of products or services.

Bridging   beginning a programme about half an hour earlier than a similar, competing programme, so as to attract audiences and keep them past the start time of the competing programme.

Cable franchise   an agreement between a local franchising authority and a cable operator allowing the former to install cable wires and supply programmes to a specific geographic area.

Cable network   service distributing a channel of programming to satellite and cable systems.

Cable operator   the person or company that manages cable facilities under a franchise.

Clone   a close copy of a prime-time show, usually on another network.

Coding   in radio, classifying songs by type or age of music and play frequency.

Commentary   background interpretation of events by radio and television analysts.

Concept testing   research into audiences asking them if they like the idea for a proposed programme.

Convergence   technological mixing of separate communication devices (television, computer, telephone, etc.) into one system.

Cookie   software that attaches to a user's computer hard drive and provides evidence of websites accessed.

Critical information pile   an amount of urgent, breaking news that causes alterations to planned news coverage.

Designated Market Area (DMA)   Nielsen's term for a local viewing area.

Diary   an instrument for recording hours of listening or viewing of a station or channel, used by research firms, such as Nielsen and Arbitron.

Double running   the practice of showing additional screenings of a programme on the same day.

Drivetime   the time when audiences are likely to listen to the radio when driving (usually 6–10 a.m. and 4–7 p.m.).

Eclectic   a mixed radio format which incorporates different types of programmes.

Endbreaks   commercial breaks following a programme's closing credits.

Flipping   changing channels frequently during programmes (also known as *grazing*).

Format   the overall programming design of a station, cable service or specific programme.

Formula   the set of elements that define a *format*.

Global brands   brand names recognized internationally, such as Disney, Microsoft and Nokia.

$\Rightarrow$

Gold   a hit song or record, usually with lasting appeal.

Group owner   an individual or company having the licence for more than two broadcast facilities.

Hammocking   positioning a weak programme between successful programmes to support it by motivating audiences to watch it.

Hard news   daily, factual reporting of national, international and local news stories. This is contrasted with *soft news.*

Hook   a plot or character element at the start of a programme that grabs audience attention.

Hyping   extended promotion of a programme to increase audience size.

Incubation strategy   launching a new network by sheltering the new service under an existing network.

Inheritance effect   research term for an audience remaining tuned in for a subsequent programme.

Intelligence boxes   television converters that give access to multiple media activities at the same time, such as watching a programme, accessing the web and telephoning.

Interactive media   media that permit users to send messages to the programme source as well as receive messages from the source.

Lead-in   a programme that precedes others in a time slot, usually intended to increase audience flow to the later programmes.

Least Objectionable Programme (LOP)   a theory maintaining that viewers select a programme that offends the least number of viewers watching together, and not the most appealing programme. It assumes that people change channels only when what is shown on the channel currently being viewed is objectionable.

Loss leader   a programme aired because management think it is worthwhile to do so as an image booster, possibly because of ethical, aesthetic or cultural leaders. This programme on the whole is not financially rewarding.

Mini-series   prime-time network television series shorter than the conventional 11 episodes.

Multiple System Operator (MSO)   owner of more than one cable system. Also known as *group owner.*

Passive meter (or passive peoplemeter)   a television meter that incorporates an automatic camera with a computer recognition system matching viewer silhouettes with stored demographic data. This allows the recording of viewing habits without needing any audience input, such as keeping a diary or pushing buttons.

Pay-Per-View (PPV)   cable or pay-TV programmes for which subscribers pay individually.

Peoplemeter   an electronic meter attached to television sets measuring both tuning and audience demographics (who watches what and when). It requires viewers to push buttons to identify themselves.

Pilot   a sample first programme of a proposed television series. It is often longer than regular episodes and introduces characters and events.

Positioning   making the audience believe that one station or cable service is different from its competitors.

Prime time   the time when television attracts the largest number of viewers, usually for three consecutive hours between 7 p.m. and midnight.

Promo   a broadcast advertising spot announcing a new programme or encouraging viewing of an entire schedule.

Public Service Announcement (PSA)   a non-commercial spot advocating a community event or a not-for-profit charity or public service activity.

Pure format   a radio format appealing to an easily definable demographic who like the same music (as opposed to mixed format).

Rating   an audience measurement unit representing the percentage of the total potential audience tuned to a specific programme or a particular time slot.

Repurposing   using content originally produced for one medium in another medium.

Resting   shelving a film or series for a time to make it seem fresh when revived.

Sample size   the number of people surveyed in radio or television research.

Scrambling altering a television transmission so that a special decoder is needed to ensure a visible picture.

Screening in research, locating individuals fitting specific age or gender criteria.

Segmentation subdividing formats to appeal to narrow target audiences.

Share a measurement unit for comparing audiences. It represents the percentage of total listening or viewing audience tuned to a given station.

Simulcast a programme airing simultaneously on two or more channels.

Soft news this consists of features and reports that do not depend on timely airing (as does hard news), and includes entertainment stories, leisure and travel, health issues and hobby material.

Stickiness the measure of time spent at a website (also called *time-spent-online*).

Streaming digital distribution of audio or video in near real-time (also called *webcasting*).

Teaser a very brief news item or programme spot intended to lure an audience into watching or listening to the subsequent programme.

Theme networks cable networks broadcasting a single type of content, such as weather, news or sports (also called *niche networks*).

Transparency the appearance of simplicity to users despite complex technical structures and processes.

Treatment this is an outline of a film, series or programme which describes the characters, plot and events before the full script is written.

Turnover changes in the number of subscribers, listeners or viewers. In pay-TV, this refers to the ratio of disconnecting to newly connecting subscribers.

Underwriter foundation or private corporation giving grant money to cover the costs of producing or airing a programme on public television or radio.

Upscale Audiences or subscribers with higher than average socioeconomic demographics (as opposed to *downscale*).

Value-added promotion contests, games and other promotions offering more publicity to the advertiser than spot advertising.

Vertical ownership ownership of both the programme supply and the means of distribution.

Webcasting digitally distributing a programme via the web (also known as *streaming*).

Zipping fast-forwarding through commercials on home-taped videocassettes.

Zoning dividing the advertising section of a cable system or network into contained geographic areas to allow local businesses to purchase ads.

Figure 8.4 Definitions of Frequently Used Terms in Broadcasting

▌Summary

◆ The internet, the fastest-growing medium ever recorded, is unique in its all-encompassing orientation and absence of in-built gatekeepers. Communication elements associated with the internet are access, community formation and convergence.

◆ The term 'globalization' describes the social, cultural and economic situation of the world as this is influenced by trade practices associated mainly with international organizations, such as the World Trade Organization (WTO). Although globalization is supposed to support free trade and provide equal access for all countries to trade agreements, many argue that it actually supports Western capitalist interests and in fact inhibits the growth and independence of developing countries. The mass media, through their global reach, play a major role in representing and disseminating the values of globalization.

◆ The influence of the media in society is determined to a large extent by who owns and regulates them. Three categories of ownership are distinguished: publicly owned media, privately owned media, and community-based media.

◆ The term 'synergy' describes the business strategy that brings together different sectors of the media industry. Synergy is facilitated by technological developments, and by the fragmentation of audiences, which creates different tastes and the need for a range of media products.

◆ Media corporations can be integrated vertically or horizontally. In vertical integration, corporations own a number of companies that produce and distribute a product. In horizontal integration, corporations own different types of media products.

◆ The management of media companies is organized into top management roles, which usually outline the long-term strategy of the company, middle management roles, which generally initiate projects and coordinate the functioning of different departments, and low management roles, which tend to focus on the running and administration of a particular department or sector.

Topics for discussion

▶ Visit the websites of three major media corporations, such as Vivendi, Warner and Disney. Write a comparative profile, focusing on products and company organization. Although you are studying these companies as outsiders with only public documents for sources, you can still trace patterns and salient features through close reading. For example, you could follow this strategy:

- Check the employment sections and see what jobs are advertised. How are these jobs described? What does this indicate about the company?

- Check the media releases sections, noting major developments that the companies have advertised in the last couple of years. Can you trace similarities and differences between companies?

- Check to see if the companies publicize annual reports. How much information does each company provide to the public about its revenue and management? What does this indicate about the company?

▶ Choose a PR venture of a company (not necessarily restricted to media companies) and analyse the documents produced as part of the venture and the approach that the company followed to sustain its image. Examples of this include the Warner–AOL merger of 2000, and Microsoft's long-running antitrust case. An effective procedure to accomplish this is to check the company's press releases at the time of the venture or event, then to follow up the story in specialist magazines such as *The Economist, Business Weekly* and *Wired*. If these sources are not enough for you to draw up a picture of how the PR venture was implemented, they should at least point to other leads through their references to publications and people. In your discussion, note how the company's version of the situation differed from external versions, and the strategies that the company used to counteract accusations or criticisms.

▶ Discuss how pervasive the effects of globalization are in contemporary society. Find out the views of those who protest against globalization and the responses to these views by supporters of free trade. Write a list of areas where globalization can be felt, and speculate some possible consequences of this for developing countries as well as for the developed world.

■ References and further reading

Abercrombie, N. (1996) *Television and Society*. Cambridge: Polity Press.

Blumler, J. (ed.) (1992) *Television and the Public Interest: Vulnerable Values in West European Broadcasting*. London: Sage.

Bolter, J. D. and Grusin, R. (1999) *Remediation: Understanding New Media*. Cambridge, MA: MIT Press.

Browning, J. and Reiss, S. (1998) 'Encyclopedia of the New Economy', *Wired*, May.

Compaine, B. M. and Gomery, D. (2000) *Who owns the media? Competition and Concentration in the Mass Media Industry*, 3rd edn. Mahwah, NJ: Erlbaum.

Craft, J. E., Leigh, F. A. and Godfrey, D. G. (2001) *Electronic Media*. Belmont, CA: Wadsworth.

Croteau, D. and Hoynes C. (2000) *Media Society: Industries, Images and Audiences*. Thousand Oaks, CA: Sage.

Cunningham, S. and Turner, G. (eds) (2002) *The Media and Communications in Australia*. Sydney: Allen and Unwin.

Cyberatlas (2004) 'The World's Online Populations'. Retrieved 10 September from www.clickz.com/stats/big_picture/geographics

Davis, A. (2004) *Mastering Public Relations*. Basingstoke: Palgrave Macmillan.

Dizard, W. Jr. (2000) *Old Media, New Media: Mass Communications in the Information Age*, 3rd edn. New York: Longman.

Eastman, S. T. (2000) (ed.) *Research in Media Promotion*. Mahwah, NJ: Erlbaum.

Eastman, S. T. and Ferguson, D. A. (2002) *Broadcast/Cable/Web Programming: Strategies and Practices*, 6th edn. Stanford CT: Wadsworth.

Fearn-Banks, K. (1996) *Crisis Communications*, Hillsdale, NJ: Erlbaum.

Flew, T. (2005) *The New Media*. 2nd edn. Oxford: Oxford University Press.

Giddens, A. (1999) *Runaway World: How Globalization is Reshaping our Lives*. London: Profile Books.

Grant, A. E. (ed.) (2000) *Communication Technology Update*, 7th edn. Boston: Focal Press.

Grunig, J. E. (ed.) (1992) *Excellence in Public Relations and Communication Management*. Hillsdale, NJ: Erlbaum.

Grunig, J. E. and Hunt, T. (1984) *Managing Public Relations*. New York: Holt, Rinehart and Winston.

Hartley, John (1999) *Uses of Television*. London and New York: Routledge.

Herman, A. and Swiss, T. (eds) (2000) *The World Wide Web and Contemporary Cultural Theory*. London: Routledge.

Jankowski, G. F. and Fuchs, D. C. (1995) *Television Today and Tomorrow: It Won't Be What You Think*. New York: Oxford University Press, p. 37.

Kisselof, J. (1995) *The Box: An Oral History of Television, 1920-1960*. New York: Viking Press.

Leblang, S. (2004) Personal interview. Los Angeles, CA.

McLuhan, M. (1964) *Understanding Media*. London: Routledge and Kegan Paul.

McQuail, D. (1992) *Media Performance*. Newbury Park, CA and London: Sage.

Nadin, M. and Zakia, R. (1994) *Creating Effective Advertising Using Semiotics*. New York: Consultant Press.

Newcomb, H. (ed.) (2000) *Television: The Critical View*. New York: Oxford University Press.

NUA internet Survey (2004) retrieved 10th May from www.nua.ie/surveys/how_many_online

Pringle, P. K., Starr, M. F. and McCavitt, W. (1995) *Electronic Media Management*, 3rd edn. Boston: Focal Press.

Schumann, D. W. and Thorson, E. (1999) *Advertising and the World Wide Web*. Mahwah, NJ: Erlbaum.

Shenton, K. and McNeely, T. (1997) *The Virtual Communities Companion*. Albany, NY: Coriolis Group.

Smith, A. (ed.) (1995) *Television: An International History*. New York: Oxford University Press.

Stefik, M. (1999) *The Internet Edge: Social, Technical and Legal Challenges for a Networked World*. Cambridge, MA: MIT Press.

Stone, N. (1995) *The Management and Practice of Public Relations*. Basingstoke: Palgrave Macmillan.

Turow, J. (1992) 'The Organizational Underpinnings of Contemporary Media Conglomerates', *Communication Research* 19, 6, pp. 682–704.

Watson, J. (2003) *Media Communication*, 2nd edn. Basingstoke: Palgrave Macmillan.

Witherspoon, J. and Koitz, R. (eds) (2000) *The History of Public Broadcasting*. Washington, DC: Current.

Bibliography

Abercrombie, N. (1996) *Television and Society*. Cambridge: Polity Press.

Abercrombie, N. and Longhurst, B. (1998) *Audiences*. London: Sage.

Abrams, D. and Hogg, M. A. (1988) 'Comments on the Motivational Status of Self-Esteem in Social Identity and Intergroup Discrimination', *European Journal of Social Psychology*, 18, pp. 317–34.

Adams, Michael H. (1995) *Introduction to Radio: Production and Programming*. Madison, WI: Brown and Benchmark.

Akmajian, A., Demers, R. A., Farmer, A. K. and Harnish, R. M. (2001) *Linguistics: An Introduction to Language and Communication*. Cambridge, MA: MIT Press.

Albaran, A. B. (2002) *Management of Electronic Media*, 2nd edn. Belmont, CA: Wadsworth.

Anderson, C. A. (1997) 'Effects of Violent Movies and Trait Hostility on Hostile Feelings and Aggressive Thoughts', *Aggressive Behavior*, 23, pp. 161–78.

Ang, Ien (1985) *Watching Dallas: Soap Opera and the Melodramatic Imagination*. London: Methuen.

Ang, Ien (1991) *Desperately Seeking the Audience*. London: Routledge.

Argyle, M. (1983) *The Psychology of Interpersonal Behaviour*, 4th edn. London: Penguin.

Aristotle (1991) *The Art of Rhetoric*, trans. by H. Lawson-Tancred. London: Penguin.

Aristotle (1996) *Poetics*, trans. by M. Heath. London: Penguin.

Armes, R. (1985) *French Cinema*. New York: Oxford University Press

Ashley, S. (2004) 'Penny Wise Smart Labels', *Scientific American*, August, pp. 30–1.

Asllani, A. and Luthans, F. (2003) 'What Knowledge Managers Really do: An Empirical and Comparative Analysis', *Journal of Knowledge Management*, vol. 7, no. 3, pp. 53–66.

Astruc, A. (1968) [1948] 'The Birth of a New Avant-Garde: La Camera-Stylo', in P. Graham (ed.), *The New Wave*. London: Martin Secker and Warburg.

Bal, M. (1985) [1977] *Narratology: Introduction to the Theory of Narrative*, trans by C. Van Boheemen. Toronto: Toronto University Press.

Bal, M. (1991) *On Story-telling: Essays in Narratology*. Sonoma, CA: Polebridge Press.

Barker, Martin and Brooks, Kate (1998) *Knowing Audiences: Judge Dredd, its Friends, Fans and Foes*. Luton: University of Luton Press.

Barlow, J. D. (1982) *German Expressionist Film*. Boston, MA: Twayne Publishers.

Barthes, R. (1968) *Elements of Semiology*. London: Cape.

Barthes, R. (1984) [1957] *Mythologies*. New York: Hill and Wang.

Barthes, R. (1990) [1966] 'The Structural Analysis of Narrative', in S. Sontag (ed.) *A Barthes Reader*. New York: Farrar, Straus and Giroux.

Baudrillard, J. (1988) *Selected Writings*, ed. by M. Poster Cambridge: Polity Press.

Bazerman, C. and Paradis, J. (eds) (1991) *Textual Dynamics of the Professions*. Madison, WI: University of Wisconsin Press.

Bazin, A. (1967) [1958] *What is Cinema?*, trans. by H. Gray. Berkeley, CA: University of California Press.

Bazin, A. (1968) [1957] The Evolution of Film Language, in P. Graham (ed.), *The New Wave*. London: Martin Secker and Warburg.

Belbin, R. M. (2000) *Beyond the Team*. London: Butterworth Heinemann.

Bennett, T. and Woollacott, J. (1987) *Bond and Beyond: The Political Career of a Popular Hero*. New York: Methuen.

Berelson, B. (1952) *Content Analysis in Communication Research*. Glencoe, IL: Free Press.

Berger, A. A. (1996) *Manufacturing Desire: Media, Popular Culture, and Everyday Life*. New Brunswick, NJ: Transaction.

Berger, A. A. (1999) *Signs in Contemporary Culture: An Introduction to Semiotics*, 2nd edn. Salem, WI: Sheffield.

Berger, A. A. (2000) *Media and Communication Research Methods: An Introduction to Qualitative and Quantitative Approaches*. Thousand Oaks, CA and London: Sage.

Birdwhistell, R. (1970) *Kinesics and Context: Essays on Body Motion Communication*. Philadelphia, PA: University of Pennsylvania Press.

Blumer, H. (1951) 'Collective Behavior', in A. M. Lee (ed.), *New Outline of the Principles of Sociology*. New York: Barnes and Noble.

Blumler, J. G. (ed.) (1992) *Television and the Public Interest: Vulnerable Values in West European Broadcasting*. London: Sage.

Blumler, J. G. and Katz, E. (1974) (eds) *The Uses of Mass Communication*. Beverly Hills, CA: Sage.

Bolter, J. D. and Grusin, R. (1999) *Remediation: Understanding New Media*. Cambridge, MA: MIT Press.

Booth, W. C. (1961) *The Rhetoric of Fiction*. Chicago: Chicago University Press.

Booth, W. C. (2004) *The Rhetoric of Rhetoric: The Quest for Effective Communication*. Oxford: Blackwell.

Bordwell, D. (2002) 'Intensified Continuity: Visual Style in Contemporary American Film', *Film Quarterly*, Vol. 55, 3: pp. 16–28.

Bordwell, D. and Carroll, N. (1996) *Post-Theory: Reconstructing Film Studies*. Madison: University of Wisconsin Press.

Bordwell, D. and Thompson, K. (2005) *Film Art: An Introduction*, 7th edn. New York: McGraw Hill.

Breton, A. (1969) [1962] *Manifestoes of Surrealism*, trans. by R. Seaver and H. R. Lane. Ann Arbor, University of Michigan Press.

Briggs, A. and Cobley, P. (eds) (1998) *The Media: An Introduction*. Harlow: Longman.

Browning, J. and Reiss, S. (1998) 'Encyclopedia of the New Economy', *Wired*, May.

Bryant, J. and Zillmann, D. (eds) (2002) *Media Effects*. Hillsdale, NJ: Lawrence Erlbaum.

Buñuel, L. (1968) [1947] 'Notes on the Making of "Un chien andalou"', in F. Stauffacher (ed.) *Art in Cinema*, 2nd edn. New York: Arno.

Burgelin, O. (1972) 'Structural Analysis and Mass Communication', in D. McQuail (ed.), *Sociology of Mass Communications*, pp. 313–28. Harmondsworth: Penguin.

Burton, G. (2000) *Talking Television: An Introduction to the Study of Television*. London: Arnold.

Carey, J. (1992) *Communication as Culture*. New York: Routledge.

Casetti, F. (1999) *Theories of Cinema: 1945–1995*, trans. by F. Chiostri and E. Gard Bartolini-Salimbeni. Austin, TX: University of Texas Press.

Chandler, D. (1999) *Semiotics: The Basics*. London: Routledge.

Chatman, S. (1978) *Story and Discourse: Narrative Structure in Fiction and Film*. Ithaca, NY: Cornell University Press.

Chatman, S. (1990) *Coming to Terms: The Rhetoric of Narrative in Fiction and Film*. Ithaca, NY: Cornell University Press.

Chomsky, N. (1972) *Language and Mind*. New York: Harcourt Brace Jovanovich.

Cobley, P. (ed.) (1996) *The Communication Theory Reader*. London: Routledge.

Collin, B. C. (2004) Personal interview. Los Angeles, CA.

Compaine, Benjamin, M. and Gomery, Douglas (2000) *Who Owns the Media? Competition and Concentration in the Mass Media Industry*, 3rd edn. Mahwah, NJ: Erlbaum.

Cook, P. (1999) 'I Heard it through the Grapevine: Making Knowledge Managment Work by Learning to Share Knowledge, Skills and Experience', *Industrial and Commercial Training*, vol. 31, no. 3, pp. 101–5.

Corbett, E. P. J. and Connors, R. J. (1999) *Classical Rhetoric for the Modern Student*, 4th edn. Oxford: Oxford University Press.

Coste, D. (1989) *Narrative as Communication*. Minneapolis: University of Minnesota Press.

Coupland, D. (1994) *Generation X: Tales for an Accelerated Future*. New York: St Martins.

Craft, J. E., Leigh, F. A. and Godfrey, D. G. (2001) *Electronic Media*. Belmont, CA: Wadsworth.

Croteau, D. and Hoynes, W. (2000) *Media Society: Industries, Images and Audiences*, 2nd edn. Thousand Oaks, CA: Pine Forge Press.

Cunningham, Stuart and Turner, Graeme (eds) (2002) *The Media and Communications in Australia*. Sydney: Allen and Unwin.

Currie, M. (1998) *Postmodern Narrative Theory*. New York, NY: St Martin's Press.

Danesi, M. (1995) *Interpreting Advertisements: A Semiotic Guide*. Toronto: Legas.

Danesi, M. (ed.) (2000) *Encyclopedic Dictionary of Semiotics, Media and Communications*. Toronto: University of Toronto Press.

Davenport, T. H. and Prusak, L. (2000) *Working Knowledge: How Organizations Manage What They Know*. Boston, MA: Harvard Business School Press.

Davis, A. (2004) *Mastering Public Relations*. Basingstoke: Palgrave Macmillan.

Deacon, D. Pickering, P. and Murdock, G. (1999) *Researching Communications*. London: Arnold.

Dearlove, D. (2000) *The Ultimate Book of Business Thinking*. Oxford: Capstone.

De Certeau, M. (2002) *The Practice of Everyday Life*, trans by S. F. Rendall. Los Angeles, CA: University of California Press.

Decherney, P. (2005) *Hollywood and the Culture Elite*. New York: Columbia University Press.

Devereux, E. (2003) *Understanding the Media*. Thousand Oaks, CA and London: Sage.

Dichter, E. (1985) *The Strategy of Desire*. London: Garland.

Dizard, W. Jr (2000) *Old Media, New Media: Mass Communications in the Information Age*, 3rd edn. New York: Longman.

Dunnette, M. (ed.) (1976) *The Handbook of Industrial and Organizational Psychology*. Chicago: Rand McNally.

Eastman, S. T. (2000) (ed.) *Research in Media Promotion*. Mahwah, NJ: Erlbaum.

Eastman, S. T. and Ferguson, D. A. (2002) *Broadcast/Cable/Web Programming: Strategies and Practices*, 6th edn. Stanford, CT: Wadsworth.

Eco, U. (1976) *A Theory of Semiotics*. Bloomington: Indiana University Press.

Eco, U. (1983) *The Name of the Rose*. London: Harvest Books.

Eco, U. (1984) *The Role of the Reader: Explorations in the Semiotics of Texts*. Bloomington: Indiana University Press.

Eisenstein, S. (1959) *Notes of a Film Director*. London: Lawrence and Wishart.

Elsaesser, T. (2000) *Weimar Cinema and After: Germany's Historical Imaginary*. New York: Routledge.

Erlich, V. (1981) *Russian Formalism: History and Doctrine*, 3rd edn. New Haven, CT: Yale University Press.

Evans, P. W. (1995) *The Films of Luis Buñuel: Subjectivity and Desire*. Oxford: Clarendon Press.

Fearn-Banks, K. (1996) *Crisis Communications*. Hillsdale, NJ: Erlbaum.

Febvre, L. and Martin, H. (1984) *The Coming of the Book: The Impact of Printing 1450–1800*. London: Verso.

Feyerabend, P. (1976) *Against Method: Outline of an Anarchistic Theory of Knowledge.* London: New Left Books.

Figallo, C. and Rhine, N. (2002) *Building the Knowledge Management Network.* New York: John Wiley.

Finch, G. (2003) *How to Study Linguistics*, 2nd edn. Basingstoke: Palgrave Macmillan.

Finch, G. (2005) *Key Concepts in Language and Linguistics*, 2nd edn. Basingstoke: Palgrave Macmillan.

Fiske, J. (1987) *Television Culture.* London: Methuen.

Fiske, J. (1990) *Introduction to Communication Studies*, 2nd edn. London: Routledge.

Flew, A. (ed.) (1979) *A Dictionary of Philosophy.* London: Pan.

Flew, T. (2005) *The New Media*, 2nd. edn. Oxford: Oxford University Press.

Floch, J-M. (2001) *Semiotics, Marketing and Communication*, trans. by R. Orr Bodkin. Basingstoke: Palgrave Macmillan.

Frank, T. (1997) *The Conquest of Cool: Business Culture, Counter Culture and the Rise of Hip Consumerism.* Chicago: University of Chicago Press.

Gardner, H. (2004) *Changing Minds: The Art and Science of Changing Our Own and Other People's Minds.* Boston, MA: Harvard Business School Press.

Garfinkel, H. (1967) *Studies in Ethnomethodology.* Oxford: Blackwell.

Genette, G. (1980) [1972] *Narrative Discourse: An Essay in Method*, trans. by J. E. Lewin. Ithaca, NY: Cornell University Press.

Genette, G. (1997) [1987] *Paratexts.* Lincoln: University of Nebraska Press.

Gerbner, G. (1956) 'Toward a General Model of Communication', *Audio-Visual Communication Review* 4, pp. 171–99.

Gerbner, G. (1964) 'On Content Analysis and Critical Research in Mass Communication', in L. A. Dexter and D. M. White (eds), *People, Society and Mass Communications.* New York: Free Press.

Gibson, A. (1996) *Towards a Postmodern Theory of Narrative.* Edinburgh: Edinburgh University Press.

Gibson, W. (1984) *Neuromancer.* London: Penguin.

Gibson, W. (1999) *All Tomorrow's Parties.* London: Penguin.

Giddens, A. (1999) *Runaway World: How Globalization is Reshaping our Lives.* London: Profile Books.

Glass, A. L. and Holyoak, K. J. (1989) *Cognition*, 2nd edn. New York: McGraw Hill.

Goldstein, J. H. (1998) *Why We Watch: The Attractions of Violent Entertainment.* New York: Oxford University Press.

Graber, D. (2003) *The Power of Communication: Managing Information in Public Organizations.* Washington, DC: CQ Press.

Grant, A. E. (ed.) (2000) *Communication Technology Update*, 7th edn. Boston: Focal Press.

Gray, A. (1992) *Video Playtime: The Gendering of a Leisure Technology.* London: Routledge.

Greimas, A. J. (1966) *Sémantique structurale.* Paris: Larousse.

Greimas, A. J. (1987) *On Meaning: Selected Writings in Semiotic Theory*, trans. by P. Perron and F. Collins. Minneapolis: University of Minnesota Press.

Greimas, A. J. and Courtes, J. (1982) *Semiotics and Language: An Analytical Dictionary*, trans. by L. Crist et al. Bloomington: Indiana University Press.

Grodal, T. (1997) *Moving Pictures: A New Theory of Film Genres, Feelings and Cognition.* Oxford: Clarendon Press.

Grunig, J. E. (ed.) (1992) *Excellence in Public Relations and Communication Management.* Hillsdale, NJ: Erlbaum.

Grunig, J. E. and Hunt, T. (1984) *Managing Public Relations.* New York: Holt, Rinehart and Winston.

Habermas, J. (1979) *Communication and the Evolution of Society*, trans by T. McCarthy. Boston: Beacon Press.

Hall, Stuart (1977) 'Culture, the Media and the "Ideological Effect"', in James Curran, Michael Gurevitch and Janet Woollacott (eds), *Mass Communication and Society*. London: Edward Arnold.

Hall, Stuart (1980) [1973] 'Encoding/Decoding', in Centre for Cultural Studies (ed.), *Culture, Media, Language: Working Papers in Cultural Studies, 1972–79*. London: Huchinson, pp. 128–38.

Hansen, A. Cottle, S. Negrinne, R. and Newbold, C. (eds) (1998) *Mass Communication Research Methods*. London: Palgrave Macmillan.

Hartley, John (1999) *Uses of Television*. London and New York: Routledge.

Herman, A. and Swiss, T. (eds) (2000) *The World Wide Web and Contemporary Cultural Theory*. London: Routledge.

Hofstede, G. (1991) *Cultures and Organizations*. London: McGraw-Hill.

Hofstede, G. (2001) *Culture's Consequences: Company Values, Behaviours, Institutions and Organizations Across Nations*. Thousand Oaks, CA: Sage.

House, R. J. (1998) 'A Brief History of GLOBE', *Journal of Managerial Psychology*, Vol. 13, 3–4: pp. 230–40.

House, R. J., Hanges, P. J., Javidan, M., Dorfman, P. W. and Gupta, V. (2004) *Culture, Leadership and Organizations: The GLOBE Study of 62 Societies*. Thousand Oaks, CA: Sage.

Hume, D. (2000) [1740] *A Treatise of Human Nature*. Oxford: Oxford University Press.

Hymes, D. (1974) *Foundations of Sociolinguistics: An Ethnographic Approach*. Philadelphia, PA: University of Pennsylvania Press.

Irwin, H. (1996) *Communicating with Asia: Understanding People and Customs*. St Leonards, NSW: Allen and Unwin.

Jakobson, R. (1960) 'Linguistics and Poetics', in T. A. Sebeok (ed.), *Style and Language*. Cambridge, MA: MIT Press, pp. 34–45.

Jameson, F. (1991) *Postmodernism, or the Cultural Logic of Late Capitalism*. London: Verso.

Janis, I. L. (1982) *Groupthink: Psychological Studies of Policy Decisions and Fiascoes*, 2nd edn. Boston: Houghton Mifflin.

Jankowski, G. F. and Fuchs, D. C. (1995) *Television Today and Tomorrow: It Won't Be What You Think*. New York: Oxford University Press.

Javidan, M. and House, R. (2001) 'Cultural Acumen for the Global Manager: Lessons From Project GLOBE', *Organizational Dynamics*, Vol. 29, 4: pp. 289–305.

Kane, T. (1984) *The New Oxford Guide to Writing*. Oxford: Oxford University Press.

Karriker, H. (2005) *Film Studies: Women in Contemporary World Cinema*. New York: Peter Lang.

Katz, E. and Lazarsfeld, P. F. (1955) *Personal Influence: The Part Played by People in the Flow of Mass Communication*. Glencoe, IL: Free Press.

Kaufer, D. S. and Carley, K. M. (1993) *Communication at a Distance: The Influence of Print on Sociocultural Organization and Change*. Hillsdale, NJ: Lawrence Erlbaum.

Kelly, K. and Parisis, P. (1997) 'Beyond "Star Wars"', *Wired*, Vol. 5, no. 2.

Kermally, S. (2002) *Effective Knowledge Management: A Best Practice Blueprint*. London: John Wiley.

Kierkegaard, S. (1987) [1845] *Either/Or*, ed. and trans. by H. V. Hong and E. H. Hong. Princeton, NJ: Princeton University Press.

King, G. (2000) *Spectacular Narratives: Hollywood in the Age of the Blockbuster*. London and New York: Tauris.

King, S. (1981) 'Why We Crave Horror Movies', *Playboy*, January.

Kisselof, J. (1995) *The Box: An Oral History of Television, 1920–1960*. New York: Viking Press.

Knapp, M. (1995) *Essentials of Non Verbal Communication*. Orlando, FL: Harcourt.

Kristeva, J. (1969) *Semeiotiké*. Paris: Seuil.

Lakoff, G. (1987) *Women, Fire and Dangerous Things: What Categories Reveal about the Mind*. Chicago: University of Chicago Press.

Lakoff, G. and Johnson, M. (2003) *Metaphors We Live By*, 2nd edn. Chicago: University of Chicago Press.

Lanham, R. A. (1991) *A Handlist of Rhetorical Terms*, 2nd edn. Berkeley: University of California Press.

Lasswell, H. D. (1948) 'The Structure and Function of Communication in Society', in Bryson (ed.), *The Communication of Ideas*. New York: Harper and Brothers.

Latour, B. and Woolgar, S. (1979) *Laboratory Life: The Construction of Scientific Facts*. Thousand Oaks, CA: Sage.

Lazarsfeld, P. F., Berelson, B. and Gaudet, H. (1968) [1944] *The People's Choice: How the Voter Makes up his Mind in a Presidential Election*. New York: Columbia University Press.

Lazarsfeld, P. F. and Merton, R. K. (1964) 'Friendship as a Social Process: A Substantive and Methodological Analysis', in M. Berger et al. (eds) *Freedom and Control in Modern Society*. New York: Octagon.

Lemon, L. T. and Reis, M. J. (1965) *Russian Formalist Criticism: Four Essays*. Lincoln: University of Nebraska Press.

Lester, A. (2003) *Project Planning and Control*. Oxford: Butterworth Heinemann.

Lester, P. M. (1995) *Visual Communication: Images with Messages*. Belmont, CA: Wadsworth.

Levinson, S. (1983) *Pragmatics*. Cambridge. Cambridge University Press.

Levy, Mark and Windahl, Sven (1985) 'The Concept of Audience Activity', in K. E. Rosengren, L. A. Wenner and P. Palmgreen (eds) *Media Gratifications Research: Current Perspectives*. London and Beverly Hills: Sage, pp. 109–22.

Leyda, J. (1963) (ed.) *Film Form: Essays in Film Theory*. London: Dennis Dobson.

Lindlof, Thomas (1995) *Qualitative Communication Research Methods*. Thousand Oaks, CA: Sage.

Livingstone, Sonia and Lunt, Peter (1994) *Talk on Television: Audience Participation and Public Debate*. London: Routledge.

Lyotard, F. (1984) [1979] *The Postmodern Condition: A Report on Knowledge*. Manchester: Manchester University Press.

Manovich, L. (2001) *The Language of New Media*. Cambridge, MA: MIT Press.

Marsen, S. (2003) *Professional Writing: The Complete Guide for Business, Industry and IT*. Basingstoke: Palgrave Macmillan.

Marsen, S. (2004) 'Against Heritage: Invented Identities in Science Fiction Film', *Semiotica*, 150–1/4, pp. 141–57.

Marshall, P. D. (1997) *Celebrity and Power: Fame in Contemporary Culture*. Minneapolis: University of Minnesota Press.

Maslow, A. (1987) [1954] *Motivation and Personality*, 3rd edn. New York: Harper Collins.

McKee, A. (2003) *Textual Analysis*. London: Sage.

McKee, A. (2005) *The Public Sphere: An Introduction*. Cambridge: Cambridge University Press.

McLuhan, M. (1964) *Understanding Media*. London: Routledge and Kegan Paul.

McLuhan, M. and McLuhan E. (1988) *Laws of Media: The New Science*. Toronto: University of Toronto Press.

McQuail, D. (1975) *Communication*. London: Longman.

McQuail, D. (1992) *Media Performance*. Newbury Park and London: Sage.

McQuail, D. (1994) *Mass Communication Theory: An Introduction*, 3rd edn. London: Sage.

McQuail, D. (1997) *Audience Analysis*. Thousand Oaks, CA and London: Sage.

McQuail, D. and Windahl, S. (1993) *Communication Models for the Study of Mass Communication*. 2nd edn. London: Longman.

McQueen, D. (1998) *Television: A Media Student's Guide*. London: Arnold.

Medhurst, M. J. and Benson, T. W. (eds) (1984) *Rhetorical Dimensions in Media: A Critical Casebook*. Dubuque: Kendall-Hunt.

Merton, R. (1949) *Social Theory and Social Structure*. New York: Free Press.

Merton, R. K. and Kendall, P. L. (1946) 'The Focused Interview', *The American Journal of Sociology*, 51, 6, pp. 541–57.

Metz, C. (1974) *Film Language: A Semiotics of the Cinema*, trans. by M. Taylor. New York: Oxford University Press.

Meyrowitz, J. (1985) *No Sense of Place: The Impact of Electronic Media on Social Behavior*. Oxford: Oxford University Press.

Mitry, J. (2000) [1987] *Semiotics and the Analysis of Film*. London: Athlone.

Monaco, J. (1981) *How to Read a Film*. New York: Oxford University Press.

Morley, D. (1980) *The 'Nationwide' Audience: Structure and Decoding*. London: British Film Institute.

Nadin, M. and Zakia, R. (1994) *Creating Effective Advertising Using Semiotics*. New York: Consultant Press.

Nelmes, J. (1996) *An Introduction to Film Studies*. London: Routledge.

Newcomb, H. (ed.) (2000) *Television: The Critical View*. New York: Oxford University Press.

Newson, E. (1994) 'Video Violence and the Protection of Children', *Journal of Mental Health*, 2.

NUA Internet Survey (2004) retrieved 10 May from www.nua.ie/surveys/how_many_on_line

Peirce, C. S. (1931) *Collected Papers of Charles Sanders Peirce*. Cambridge, MA: Harvard University Press.

Pepper, S. (1942) *World Hypotheses: A Study in Evidence*. Berkeley, CA: University of California Press.

Pettinger, R. (2002) *Introduction to Management*. Basingstoke: Palgrave Macmillan.

Phillips, W. H. (1999) *Film: An Introduction*. New York: Bedford St Martins.

Plate, T. (2002) 'Hollywood Faces New Competition: World Film Industry is Globalization at its Best'. UCLA International Institute. Retrieved 2 September 2005 from http://www.international.ucla.edu/article.asp?parentid=2059

Prachter, B. (2002) *When the Little Things Count . . . and They Always Count: 601 Essential Things that Everyone in Business Needs to Know*. New York: Marlowe & Co.

Preston, P. (2005) 'Nonverbal communication: Do You Really Say What You Mean?', *Journal of Healthcare Management*, Vol. 50, 2, pp. 83–8.

Price, S. (1997) *Communication Studies*. London: Longman.

Prince, G. (1982) *Narratology: The Form and Functioning of Narrative*. Berlin: Mouton.

Prince, G. (1987) *A Dictionary of Narratology*. Lincoln: University of Nebraska Press.

Pringle, P. K., Starr, M. F. and McCavitt, W. (1995), 3rd edn. *Electronic Media Management*. Boston: Focal Press.

Propp, V. (1968) [1928] *Morphology of the Folktale*. Austin, TX: University of Texas Press.

Qubein, N. R. (1986) *Get the Best from Yourself*. New York: Berkley.

Robbins, S. and Barnwell, N. (2002) *Organisation Theory: Concepts and Cases*. Sydney: Prentice-Hall.

Rogers, E. M. (1995) *Diffusion of Innovations*, 4th edn. New York and London: Free Press.

Rogers, E. M. (2003) Diffusion of News of the September 11 Terrorist Attacks, in A. M. Noll (ed.) *Crisis Communications: Lessons from September 11*. London and New York: Rowman and Littlefield.

Root, R. L. Jr (1987) *The Rhetorics of Popular Culture: Advertising, Advocacy and Entertainment*. New York: Greenwood.

Rosengren, K. E., Wenner, L. A. and Palmgreen, P. (eds) (1985) *Media Gratifications Research: Current Perspectives*. London and Beverly Hills: Sage.

Salt, B. (1992) *Film Style and Technology: History and Analysis*, 2nd edn. London: Starword.

Saussure, F. de (1966). *Course in General Linguistics*. New York: McGraw Hill (original published in 1916).

Saville-Troike, M. (2002) *The Ethnography of Communication*. Oxford: Blackwell.

Schank, R. and Abelson, R. (1977) *Scripts, Plans, Goals and Understanding: An Inquiry into Human Knowledge Structures*, Hillsdale, NJ: Lawrence Erlbaum.

Schumann, D. W. and Thorson, E. (1999) *Advertising and the World Wide Web*. Mahwah, NJ: Erlbaum.

Schutz, W. (1966) *The Interpersonal Underworld*. London: Science and Behaviour Books.

Shannon, C. and Weaver, W. (1949) *The Mathematical Theory of Communication*. Urbana: University of Illinois Press.

Shenton, K. and McNeely, T. (1997) *The Virtual Communities Companion*. Albany, NY: Coriolis Group.

Smith, A. (ed.) (1995) *Television: An International History*. New York: Oxford University Press.

Stam, R. (2000) *Film Theory: An Introduction*. Oxford: Blackwell.

Stam, R. and Miller, T. (2000) (eds) *Film and Theory: An Anthology*. Oxford: Blackwell.

Stanzel, F. K. (1984) *A Theory of Narrative*, trans by C. Goedsche. Cambridge: Cambridge University Press.

Stefik, M. (1999) *The Internet Edge: Social, Technical and Legal Challenges for a Networked World*. Cambridge, MA: MIT Press.

Steiner, P. (1984) *Russian Formalism: A Metapoetics*. Ithaca, NY: Cornell University Press.

Stewart, D. W. and Shamdasani, P. N. (1990) *Focus Groups: Theory and Practice*. Newbury Park, CA: Sage.

Stone, N. (1995) *The Management and Practice of Public Relations*. Basingstoke: Palgrave Macmillan.

Strauss, W. and Howe. N. (1991) *Generations: The History of America's Future 1584 to 2069*. New York: William Morrow.

Surowiecki, J. (2005) *The Wisdom of Crowds: Why the Many are Smarter than the Few*. London: Abacus.

Sutherland, J. and Canwell, D. (2004) *Key Concepts in Management*. Basingstoke: Palgrave Macmillan.

Takeuchi, H. and Nonaka, I. (2004) *Hitotsubashi on Knowledge Management*. New York: John Wiley.

Tannebaum, R. and Schmidt, W. H. (1973) 'How to Choose a Leadership Pattern', *Harvard Business Review*

Thompson, K. (1999) *Storytelling in the New Hollywood*. Cambridge, MA: Harvard University Press.

Trenholm, S. (1999) *Thinking through Communication*. Boston: Allyn and Bacon.

Turow, J. (1992) 'The Organizational Underpinnings of Contemporary Media Conglomerates', *Communication Research* 19, 6, pp. 682–704.

Verderber, R. and Verderber S. (1992) *Inter-Act: Using Interpersonal Communication Skills*, 6th edn. Los Angeles, CA: Wadsworth.

Vernet, M. (1992) *Aesthetics of Film*, trans. by R. Neupert. Austin, TX: University of Texas Press.

Wasko, J. (2003) *How Hollywood Works*. Thousand Oaks, CA: Sage.

Watson, J. (2003) *Media Communication*, 2nd edn. Basingstoke: Palgrave Macmillan.

Wiener, N. (1965) [1948] *Cybernetics: Or Control and Communication in the Animal and the Machine*. 2nd edn. Cambridge, MA: MIT Press.

Wiener, N. (1988) [1954] *The Human Use of Human Beings: Cybernetics and Society*, 2nd edn. Boston: Da Capo.

Wilenski, H. (1967) *Organizational Intelligence*. New York: Basic Books.

Williams, R. (1974) *Television: Technology and Cultural Form*. London: Fontana.

Williams, R. (1980) *Problems in Materialism and Culture*. London: Verso.

Wilson, G. M. (1986) *Narration in Light: Studies in Cinematic Point of View*. Baltimore, MD: Johns Hopkins University Press.

Witherspoon, J. and Koitz, R. (eds) (2000) *The History of Public Broadcasting*. Washington, DC: Current.

Wollen, P. (1998) [1968] *Signs and Meaning in the Cinema*. London: British Film Institute.

Yule, G. (1996) *Pragmatics*. Oxford: Oxford University Press.

Index